808.869
Boo   The Book of love

JAN   1993

DUE DATE

THE
BOOK
OF LOVE

Writers and Their
Love Letters

ALSO BY CATHY N. DAVIDSON

Revolution and the Word: The Rise of the Novel in America

The Experimental Fictions of Ambrose Bierce

EDITED BY CATHY N. DAVIDSON

Reading in America: Literature and Social History

The Lost Tradition: Mothers and Daughters in Literature
(*with E. M. Broner*)

THE
BOOK
OF LOVE

Writers and Their Love Letters

Selected and Introduced by
CATHY N. DAVIDSON

POCKET BOOKS
New York   London   Toronto   Sydney   Tokyo   Singapore

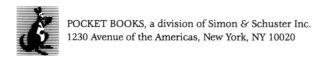

POCKET BOOKS, a division of Simon & Schuster Inc.
1230 Avenue of the Americas, New York, NY 10020

The Book of love : writers and their love letters / [edited by] Cathy
    N. Davidson.
        p.   cm.
    Includes bibliographical references.
    ISBN: 0-671-70133-9
    1. Love letters. 2. Authors—Correspondence. I. Davidson, Cathy
N.
    PN6140.L7B58   1992
    808.86′9354—dc20   92-9736
                                                            CIP

First Pocket Books hardcover printing December 1992

10   9   8   7   6   5   4   3   2   1

POCKET and colophon are registered trademarks of
Simon & Schuster Inc.

Printed in the U.S.A.

PERMISSIONS

Grateful acknowledgment is made for permission to quote from materials listed below:

The Letters of Abelard and Héloïse, translated by Betty Radice (Penguin Classics, 1974), copyright © Betty
    Radice, 1974. Reproduced by permission of Penguin Books Ltd.
Correspondencia íntima de Delmira Agustini y tres versiones de "Lo inefable," ed. Arturo Sergio Visca,
    Montevideo: Biblioteca Nacional, Publicaciones del Departamento de Investigaciones, 1978.
Selected Letters of Conrad Aiken, edited by Joseph Killorin, New Haven: Yale University Press, 1978. By
    permission of Mary H. Aiken and Joseph Killorin.
Nelson Algren: A Life on the Wild Side, by Bettina Drew. Copyright © 1989 by Bettina Drew. Reprinted by
    permission of the Putnam Publishing Group.
Sherwood Anderson's Love Letters to Eleanor Copenhaver Anderson, reprinted by permission of Harold
    Ober Associates Incorporated. Copyright © 1989 by Charles E. Modlin, Hilbert H. Campbell, and
    Christopher Sergel, Trustees, Sherwood Anderson Literary Estate Trust.

(con't. on page 300)

For Ted, of course.

And for Charles and Susan.

A NOTE TO THE READER

Wherever possible, these letters have been reprinted from the most definitive edition available. Some of the best writers are notoriously bad spellers. Their errors remain and contribute to the charm and spontaneity of the letters.

However, in a few instances, paragraph indentations have been added and spellings modernized in order to make some of the older letters more accessible to contemporary readers. Where an exceptionally long letter has been condensed or where purely topical or extraneous matter has been omitted, ellipses have been inserted in the text to indicate deletions.

Transliterations of foreign names (such as "Fyodor Dostoyevsky") follow the usage of the collection from which the letter has been reprinted. Finally, brief explanations of important references are sometimes supplied in brackets in the text while longer explanatory material can be found in the end notes.

ACKNOWLEDGMENTS

My friend Alice called one day excited about an "oldie" she'd just heard on the radio.

"Remember 'The Book of Love'?" she asked, and proceeded to sing the lyrics, which, chapter by chapter, recount the course of love's progress.

"It's *your* book!" she exclaimed.

My first acknowledgment therefore goes to Alice Kaplan for providing me with my title. I also thank her, Jane Tompkins, and Marianna Torgovnick (members of our writing group) for reading this manuscript with exemplary insight, care, wit, wisdom, and, most of all, friendship (which has its own chapter in the book of love).

My gratitude, too, to Jennifer Huntley for her diligence in typing much of the manuscript, and to Kathryn West, who helped me to locate well over a thousand volumes of letters, biographies, autobiographies, and reference works relevant to this project, and who expertly managed the extensive correspondence required to reprint the following letters. This book, quite simply, could not have been completed without her.

Cynthia Davis provided expert research and editorial assistance at the eleventh hour, as did Glenn Willmott, and Donna Ng. Jan Freeman, Karina Davidson, and Dana D. Nelson offered valuable comments on the introduction while Sam S. Baskett, Louis J. Budd, Tanner Davis, Merlin Holland, Melody Ivins, Alphonse Juilland, Michael Moon, Silvia Tandeciarz, Linda Wagner-Martin, and Pablo Yanez supplied useful information about individual letters and authors. My editor, Jane Rosenman, and my agent, Geri Thoma, were a continuing source of editorial acumen and enthusiastic support. More personally, I'm grateful to my family, especially Paul Notari and Marlene Fineman Notari, and my grandparents, Lillian Fineman and the late David Fineman, for their loving example and constant care. Ted Davidson, Charles Davidson, and Susan Brown have inspired many of my ideas about love and letters.

Finally, all of the letters in this volume have been published previously, and most of the authors represented have been the subject of numerous (and sometimes contradictory) biographies. I would like to express my general sense of admiration for and indebtedness to the many editors and biographers whose work is cited in the endnotes as well as on the permission pages of this volume.

My individual chapters don't correspond exactly to those outlined by the Monotones in 1958, but my basic point is the same. There *is* a book of love. Who writes it? We all do.

Hillsborough, NC
April, 1991

CONTENTS

2 LOVE'S INFINITE VARIETY

LOVE IS TENDER

LOVE IS PASSIONATE

TRIANGLES

DECEMBER LOVE

3   ABSENCE

SEPARATION

THE FINAL SEPARATION

4 LOVE HURTS

UNREQUITED LOVE

OBSTACLES

THE GOOD FIGHT

5 THE END OF LOVE

DEAR JOHN/DEAR JANE

BETRAYED AND ABANDONED

AFTER GREAT PAIN

REMEMBRANCE OF LOVE PAST

6 FALLING IN LOVE AGAIN

Going to Him! Happy letter!
Tell Him—
Tell Him the page I didn't write—
Tell Him—I only said the Syntax—
And left the Verb and the pronoun out—
Tell Him just how the fingers hurried—
Then—how they waded—slow—slow—
And then you wished you had eyes in your pages—
So you could see what moved them so—

—*Emily Dickinson*

INTRODUCTION

Early in the twentieth century, novelist Edith Wharton fell in love. She was in her mid-forties, famous from the publication of *The House of Mirth* (1905), admired for her grace and taste, envied for her family's position in New York society, and miserable in a debilitating marriage to Teddy Wharton, a man both emotionally unstable and ostentatiously unfaithful. Then she met W. Morton Fullerton, an American journalist also living in Paris. "The moment my eyes fell on him," she wrote, "I was content."

Wharton's letters to Fullerton have survived and provide as good a testimony as any I know to the compelling power of love letters. "Do you want to know some of the things I like you for?" Wharton asks rhetorically in a letter written in June of 1908. "I like the way in which you instantly discriminate between the essential & the superfluous, in people & things—& your feeling as I do about the 'green worms' of life—caring about the waitress's losing her tip if we moved our table, & being worried lest the taxi-man you sent back to me at the R. des Deux Mondes should have waited & missed a fare—if you knew how every little thing like that *sank in!*"

Her letters are filled with such loving "little things." By turns tender and wryly witty, rapturous and tinged with regret, they chronicle passion's erratic progress. In the same letter that brims with love for Fullerton's solicitude toward waitresses and taxi drivers, Wharton confesses: "I vowed I wouldn't write you again until I had overcome my black mood . . . but yesterday, in my despair, I very nearly cabled you the one word: *Inconsolable.*" On another day, a flash of ecstasy: "I am like one who went out seeking for friendship, & found a kingdom." Taken together, the letters are an exquisite rendition of the moods and motives of love, as finely tuned as any Wharton novel.

The affair between Wharton and Fullerton lasted several years but with different degrees of intensity and commitment for each lover. To a modern reader perusing the Wharton half of this correspondence, it is obvious that the passion of her life was a dalliance in his. Yet in defeat, too, Wharton's letters are moving classics of the love letter genre. Her words swirl in a maelstrom of despondency following Fullerton's sudden leavings and unannounced returns, his lingering and inarticulate defection. "I don't know what you want, or what I am! You write me like a lover, you treat me like a casual acquaintance!" The tone of her letters ranges from incredulity to despair, a wrenching taxonomy of grief.

Since Fullerton's portion of the correspondence has been lost, we can only guess at his words and actions from her half. As far as one can tell, he dropped her but refused to oblige her with the courtesy of a contrived rejection, the ritualized Dear John ("You are the best thing that ever happened to me") that she needed. There seem to have been indecisive and contradictory conversations but no satisfactory closure. Wharton had to supply her own ending because Fullerton did not. A love affair that has been orchestrated by letters demands the terminal Dear John/Dear Jane that is as much a climax to an epistolary love affair as is the final act in classical drama.

Through post-amour epistles, Wharton writes Fullerton out of her life—slowly, painfully, beseechingly, imploring some response, some acknowledgment that so much emotion was not entirely in vain. "My life was better before I knew you," she writes, almost begging him to prove her wrong. "That is, for me, the sad conclusion of this sad year. And it is a bitter thing to say to the one being one has ever loved *d'amour*." Finally admitting to herself that she will receive not even the smallest consolation from Fullerton, she tidies the relationship into a proper friendship, trying to be civil about it all, returning his letters (even as he ignores her repeated request that he return hers). Ever polite, ever the lady, Wharton's bitterness shines through only by indirection and inference: "I enclose yr letters in another envelope—no, after all, I find they will fit in this."

Throughout it all Wharton retains her dignity despite Fullerton's humiliating silence, his refusal to acknowledge her as a lover or a person. Exhausted with the responsibility of thinking through (and *writing* through) their love and its end, she finally has her literary assistant, Anna Bahlmann, write to Fullerton on her behalf:

Mrs. Wharton begs you to excuse her not writing herself, as she is up to her eyes in work & has Mrs. Jones [Wharton's mother] staying here besides. She asks me to ask you if you could conveniently send for your books, as she has to find

room for a lot of furniture. Of course she has been delighted to
keep the books for you, but now she is herself pressed for
room. . . . They have been carefully packed in 25 or 30 boxes.
Could you make it convenient to send for them on Wednesday
morning? That would solve her problem nicely, though she
regrets having to give you the trouble.

Solving problems nicely. It's enough to break one's heart.

~

I dwell on Wharton's case at length because in both quality and
effect her love letters are archetypal. In fact, the idea for this book
came from reading these letters. They are so moving in their own
right that they made me think about other writers similarly disappointed in love. I began to contemplate the reasons why so many
writers fall passionately in love with men and women physically distant, and distant in their emotional responses as well. Wharton, to be
sure, wanted a real person (although not, perhaps, the real—and
markedly flawed—Fullerton). But it seems as if at least some of the
writers in this volume actually preferred the passion of words (the
inevitable ecstasies and despairs of a love marked by absence) to the
less tumultuous satisfactions of steady companionship. After reading
literally thousands of letters, I began to wonder if writers don't
choose to love long-distance, a sure way of blending passion and
prose. The love letter seems perfectly suited to the contradictions of
a writer's life. Writers are both isolated and yet excruciatingly aware
of their audience. If literature is a "letter to the world," in Emily
Dickinson's phrase, then the love letter may be the emblem of a vo-
cation that demands solitude but desires communication. Like literature, a love letter is intimacy by proxy.

At the end of their relationship, Wharton wrote most of the letters
to Fullerton because her only other choice was to conspire in a silence that felt like death. But from the very beginning, Wharton's
passion was as much epistolary as physical, as if one who lives by the
letter, loves by the letter. For her, love was articulate. It opened a
floodgate of words. In love, she wanted to write everything to Fullerton and wanted to write Fullerton into everything, as if their love were
one of her novels. In this, again, she is typical. For many professional
writers, the love letter incarnates passion; prose takes love's measure. It is as if the writer requires the letter to make the love real.

Love letters are a logical extension of the craft of writing. To state
the matter as simply as possible, literature wouldn't exist without
people who felt compelled to communicate their own view of their

world in words. Letters of all kinds (especially prior to the invention of the telephone) are one of the literary profession's chief occupational hazards. Victor Hugo is said to have received as many as fifty letters a day. Once in 1924, returning from a trip of only three days, Edith Wharton found sixty-five letters waiting for her. Conrad Aiken is estimated to have written twelve thousand letters over the course of his life; Virginia Woolf some twenty thousand. To publish the complete correspondence of Henry James would require over fifty large volumes. But the love letter occupies a special place even within the most prolific correspondence because of its intensity, focus, and self-absorption as well as its implicit license. In a love letter, the writer can indulge in the kind of stratospheric prose that might be censored from more usual correspondence and edited out of more finished literary productions.

Not only do writers write more letters than most people, what they write tends to survive. Admiring readers, proud progeny, responsible literary executors, and even old enemies and jilted lovers all save writers' letters. Although the more passionate letters are sometimes suppressed out of a sense of decorum, even these letters sometimes manage to find their way into print. As a young man still in his teens, Ernest Hemingway loved and was jilted by Agnes von Kurowsky. A number of his biographers have argued that his bitter reaction to the end of what for Agnes was mostly a wartime fling scarred his relationships with women until the end of his life and directly colored the presentation of women and love in his fiction. The lovestruck letters between Hemingway and Kurowsky were first published in 1989, yet they recreate that ill-fated romance as if it happened yesterday: "I dreamed an awfully nice dream last night," Ag wrote to Hem on October 30, 1918. "I dreamed . . . I spied you thru a lighted window shaving & fixing yourself all up in your best uniform. I was sitting on a bench outside waiting for you."

In another letter to Hemingway, Agnes openly expresses her nervousness about letters. "Writing has always made me draw into a shell—it seemed so irrevocable. Once written you can't take back what you have said." She was right, as the fate of her letters, seventy years later, suggests. Similarly, Fullerton never did return Wharton's letters, nor did he destroy them. At the age of eighty-six, he sold off twenty-two of her letters. Another three hundred turned up in the hands of a Parisian book dealer after Fullerton's death. Dull-minded critics had previously dismissed Wharton as a "frigid" woman remembered chiefly for her friendship with Henry James. Wharton would have found it ironic indeed that the revelation of her affair with Fullerton contributed to a revaluation of her literary reputation.

Writers write. That's obvious enough. However, the relationship between love letters and literature is as diverse as the writers themselves. For Hemingway, the relationship was inverse. He was often apologetic about the poor quality of his love letters, yet believed that he wrote his best fiction when he was in love. He was far too busy writing the heroines into his fiction to write beautiful words to the actual women who were the models for those characters—one of the more intriguing paradoxes among literary lovers.

At other times there is a direct relationship between love letters and literature. The three "Master" letters that Emily Dickinson scrawled to someone who remains mysteriously anonymous today are full of the breath-stopping pain that characterizes many of her finest poems. Writing of herself in the third person, she describes "a love so big it scares her, rushing among her small heart—pushing aside the blood—and leaving her faint and white in the gust's arm." In her final letter to "Master" she writes: "If you saw a bullet hit a Bird—and he told you he wasn't shot—you might weep at his courtesy, but you would certainly doubt his word—One drop more from the gash that stains your Daisy's bosom—then would you *believe?*" Are these love letters or poetry? Is there a difference? The anguish scans like Dickinson's verse.

Sometimes love letters rank among a writer's finest achievements, as if the particular Beloved is required to inspire the best poetry. Sometimes I even find myself wondering which is more important, the love or the letter? A number of famous writers—including Kafka, Rilke, and Kleist—had love affairs that existed *only* in correspondence. Reading their letters, I'm filled with impatience. When will this writer stop writing and start loving? Although for some writers represented in this volume separation is real, unavoidable, and devastating, for others separation is quite preventable and occasionally seems contrived to afford an opportunity for more love letters. In these cases, the love letter is not an expression of intimacy but a way of avoiding intimacy, a way of using beautiful words on paper to avoid making the ultimate commitment of the self to another.

Writers may not love any worse or better than anyone else. What they do differently is write about it, and a good number of writers have used their failed loves as the basis for good plots. After French writer Francis Carco briefly wooed Katherine Mansfield, she transformed her disillusionment with him into a notably unflattering story, "Je ne parles pas français." Carco returned the compliment by using Mansfield as the model for Winnie in *Les Innocents*, a writer who falls in love in order to glean material for future short stories. Similarly, in the Paris of the twenties, Ford Madox Ford had an adulterous affair with ingenue-writer Jean Rhys, and then he, she, and their respective partners (artist Stella Bowen and forger Jean Lenglet) all provided their own versions of that romance in various competing memoirs and *romans à clef*. The symbiosis of literary love and letters makes it difficult to untangle a writer's love letters from her or his fiction. How, for example, can we separate the intertwining love letters and love fictions of F. Scott Fitzgerald, Zelda, and Sheila Graham? They all loved; in different ways, they all lost; they all wrote about it, sometimes inserting one or another's letters directly into their books.

Of course not all writers are cads who fall in love in order to write letters that inspire novels about failed love affairs. Many love deeply and use letters as a way to communicate that love. Samuel Clemens (Mark Twain) knew even before he married that he wanted a wife who would be a "companion." He courted Olivia Langdon assiduously, recreating himself as the kind of socially responsible and sensitive young writer that she admired. The reader of *The Adventures of Huckleberry Finn* might be surprised by the lover's passion (and his purple prose style): "For I *do* love you, Livy—as the dew loves the flowers; as the birds love the sunshine; as the wavelets love the breeze; as mothers love their first-born; as memory loves old faces; as the yearning tides love the moon; as angels love the pure in heart."

~

As the letters in this collection attest, the love letter blurs distinctions between "private" and "public" expression. These letters are intriguing for the insights they give into a writer's biography; they are satisfying as literature; but they are most important for the way they speak to all readers, even though they originally address only one. Love letters fulfill a need to confide, to testify, and to articulate what is ordinarily left unspoken. The same need underlies the craft of writing. Writers are not only characterized by a heightened sensibility or an acuity about the emotional realm (although this certainly helps). They are also (except in rare cases such as Dickinson) impelled to express that sensibility in a public way. Composing fiction or poetry is a special form of communication that is both intimate and remote. It is intimate in the sense that the bond between writer and readers is intense—often nearly as intense as love. It is remote in the sense that writers seldom meet their actual readers, and when they do, there is often disappointment on both sides. A writer is not the hero or heroine with whom the reader identifies. Nor does the reader typically care about the mechanics of the writing process (transitions, chapter endings and beginnings, even commas, the nuts and bolts of writing). Readers get the final product, and (selfishly?) that is what they are concerned about.

With love letters the writer displays her or his craft before an actual (and often adoring) audience. The collective "reader" is particularized, symbolized by the Beloved. What more flattering, sympathetic reader than an actual lover? Nor can one separate the private love from the public literature it produces. Writers as diverse as Robert Burns, Charles Baudelaire, Paul Laurence Dunbar, Lady Augusta Gregory, Carl Sandburg, Wallace Stevens, and Pablo Neruda enclosed love poems with their love letters, stressing the simultaneity of inspiration and creation. These writers explicitly record the relationship between passion and composition, how love inspires work or how longing interferes. For them, the Beloved serves as muse and principal reader. In those cases where the poet goes on to publish the love poems, the general reader becomes a surrogate for the actual lover; where the poet intended to publish the poems all along, the actual lover was initially a stand-in for the general reader.

For at least some writers, the love letter may well be the ultimate literary act. The craft of literature teaches how to entice through words, how to make a reader assent, for the duration of the reading experience, to the writer's view of the world. As Ross Chambers reminds us, literature is a kind of seduction. Like taking a lover, reading literature is a secret pleasure, engaged in privately and demanding stolen time. It is a refuge from or a revolt against the demands of ordinary life. Writers know this. They know the competition for a reader's attention and affections is tough. For some writers, the love letter is the perfect vehicle for honing and testing the skills of print seduction. "Writing," as Jean Cocteau said, "is an act of love. Else it is nothing but scribbling." In a literary love letter, that act of love is real; the metaphoric seduction of narrative is literalized. The rewards of authorship become palpable. The reader has a body. The word becomes flesh.

A love letter is also a good place to perfect one's literary skills, since so much literature is about love, especially the ill-fated variety. To apply to love Tolstoy's formulation about the sameness (and dullness) of happy families, everyone knows that unsuccessful love affairs make for successful plots. "They lived happily ever after" is a standard ending because it would make a very boring beginning. In *Pride and Prejudice,* Elizabeth's prejudices have to clash with Darcy's pride or there's no book. Emma Bovary has to marry the cloddish Charles or *Madame Bovary* doesn't exist. If Cathy runs off at the start with Heathcliff, then *Wuthering Heights* necessarily devolves into extended marital squabbles—bills to pay, a roof that needs shingling, conflicting ideas on child-rearing, insufferable table manners. As Carolyn Heilbrun has recently suggested, it probably would be better if women read such sobering accounts of the domesticity that follows romantic love. But until the contemporary era in women's fiction, larger-than-life passionate love—often unrequited or betrayed—has provided some of the best literary material. What this means in biographical terms is that the writer-lover who loses badly in love still wins, in the sense that he or she now has something to write about.

Again the example of Edith Wharton is paradigmatic. She was not just a woman who loved and lost; she was a novelist who wrote throughout her long and distinguished career about women who loved and lost, about impressive women in love with ineffectual men. Wharton's passionate letters to Fullerton partly parallel the botched love affair in Wharton's bestseller, *The House of Mirth*, the tragic tale of the beautiful Lily Bart and the ineffectual and Fullerton-ish Lawrence Selden. Their love affair is also reminiscent of plots and characters in *The Fruit of the Tree* and *The Touchstone*. Yet all of these books were written before Wharton ever met Fullerton. The man may resemble the fictional characters—but the characters got there first. In both a literal and a figurative sense, Wharton *invented* Fullerton, the love of her life, and, with exacting logic, he played out the imperfect part that had already been written for him. A decade later, she could then use the affair as source material for her masterpiece, *The Age of Innocence*, a development predicted by Fullerton, who told her once that she "should write better for this experience of loving." Nor is Wharton's case unusual. Poe, Ford, Colette, Hemingway, Langston Hughes, Katherine Anne Porter, and Fitzgerald, to name just a few, all anticipated and rehearsed in their fiction the love plots of their lives.

By trade and by training, writers are susceptible to the Pygmalion imperative—falling in love with the objects of their creation—and they are eloquent in describing its typically disastrous consequences. And maybe that's the point. Writers articulate (even *over*-articulate) what anyone who has ever been in love suspects: Falling in love is an act of creation. "Your sonnet is quite lovely," Oscar Wilde writes encouragingly, if a bit patronizingly, to his young lover, Lord Alfred Douglas, and then goes on to show the lad what real poetry—the poetry of love letters—is all about: "It is a marvel that those red rose-leaf lips of yours should be made no less for the music of song than for the madness of kissing. Your slim gilt soul walks between passion and poetry." For most of us, love letters are as close as we come to art. For writers, love is a first draft.

∿

Although love itself is a very real and powerful emotion, its written form—the love letter—is a genre with its own set of rules and conventions, less defined than a sonnet perhaps, but at least as prescribed as a short story or a novel. The variations in the formula that have taken place across centuries and continents and even, surprisingly, across the great divide of the sexes are relatively minor when compared to the features of the love letter that persist relatively unchanged. In cuneiform or hieroglyphics, lovers declared themselves in terms still recognizable today. In ancient or modern civilizations, love has its imperatives. "I beg you, Lord, if it seems good to you, to send for me, else I die because I don't behold you daily," Taus wrote to Appolonios from second-century Rome. Nearly two millennia later, the urgency is the same even though a partial solution, the telephone, is immediately at hand: "God knows when [we'll] meet," John Cheever writes to his lover, "but I'll call soon or call me. Call me collect and when the operator asks if I'll accept the charges on a call from [you], I'll say yes, yes, yes, yes."

Ten essential features define the love letter as a genre. Not every individual letter demonstrates all ten features, of course, but they are present in virtually every sequence of letters. Anyone who has written a love letter will recognize them. Great love-letter writers merely elevate them to an art form.

1) *The love letter records a lack.*

As Roland Barthes has suggested, absence is the love letter's primary requirement. Without separation, the letter has no reason to exist. The love letter is, then, a substitute for intimacy.

Sometimes the absence is necessary, as when John Steinbeck, away at war, writes to his wife Gwyndolyn about "these thousands of lonely soldiers here [in London] . . . looking for something," and then goes on to tell what he is looking for. "Darling, you want to know what I want of you . . . I want you to keep this thing we have inviolate and waiting—the person who is neither I nor you but us. It's a hard thing this separation but it is one of the millions of separations at home and many more millions here." Writing only a few years later to the new woman in his life, Elaine Scott, Steinbeck is more direct about his sense of lack: "Parting is not sweet sorrow to me but a dry panic."

Many writers try to transcend separation through the power of the love letter, as when Zelda writes Scott: "I look down the tracks and see you coming—and out of every haze & mist your darling rumpled trousers are hurrying to me."

Occasionally separation itself is the object of desire. Anaïs Nin's biographer notes that she could hardly wait for Henry Miller to leave so that she could write about him in her diary as well as in love letters she would send to both him and his wife June (with whom she was also in love). A passionate long-distance correspondence sometimes substitutes for a more conventional relationship. Simone de Beauvoir wrote voluminously to Nelson Algren, yet repeatedly declined his pressing proposals of marriage out of feelings of obligation, she says, to "poor Sartre." In the twelfth century, Héloïse and Abelard sustained their relationship through love letters after God (and the more immediate powers-that-be) ordained they be apart. Separation can derive from either intractable or flimsy reasons—Héloïse's convent-prison, Beauvoir's Sartre—but it must be there. Sometimes, indeed, the participants suspect that their love can survive only in letters and only because the lovers are apart in life. Just try to imagine Simone de Beauvoir as "Mrs. Nelson Algren of Chicago, Illinois."

2) *The love letter is a performance.*

The love letter is the surrogate for the missing self. It is also its own kind of sex. We can call it literal sex. As with all other varieties, technique is essential. A love letter can't just mean but also has to *be.* In some very real sense, every lover is a poet and every poet a lover. "I wish I had the gift of making rhymes, for methinks there is poetry in my head and heart since I have been in love with you," Nathaniel Hawthorne wrote Sophia Peabody. "You are a poem. Of what sort, then? Epic? Mercy on me, no! A sonnet? No; for that is too labored and artificial. You are a sort of sweet, simple, gay, pathetic ballad, which is nature singing."

As in a performance, the audience, too, has certain expectations for a love letter. The lover wants an opening night gala—not the dress rehearsal. Consider our own era's Hallmark cards with their soft-focus photographs and something pithily profound inside. Love Letters Ink, a California (of course) organization, has even made a business of writing love letters in calligraphy on fine handmade papers, while Computers On-Line will "message" a prepared love letter (even a Dear John) to a beloved's word processor. The point is that the language of a love letter must embody a kind of verbal foreplay. "I love you" is nice, but "I love you laughingly" (Henry Miller's line to Anaïs Nin) is much, much better. Love letters allow even those you'd least expect (perhaps especially those you'd least expect) to go all poetic in love. "The hour is already too big to become anything less than the biggest," Jack London, he-man of the arctic, adulterously wooed adventurer Charmian Kittredge. "We cannot fail, diminish, fall back into night with the dawn thus in our eyes."

3) *The love letter is an instant make-over.*

As in a before-and-after ad, the lover feels *changed* by the act and process of love. The love letter is the conduit of that change—like a face-lift or a health club membership. "I may be thinking of turnip greens with dumplings, of more royalty checks," Zora Neale Hurston wrote derisively about the blind romanticism of the lover, "and here is a man who visualizes me on a divan sending the world up in smoke."

But others do not view love quite so cynically. Many lovers feel renewed by love and record that rebirth in love letters. Part of the ritual of love letters is the rehearsal of the life B.L. and A.L. (Before Love and After Love). Nothing made sense before; I was a goner; now I am saved. Epiphanies, conversion experiences, even resurrections from the dead are part of the iconography of the love letter, as when Jean Toomer writes of his love for Margaret Naumburg: "Here was beauty. Here was wonder. Here was meaning . . . Here was the resurrection of my deepest life out [of] its long death." John Steinbeck tells Elaine Scott about how she revived him from "a kind of dark and deathly cynicism." Now, he writes, "the energy is washing back into me and I'm not dried up. I feel wonderful. . . . Good night, dear, I'll kick some worlds around now." Elizabeth Barrett writes to Robert Browning that "my life was ended when I knew you, & if I survive myself it is for your sake." Lazarus images figure prominently in love letters, as in Conrad Aiken's to Clarissa Lorenz: "You have no idea what you have done for me, and what you are still doing, and what I hope you will always do. I have come alive again, when I thought I was dead. I am Lazarus coming up out of his tomb, still with the cobwebs on him."

4) *The love letter transforms daily life.*

Love letters demand and enact transformation, metamorphosis. Nothing can be mundane for lovers; nor can love be mundane. E. L. Doctorow terms this the "lover's rhetoric of cosmic conviction." We are the world—no, the whole cosmos. (What lover hasn't started reading the daily horoscopes?) Narcissism, the unself-consciously self-conscious lovestruck narcissism of mutual attention, transforms the minutiae of one's everyday life into something suddenly significant and real. All the discrete incidents of life, however minor, are incorporated into a narrative of love—as if nothing in life matters but those love moments. "But I see you in many another unforgettable guise," Robert Schumann wrote to Clara Wieck in 1838, recasting earlier chance meetings into a catalogue of significant encounters fraught with now-revealed meaning. "Once you were in a black dress, going to the theatre with Emilia Liszt; it was during our separation. I know you will not have forgotten; it is vivid with me. Another time you were walking in the Thomasgasschen with an umbrella up, and you avoided me in desperation. And yet another time, as you were putting on your hat after a concert, our eyes happened to meet, and yours were full of the old unchanging love." Daily, mundane life is superseded by a master narrative of love in which otherwise discrete and meaningless events—wearing a black dress to the theater, walking in the park under an umbrella, putting on a hat after a concert— are all connected, all transformed by the story of love. The person in love finds that everything, all the details of life, have a purpose, a teleology that suddenly makes life explicable. This is one reason why love is so intoxicating, so consuming, and why writers as disparate as Victor Hugo, Emily Dickinson, T. S. Eliot, and Maya Angelou have all compared love to religion.

The smallest actions are imbued with love: "I began observing all sorts of little details in a way that I had not done for eight years," Conrad Aiken wrote to Clarissa ("Joan") Lorenz. "There was only one thin blanket on my bed, and I thought, 'What fun to find another blanket in the bureau and spread it out on the bed, and then afterwards to tell Joan about it!' " And the greatest are subsumed by love: "If I am moving away from you with the speed of the Rhone torrent," writes Napoléon to Josephine on his way to Moscow, "it is only that I may see you again more quickly."

5) *The love letter is timeless.*

Virtually every writer has noted how time disappears during the creative process, as if the imagined universe of the work-in-progress is the only world that exists, suspended and timeless and crucial in the midst of the mundane. Like love. *Exactly* like love.

Love, like writing, subsumes quotidian events and usurps clock time, yearning instead for infinity. Love Time becomes real time for lovers; the only measure of existence is the moment's desire. For Katherine Anne Porter, Love Time is the test of love's authenticity: "Love that does not touch the whole life of the lovers is nothing. Love that can put itself off until all the other business of life is settled is not love at all, it is a mere convenience of emotion." Business? Agendas? Schedules? Time? "While I sit here writing to you," Katherine Mansfield wrote John Middleton Murry, "time is not."

Keats distills this sense of love's eternal timelessness into one of the most beautiful images in any love letter: "I want a brighter word than bright, a fairer word than fair," he wrote to Fanny Brawne. "I almost wish we were butterflies and liv'd but three summer days— three such days with you I could fill with more delight than fifty common years could ever contain." Fanny herself well might have preferred the fifty common years. But for the Romantic poet the epiphanic moment is all that counts, for catharsis craves excess and love depends on butterflies.

6) *The love letter erases difference.*

In the best love letters, difference, like distance, disappears. The writer and the recipient speak as if one. "You are the voice," is the way Wallace Stevens voiced his identification with Elsie Moll. Gertrude Stein explored this idea in her "autobiographical" writings about Alice B. Toklas:

> I love she
> she is adorably me.
> When it is she
> she is me.
> She embroiders
> beautifully.

Sometimes the shared voice is not just poetic but almost literal, as with Walt Whitman and Fred Vaughan, one of Whitman's nonliterary (and at first barely literate) lovers. In teaching Vaughan to read and write, Whitman also taught him to love—and vice versa. The remarkable harmony of the two voices is not coincidental. Fred Vaughan sounds like Whitman in his letters, and, in turn, Whitman was inspired by the simple eloquence of Vaughn's love letters when he wrote his poetry. A decade after Vaughn's marriage, he wrote to Whitman:

> There is never a day passes but what I think of you. So much
> that you left to be remembered by a Broadway stage—a Fulton
> ferry boat, a bale of cotton on the dock. The "Brooklyn Daily
> Times"—a ship loading or unloading at the wharf. —a poor
> man fallen from the roof of a new building, a woman & child
> suffocated by smoke in a burning tenement house. All—all
> speak to me of thee Dear Walt.

The point here is that love is such a powerful identifying force that the lover feels doubled by love—twice as good, twice as powerful, twice as wise, and, of course, twice as skillful a writer as ever before. Hemingway said as much to Katherine Anne Porter, who responded, more realistically: "I don't know whether you write better [when you're in love], but you feel so good you think you're writing better!"

7) *The* cogito *of the love letter is: "I write, therefore you are."*

The downside of passionate identification is loss of identity. The famous Cartesian *cogito* ("I think therefore I am") becomes the lover's "I write, therefore you are." The resulting love can be dangerous, even obliterating, for the Beloved. The young poet Anne Gray Harvey (later Anne Sexton) once wrote to an older poet on whom she had a crush: "I am glad that you wrote me. I thought I had died or something"; and then a decade later she wrote to a younger poet who was infatuated with her: "Yes we love each other—but it's a mirror—of sorts—it's the male of the female and the female of the male. In other words, you're me. Also, I'm you." Or Anaïs Nin could write to June Miller: "You carry away with you a reflection of me, a part of me. I dreamed you, I wished for your existence." In a far more extreme version, Julie de l'Espinasse equated her life with her love, insisting that she loved Hippolyte de Guibert "to excess, to distraction, with rapture, with despair." When he married another woman, she wasted away and died: "By what fatality have you held me to life, and now you make me die of anxiety and of pain?"

Keats feared the unhealthy longings of his readers. "I have met with women," Keats laments to Fanny Brawne, "whom I really think would like to be married to a Poem and to be given away by a Novel." But more often it is the writer who objectifies the Beloved, preferring a muse to a person. Especially where one partner in the love affair is a professional writer and the other not, it can sometimes feel as if the nonwriter is being swallowed whole, allowed existence only as the emanation of the writer's imagination. The Beloved gets projected as some fantasy of the lover, a player in a larger literary work created by the lover in her or his letters. Byron and Goethe, to name two prominent examples, were "serial lovers" who recreated the same mythical Beloved in letters directed to very different women, abandoning woman after woman in the quest for the ideal woman of their literary dreams. "Writers make love," Anaïs Nin wrote in her diary, "to whatever they need."

Not surprisingly, many love affairs in this mode end when the real Beloved fails to meet the expectations of the creating lover, or when the Beloved finally demands to be acknowledged as a person, not a fictional creation. For writers, the love gone bad can provide the pulsing poetic subject, the blood after the barbs. But what happens to the cast-off Beloved—no longer muse, no longer god or goddess, no longer Beloved, and without even literary consolations to salvage the remains? "The man I once loved is dead. This is a vampire," Harriet Shelley, eight months pregnant, wrote of her desolation in a letter to a friend. The image of having one's life sucked from one's body is apt in Harriet's case. Shelley had eloped with her when she was only sixteen; they lived a nomadic life together, and at one point he offered to "share" her with a friend; then in 1814 he abandoned her entirely when he ran off with Mary Godwin. Harriet did not recover. In 1816 she wrote a suicide note to her sister, with whom she entrusted her two small children: "Too wretched to exert myself, lowered in the opinion of everyone, why should I drag on a miserable existence?"

8) *Everyone who writes a love letter becomes a woman.*

When I began this book, I assumed that there would be a dramatic difference between the love letters written by women and those written by men. The more letters I read, the less I was able to generalize about female versus male ways of loving or expressing that love. Sadly, both sexes engage in their share of deceit, dishonesty, and betrayal. If I could make one generalization on the basis of gender, it is that when madly and passionately in love, *everyone* sounds the way we have come to expect women to sound.

The love letter is one of the few places in Western society where men are allowed—even required—to express the kind and intensity of emotion regularly expected from women. The love letter, above all, exposes vulnerability, openness. It is a laying of oneself bare to the Beloved and requires the dizzying courage to reveal oneself entirely to the lover, however worthy or unworthy that lover might prove to be. It is like a flaying of the soul.

In almost all other contexts, only women are called upon to be spiritually stripped, to expose the blood flowing through. The love letter allows men to act in this nakedly "female" manner. "The woman in me pleads, but my manhood reasons," Jack London (whose fiction did not exactly acknowledge feminine traits) demurs to Anna Strunsky. "Maybe I am having my menstrual period," the aged libertine Henry Miller confides to Brenda Venus. "Men have them too, you know, only when they do they bleed from all the pores in their body, and the brain included."

A number of male writers who rely on gender stereotypes in their fiction (the effusively cloying female, the silently aloof male) write love letters very much in the "feminine" mode. Even Hemingway—to go to the heart of the matter—can be gushy in his love letters in a way that no "Hemingway hero" would ever be. Writing to Pauline Pfeiffer, Hemingway complained that his separation from her resulted in "horrors at night and a black depression." In contrast to his macho, laconic Jake Barnes ("Isn't it pretty to think so?"), Hemingway often gives way to an epistolary torrent of spring.

Curiously, gender stereotypes submerged during the epistolary courtship sometimes emerge again with full force in the real-life aftermath of epistolary love. To simplify, when rejected in love, many women feel self-hatred; they internalize the rejection, blaming some (imagined or real) shortcoming in themselves. Being dumped—to put it bluntly—accentuates the culturally scripted inferior role for women and encourages stereotypically feminine feelings of submission and worthlessness. The rejected woman becomes the antithesis of the Promethean, powerful in-love woman who so often flourishes in love letters. Instead, she feels annihilated. For many women writers, an agonizing period of soul-searching must follow rejection; a healing must take place before the woman can find the self-esteem and equilibrium to write again. When she does begin to write again, it is sometimes to refigure the romance with a happier ending (or, as in *The Age of Innocence,* one less demeaning for the female protagonist).

By contrast, many (certainly not all) male writers use their torment as an immediate inspiration for writing. They cope with rejection by externalizing it, refusing blame, and writing it away. Some of the most misogynistic literature ever written has been inspired by a personal rejection (again it's hard not to think of Hemingway). Similarly, because men are usually encouraged to ignore the nuances of emotions, the male writer sometimes finds even his most devastating, humiliating love experience to be a *new* experience. It becomes "material." His response to the end of love then seems to work according to another cultural script: No pain, no gain.

Nor does gender remain invisible in a relationship that ends happily. Part of the love letter's rhetoric is the meeting and melding of souls, hearts, and minds, all of which implies an equality of the partners. Too often, once the marriage vows are pronounced the partnership gives way to the power prerogatives of "The Husband." The epistolary lover who was willing to defy all bounds for love devolves into the guy who wants his socks sorted and his dinner on time. As Margaret Atwood laments in *Lady Oracle*: "Is every Heathcliff a Linton in disguise?"

9) The primary relationship in love letters is between the letter writer and the page.

Just as a novel is written for readers but must on some more immediate and primary level meet the demands of the novelist (the novel's first audience), so, too, does the love letter also exist on its own, apart from the lover. A literary performance that transforms life, stops time, imagines the future, bridges difference, and privileges a vulnerability usually derided as "feminine," the love letter is also an ultimate work of art. Even amateurs know this—which is why anyone who has ever written a love letter knows the anxiety of waiting for the lover to receive it. "Did you get my letter?" we ask, anxious for some sign of appreciation. To extend the implicit analogy: If the lover is the artist and the letter is the art, then the Beloved is necessarily the critic.

This is perhaps why the ultimate end of a relationship is not just the requisite Dear John/Dear Jane letter, but also the request that one's own letters be returned. To be denied one's letters is to be denied part of one's self (and one's self's creation). After love ends, the Beloved now becomes entirely the critic. The letters testify only to failure. Yet all too frequently, the lover's urgent request that letters be returned is denied. Power? Nostalgia? Vindictiveness? The motives are many and mixed. Over and over, Wharton asked Fullerton to return her letters: "Can you arrange, some day next week—before Wednesday—to bring, or send, me such fragments of correspondence as still exist? In one sense, as I told you, my love of order makes me resent the way in which inanimate things survive their uses."

10) *Every reader of a love letter is a voyeur.*

And that means you and me, dear reader. As Wharton intuited, that "inanimate thing," the love letter, surviving its original purpose, does find a life of its own, as the letters in this volume amply attest. Divorced from their original, intimate context, which no outsider can ever fully fathom, devoid of the passion prompting the moment's expression, frozen in the official biographical account of the writer's life and *oeuvre*, love letters can sometimes seem pretty depressing, even grotesque. Reading the biographies and love letters of the Romantic poets, I began to wonder if any writer had ever managed to love wisely or well!

That, too, is partly why we read love letters. We read greedily, hoping that in reading of the joys and pains of others we might learn something about ourselves and possibly even find a validation for our own feelings. Or so we might rationalize our fascination with literary gossip. Sometimes writers know this. They are aware that their own lives (again think of the Romantic poets) are gigantic canvases there for all the public to see. Wharton was all too aware of the public's interest, which is why she feared the use to which her love letters might be put. Her friend Henry James was so afraid that his private life would become public record that he went from friend to friend, retrieving letters he had written, then ceremoniously burning them all. He also destroyed hundreds, maybe thousands, of letters written to him.

In the past, descendants of any number of writers decided which letters should be published. They often weeded out "personal" or "nonliterary" items such as love letters. In the present permissive era, however, progeny are more likely to publish scandalous letters, the ones most likely to sell. Yet still areas of decorum remain. Biographies of black writers sometimes emphasize the political or social significance of the work and downplay the emotional complexities of the life. A desire to counteract racist stereotypes about black sexuality as well as a desire to present positive role models often leads to an "authorized" presentation of the life far less candid than is the writer's own work. The same is also frequently true for women writers (of any race) who led sexually adventurous lives, and for writers who were gay. Timing is another factor. Rarely does one publish one's own love letters. Death makes revelation permissible. Since letters have receivers as well as senders, they are sometimes "sealed" (preserved at a library but not open to the public) for decades after a writer's death.

When *The Letters of John Cheever* was published, the man who received many of Cheever's most beautiful letters was left anonymous, designated only as "Dear ——— ." The blank signals more than privacy. It is a symbol of the personal violation that occurs when one's most intimate and vulnerable self is put on display for anyone willing to plunk down the price of the book. Emma Goldman expressed it best. Asked if she might consider making public any of the passionate letters she had written to her lover Ben Reitman, Goldman adamantly refused. It would be, she said, "like tearing off my clothes."

Yet there are cases in which privacy hardly seems to be at issue. In some love letters, it even seems as if *we*—the reading public—were the intended audience all along. We may be voyeurs, but sometimes the lover-writer is the impresario of the literary peep show. The writer knows that his or her "papers" are valuable and will eventually be sold to libraries, pored over by biographers, and finally published. The letters have about them a posturing, an exhibitionism. Ford Madox Ford is as good an example as any. It is hard not to be cynical about his love life. He seemed to manufacture his various (and usually messy) affairs at least as much for the letters and literature they would produce as for more direct, emotional reasons. With precisely such economy in mind, he once advised Hemingway that a man "should always write a letter thinking of posterity." It was a sentiment that angered Hemingway so much that Hemingway went home and "burned every letter in the flat including Ford's."

~

The love letter, I have suggested, is a form of literature. It is a genre whose language may have changed over the past two thousand years but whose basic form and content remains the same. Because of the universal quality of the love letter, I have arranged the following examples as if they are all part of one romance, a romance in which any of us may have once (or more than once) played our own part.

Chapter One of *The Book of Love* presents letters about "Falling in Love." Historically, the letters span the era from Sappho to John Cheever; that is, from mid–seventh century B.C. to 1977. Emotionally, the distance is smaller. Sappho writes to Anactoria, a woman about whom nothing is now remembered. For Sappho, Anactoria was one "whose footfall I would rather hear" and "brightness of whose shining face I would rather see than all the chariots and mail-clad footmen of Lydia." Coincidentally, we know nothing of Cheever's lover either, not even his name. All we know is how Cheever feels about a young man who can "lift from my shoulders, an aloneness that I was happy to lose. . . . I wanted only that you be there."

Chapter Two fleshes out the story of romance's progress by documenting "Love's Infinite Variety," the many different kinds of love expressed in letters. Love triangles, passionate affairs, and tender marriages are the subject of different letters. In addition, there are letters written by people who love each other exclusively in letters rather than in person ("Epistolary Love"), letters written across the generational divide ("December Love"), letters between friends, and letters between parents and children. When Herman Melville writes to his friend and mentor Nathaniel Hawthorne, the love he expresses is no less passionate for being Platonic: "Your heart beat in my ribs and mine in yours, and both in God's." The nineteenth century's "female world of love and ritual" that historian Carroll Smith-Rosenberg has described was also a world of passionate friendships and rapturous letters. Molly Hallock Foote wrote to her friend Helena DeKay Gilder: "I wanted so to put my arms round my girl of all the girls in the world and tell her . . . I love her as wives do love their husbands, as *friends* who have taken each other for life—and believe in her as I believe in my God."

The third chapter of *The Book of Love* resumes the progress of a universal love affair with letters about absence—sometimes unavoidable, sometimes carefully contrived; sometimes welcome, other times deeply tragic. Even those whose love lasts must some day face the death of a loved one. As Vita Sackville-West wrote to Harold Nicolson, to whom she had been married for nearly fifty years: "In our advancing years we love each other more deeply than ever, and also more agonizingly, since we see the inevitable end. It is not nice to know that one of us must die before the other." The letters in "The Final Separation" are certainly among the most moving in this collection.

"Love Hurts," Chapter Four, charts the many ways in which love can go wrong, while Chapter Five, "The End of Love," includes ritual "Dear John/Dear Jane" notes, anguished letters by those who have been "Betrayed and Abandoned," and philosophical letters by those who reflect back upon the end of a love affair and who strive to get their lives in order again. Such a grim, brave note is not the one on which this romance ends, however. A final chapter, "Falling in Love Again," tells the story of those who have loved and lost but dared to take another turn.

Arranged here as one continuous narrative charting the evolution and devolution of love, these love letters explore the reasons we are willing to stake so much—our selves—on little more than a promise and an act of faith. The course of true love never did run smooth, and neither did the course of love letters. But what I am suggesting is that the course has been run many times by many runners, and, given the chance, who wouldn't round the track again? Even the most decimated of lovers in this collection might admit the wisdom of Tennyson's adage about its being better to have loved and lost than never to have loved at all. As William Faulkner once wrote, "Between grief and nothing, I would choose grief."

These letters document the swirl of emotions that characterizes literary love letters and energizes both love and art. It's a heady combination, as Colette—one of the world's greatest literary lovers—knew full well. "What am I doing?" she asked incredulously, late in her life and on the brink of yet another love affair. "What am I doing? Heavens, I'm spinning."

1

FALLING IN LOVE

Sappho to
Anactoria

Sappho was born in the mid–seventh century B.C. on the isle of
Lesbos, Greece. In an era when lyric poetry was considered the highest, most demanding art, she was known as the form's foremost prac-
titioner, and poets came from all over the ancient world to study with
her. Hundreds of years after her death, Alexandrine scholars carefully
studied her poems, dividing the body of her work into nine volumes
according to different metric patterns. After a great fire destroyed the
library at Alexandria, virtually all of her poetry was lost. Today only
fragments of her poetry, written on papyrus, survive.

Relatively little is known of Sappho's life and virtually nothing of
the women to whom she addressed her famous letters and verse. We
know she was married to a wealthy man and had a daughter, Clais. It
is speculated that political turmoil on Lesbos forced her to flee the
island. The remainder of her life was spent in Sicily, where she was
surrounded by other poets, mostly young women who came to study
with her. Dismayed that her powerful expressions of love were addressed to women, later Athenian writers insinuated that Sappho
passed her days in Sicily in an endless lesbian orgy, while they also
invented the (seemingly contradictory) fable that she once threw herself from a high cliff, all for unrequited love of a local boatman. Neither story is based on the slightest evidence or testimony from Sappho's time.

Subsequent generations of poets have been far less concerned than
the Athenians that the "greatest poet of antiquity" was a lesbian, and,
indeed, many generations of poets have found in Sappho's verse an
inspiration for their own. As one Victorian scholar summarized, "For
about two thousand five hundred years Sappho has held her place as

. . . the chief lyrist of all lyrists." Another nineteenth-century scholar continues: "Never before these songs were sung, and never since did the human soul, in the grip of a fiery passion, utter a cry like hers." But Elizabeth Barrett Browning wrote most tellingly:

> Sappho . . . broke off a fragment of her soul
> for us to guess at.

Mid–Seventh Century B.C.

Some say that the fairest thing upon the dark earth is a host of foot-soldiers, and others again a fleet of ships, but for me it is my beloved. And it is easy to make anyone understand this.

When Helen saw the most beautiful of mortals, she chose for best that one, the destroyer of all the house of Troy, and thought not much of children or dear parent but was led astray by love to bestow her heart far off for woman is ever easy to lead astray when she thinks of no account what is near and dear.

Even so, Anactoria, you do not remember, it seems, when she is with you, one the gentle sound of whose footfall I would rather hear and the brightness of whose shining face I would rather see than all the chariots and mail-clad footmen of Lydia.

I know that in this world humans cannot have the best yet to pray for a part of what was once shared is better than to forget it.

James Hackman to Martha Reay

In 1780 a small book of love letters became the literary sensation of England. The letters recount the illicit love between James Hackman, a Cambridge graduate who went on to become a clergyman, and Martha Reay, the mistress of Lord Sandwich and one of the most charming and accomplished musicians, conversationalists, and hostesses of her day. She first encountered Hackman at one of the musicales in which she performed with Lord Sandwich (she singing and playing the piano, the earl sometimes accompanying on the kettle drums). Soon the two were in love. Hackman wanted her to leave the earl. She liked the physical comforts of her life and was also concerned about the welfare of her children, but entertained a fantasy of running off with Hackman and joining the operatic stage. She stalled; his letters became increasingly urgent, hyperbolic, and even morbid. He put pressure on her to leave. Finally, she decided to refuse his offer of marriage and leave town for a while, hoping it would all blow over.

Hackman resolved on suicide. He followed her to a performance of the opera *Love in a Village*, where he planned to "die at her feet." However, when he saw that she was being attended by the handsome Lord Coleraine, Hackman became enraged with jealousy and shot her in the forehead before turning his gun on himself. He botched the job by half and proceeded to lie on the ground, beating his head with the butt of his pistol and crying out that he wanted only to die. No use. The wound was superficial. He was taken off to Newgate Prison, condemned to death by the famous Judge Blackstone, and finally executed for murder before an enormous crowd that included many of the literati of eighteenth-century England. A number of the witnesses went on to write their own accounts of this epistolary courtship that seemed to hover somewhere between tragedy and farce.

Huntingdon, Dec. 13, 1775.

My life and soul!

But I will never more use any preface of this sort, and I beg you will not. A correspondence begins with dear, then my dear, dearest, my dearest, and so on, till at last panting language toils after us in vain.

No language can explain my feelings. Oh, M. yesterday, yesterday! Language, thou liest; there is no such word as *satiety*, positively no such word. Oh thou, beyond my warmest dreams bewitching! What charms! What—

But words would poorly paint our joys. When, when?—yet

you shall order, govern everything. Only remember, I am *sure* of those we trust.

Are you now convinced that Heaven made us for each other? By that Heaven, by the paradise of your dear arms, I will be only yours!

Have I written sense? I know not what I write. This scrap of paper (it is all I can find) will hold a line or two more. I must fill it up to say that, whatever evils envious fate designed me, after those few hours of yesterday, I never will complain nor murmur.

Misfortune, I defy thee now. M. loves me, and H's soul has its content most absolute. No other joy like this succeeds in unknown fate.

John Keats to Fanny Brawne

The couple met in 1818 when Keats, grieving from the death of his brother Tom from tuberculosis, went to live with a friend in Hampstead, just north of London. Fanny Brawne lived next door. At first he thought her "graceful, silly, fashionable, and strange." Soon, he was madly in love with her. "I cry your mercy—pity—love—aye, love!" he wrote in his "Lines to Fanny." "Withhold no atom's atom, or I die."

Although Keats's love for Fanny Brawne inspired some of the most beautiful poetry in the English language, it was ill-fated from the start. The thoroughly middle-class Brawne family was not exhilarated to discover that their daughter was falling in love with the thin little neighbor with the persistent cough and the inexplicable predilection for verse. The son of a livery stable manager, Keats had abandoned a career as an apothecary-surgeon to devote himself to poetry. Yes, he had published his first volume of verse in 1817, before his twenty-second birthday. Yes, he was making something of a reputation for himself among a small circle of English literati. But who would want their daughter to marry a penniless, tubercular poet?

The couple was engaged in the winter of 1819, but their relationship was fraught with worry and indecision, exacerbated by his money and health problems and her family's persistent objections. Keats's own sense of pride made him reject the idea of marriage until he could support a family. He tried writing for the literary magazines to raise money; he considered resuming his medical career. But his health declined rapidly, and he set off to Italy for a cure, expecting never to see Fanny again. Plagued by a cough, a sore throat, and breathing problems, brokenhearted and by no means famous, Keats composed an epitaph to his brief, unhappy life: "Here lies one whose name was writ in water." He died on February 23, 1821, not yet twenty-five years of age.

Life, Letters and Literary Remains of John Keats was published in 1848 as a posthumous celebration of one of the great Romantic poets. Among the letters in this volume were those Keats wrote to Fanny Brawne. Matthew Arnold sniffed that they revealed "the abandonment of all reticence and dignity, of the merely sensuous man, of the man 'who is passion's slave,' " yet these love letters are now regarded as among the most beautiful ever written, as fine as many of Keats's sonnets.

Love, death, and beauty are themes running throughout Keats's poetry. Reading the Fanny Brawne letters personalizes Keats's poetry, giving even the most familiar lines an almost unbearable poignancy:

> A thing of beauty is a joy for ever:
> Its loveliness increases; it will never
> Pass into nothingness; but still will keep
> A bower quiet for us, and a sleep
> Full of sweet dreams, and health, and quiet breathing.

July 8, 1819.

My sweet girl—

Your Letter gave me more delight than any other thing in the world but yourself could do; indeed I am almost astonished that any absent one should have that luxurious power over my senses which I feel. Even when I am not thinking of you I receive your influence and a tenderer nature stealing upon me. All my thoughts, my unhappiest days and nights, have I find not at all cured me of my love of Beauty, but made it so intense that I am miserable that you are not with me: or rather breathe in that dull sort of patience that cannot be called Life.

I never knew before, what such a love as you have made me feel, was; I did not believe in it; my Fancy was afraid of it, lest it should burn me up. But if you will fully love me, though there may be some fire, 't will not be more than we can bear when moistened and bedewed with Pleasures.

You mention 'horrid people' and ask me whether it depend upon them whether I see you again. Do understand me, my love, in this. I have so much of you in my heart that I must turn Mentor when I see a chance of harm befalling you. I would never see any thing but Pleasure in your eyes, love on your lips, and Happiness in your steps. I would wish to see you among those amusements suitable to your inclinations and spirits; so that our loves might be a delight in the midst of Pleasures agreeable enough, rather than a resource from vexations and cares. But I doubt much, in case of the worst, whether I shall be philosopher enough to follow my own Lessons: if I saw my resolution give you a pain I could not.

Why may I not speak of your Beauty, since without that I could never have lov'd you?—I cannot conceive any beginning of such love as I have for you but Beauty. There may be a sort of love for which, without the least sneer at it, I have the highest respect and can admire it in others: but it has not the richness, the bloom, the full form, the enchantment of love after my own heart.

So let me speak of your Beauty, though to my own endangering; if you could be so cruel to me as to try elsewhere its Power. You say you are afraid I shall think you do not love me—in saying this you make me ache the more to be near you. I am at the diligent use of my faculties here, I do not pass a day without sprawling some blank verse or tagging some rhymes; and here I must confess, that (since I am on that subject) I love you the more in that I believe you have liked me for my own sake and for nothing else. I have met with women whom I really think would like to be married to a Poem and to be given away by a Novel. I have seen your Comet, and only wish it was a sign that poor Rice [Keats's friend] would get well whose illness makes him rather a melancholy companion: and the more so as to conquer his feelings and hide them from me, with a forc'd Pun.

I kiss'd your writing over in the hope you had indulg'd me by leaving a trace of honey. What was your dream? Tell it me and I will tell you the interpretation thereof.

Ever yours, my love!
John Keats

Do not accuse me of delay—we have not here an opportunity of sending letters every day. Write speedily.

Nathaniel Hawthorne to Sophia Peabody

Nathaniel Hawthorne first came to the Peabody house in 1837 at the invitation of Elizabeth Palmer Peabody, a well-known Transcendentalist who admired Hawthorne's stories. At the time he was still holed up in his mother's attic, writing but not much engaged in the literary life of the time. He began a correspondence (no longer extant) with Elizabeth in 1838–39 but was horrified by the bustle of her intellectual and social activities and by her obvious designs to make him part of her Transcendentalist circle. Possibly, she anticipated a proposal from Nathaniel, but it was to her quiet, serene, sickly younger sister, Sophia, that Hawthorne felt himself drawn.

Like many nineteenth-century middle-class women, Sophia used invalidism to escape a tedious round of social duties. In the privacy of her chamber, she read, painted, and sculpted. She was also a gifted writer. Her accounts of living on a plantation in Cuba were regarded as "gentle masterpieces" by the Peabody family and their literary friends, and were shown to Nathaniel in the course of his visits to the Peabody house. He copied passages from Sophia's journal into his notebook. They exchanged letters. They continued to meet. Soon these two shy, almost reclusive people were passionately in love.

Although Nathaniel admired Sophia's writing, after marriage he forbade her from publishing her work, insisting that such a public display betokened immodesty in a woman. Sophia complied with his request. Even when publisher James T. Fields urged her to publish, she obeyed her husband's wishes. Hawthorne didn't want a writer; he wanted a muse. Sophia became the prototype for the pale, delicate, virtuous, sexless, submissive domestic heroines idealized in his stories and novels.

After many years of marriage, he said to their maid, "I have yet to find a fault in Mrs. Hawthorne." But one wonders if Sophia found any faults in him. Did she like her role as dutiful helpmeet? Or did she secretly yearn to be more like Hester Prynne, the luxuriantly sexual and proudly rebellious adulteress who wears the scarlet "A" in Hawthorne's most famous novel?

After her husband's death in 1864, Sophia sought to remedy her financial woes by publishing a book of her own, *Notes in England and Italy* (1869). It's hard to be a full-time muse.

Boston, July 24th, 1839 — 8 o'clock P.M.

Mine Own,

I am tired this evening, as usual, with my long day's toil; and my head wants its pillow—and my soul yearns for the friend whom God has given it—whose soul He has married to my soul. Oh, my dearest, how that thought thrills me! We *are* married! I felt it long ago; and sometimes, when I was seeking for some fondest word, it has been on my lips to call you— 'Wife'! I hardly know what restrained me from speaking it— unless a dread (for *that* would have been an infinite pang to me) of feeling you shrink back from my bosom, and thereby discovering that there was yet a deep place in your soul which did not know me.

Mine own Dove, need I fear it now? Are we not married? God knows we are. Often, while holding you in my arms, I have silently given myself to you, and received you for my portion of human love and happiness, and have prayed Him to consecrate and bless the union. And any one of our innocent embraces—even when our lips did but touch for a moment, and then were withdrawn—dearest, was it not the symbol of a bond between our Souls, infinitely stronger than any external rite could twine around us?

Yes—we are married; and as God Himself has joined us, we may trust never to be separated, neither in Heaven nor on Earth. We will wait patiently and quietly, and He will lead us onward hand in hand (as He has done all along) like little children, and will guide us to our perfect happiness—and will teach us when our union is to be revealed to the world. My beloved, why should we be silent to one another—why should our lips be silent—any longer on this subject? The world might, as yet, misjudge us; and therefore we will not speak to the world; but when I hold you in my arms, why should we not commune together about all our hopes of earthly and external, as well as our faith of inward and eternal union?

Farewell for to-night, my dearest—my soul's bride! Oh, my heart is thirsty for your kisses; they are the dew which should restore its freshness every night, when the hot sunshiny day has parched it. Kiss me in your dreams; and perhaps my heart will feel it.

Gustave Flaubert to Louise Colet

Gustave Flaubert came to the studio of sculptor James Pradier in order to deliver the death mask of his sister Caroline. He was deeply depressed by her death as well as by the recent death of his father. In the studio that day, posing for the sculptor, was the beautiful, talented, articulate, and rebellious poet Louise Colet. Their meeting, Flaubert said, was "predestined." He was attracted to the "ringlets dancing on your white shoulders, your blue dress, your arms, your face, your everything." The two went off together for a few days before he returned to his home in Croisset, and therein ensued a passionate exchange of letters.

Flaubert had sworn off love before he turned twenty-five, "then

[Colet] came along and with the touch of a fingertip stirred every-thing up again." Flaubert's letters to Colet are the only erotic letters that he is known to have written. Except for these, his most open demonstrations of affection were reserved for his male friends. And considering the realistic, if not downright cynical, view of love in his most famous novel, *Madame Bovary* (1856), it is not surprising that in the exchange with Colet, Flaubert was deeply ambivalent about his attraction to her, even resentful.

He wrote her over two hundred letters. She made it clear that she would have preferred less correspondence and more love. Avoiding her physical presence, he used their epistolary exchange to fuel the furious and often painful writing of his novel. He filled her in on all the anguished details of fictional composition, and she soon came to realize that the novel had become her rival for his attentions.

Cynical about love, Flaubert was fully devoted to his art. "What seems to me the highest and most difficult achievement of Art," he wrote to Colet a year before the publication of *Madame Bovary*, "is not to make us laugh or cry, nor to arouse our lust or rage, but to do what nature does—that is, to set us dreaming."

Tuesday midnight
Croisset, August 4–5, 1846

Twelve hours ago we were still together, and at this very moment yesterday I was holding you in my arms! Do you remember? How long ago it seems! Now the night is soft and warm; I can hear the great tulip tree under my window rustling in the wind, and when I lift my head I see the moon reflected in the river. Your little slippers are in front of me as I write; I keep looking at them.

Here, locked away by myself I have just put away everything you gave me. Your two letters are in the little embroidered bag, and I am going to reread them as soon as I have sealed mine. I am not writing to you on my ordinary writing-paper—that is edged with black and I want nothing sad to pass from me to you. I want to cause you nothing but joy, and to surround you with a calm, endless bliss—to repay you a little for the overflowing generosity of the love you have given me.

I am afraid of being cold, arid, selfish—and yet, God can see

what is going on within me at this moment. What memories!
And what desire! Ah! Our two marvelous carriage rides; how
beautiful they were, particularly the second, with the lightning
flashes above us. I keep remembering the color of the trees lit
by the streetlights, and the swaying motion of the springs. We
were alone, happy: I kept staring at you, and even in the
darkness your whole face seemed illumined by your eyes.

I feel I am writing badly—you will read this without
emotion—I am saying nothing of what I want to say. My
sentences run together like sighs, to understand them you will
have to supply what should go between. You will do that, won't
you? Every letter, every turn of my handwriting will set you
dreaming? The way the sight of your little brown slippers
makes me dream of the movements of your feet when they
were in them, when the slippers were warm from them. The
handkerchief, too, is there; I see your blood. I wish it were
completely red with it.

My mother was waiting for me at the station. She wept at
seeing me return. You wept to see me leave. In other words,
such is our sad fate that we cannot move a league without
causing tears on two sides at once! Grotesque and sombre
thought! Here the grass is still green, the trees are as full, the
river as placid, as when I left; my books are open at the same
pages; nothing is changed. External nature shames us, her
serenity is a rebuke to our pride. No matter—let us think of
nothing, neither of the future nor of ourselves, for to think is
to suffer. Let the tempest in our hearts blow us where it will at
full sail, and as for reefs—we'll simply have to take our chance
with them.

. . . On the train I read almost an entire volume. More than
one passage moved me, but of that I will talk with you more
fully later. As you can well see, I am unable to concentrate.
Tonight I am far from being a critic. I wanted only to send you
another kiss before sleeping, to tell you I love you. No sooner
had I left you—and increasingly as I was borne further and
further away—than my thoughts flew back towards you, more
swiftly even than the smoke I saw billowing back from the
train. (My metaphor implies the idea of fire: forgive the

allusion.) Here: a kiss, quickly—you know the kind—the kind Ariosto speaks of—and another, and another! Still another, and finally one more just under your chin on the spot I love, where your skin is so soft, and another on your breast, where I lay my heart. Adieu, adieu. All my love.

Juliette Drouet to Victor Hugo

Over the course of an affair that lasted for fifty (yes *fifty*) years, Juliette Drouet wrote Victor Hugo over twenty thousand letters, enough to fill forty or fifty volumes. From any ordinary perspective, it would seem that she gave up everything for him. Her missives document her time in the cramped quarters she lived in after Hugo, in his jealousy, forced her to choose between him and her successful career on the stage. Certainly his output as one of France's most prolific poets and novelists (*Les Misérables* is probably his best known work) is matched by her enormous body of beautiful letters, some of them masterpieces of the love letter genre. The difference, of course, is that he enjoyed fame and fortune; she passed her time writing letters to him and waiting for him to visit.

Besides writing letters, her chief occupation was keeping detailed records of every franc she spent, accounts that Hugo scrutinized. She lived on eggs, milk, bread, cheese, and apples, except when he came to dinner, at which time she tried to prepare an elegant table. Sometimes she told her maid that there was not even enough money to buy firewood. Yet Hugo claimed that he gave her up to six or seven hundred francs a month, which he later raised to a thousand francs, far more than she ever actually spent. Hers was a strange, almost monastic life based on a complicated, inexplicable form of love. She helped him to flee France when his political writings were condemned by Napoléon III during the Second Empire. He took his wife and family into exile, with Juliette settling nearby (this letter, for example, is written during their time on Jersey). He had other affairs; she eventually became friends with his wife and children. He dedicated poems to her. And she wrote thousands and thousands of extraordinary, sometimes even exquisite letters, letters that were, in a very real sense, both her life and her passion. In her last letter to Hugo, dated January 1, 1883, and addressed to "Dear adored one," she wrote: "I do not know where I may be this time next year but I am proud and happy to sign my life-certificate for 1883 with this phrase: I love you."

8 A.M., Monday, December 29th, 1852.
JERSEY.

Good morning, my too dearly loved little man. I am cleverer than you, for I do not need lenses, paper, chemicals, and sunshine, to reproduce you in every form within my heart. Love is a splendid stereoscope; it throws all the photographs and daguerreotypes in the world into the shade. It can even, if the need exist, convert black jealousy into white confidence, and force into relief the smallest modicum of happiness, the slightest mark of love. That being so, I hardly know why I desire so ardently to multiply your dear little pictures around me, unless it is that I wish to compare them with those of my inner shrine. Whatever be the reason, I do implore you, my dear little man, to give me one as soon as possible; it will be such a pleasure to me. Meanwhile, my poor persecuted hero, I cannot tell what trials the future may have in store for you, but I know that as long as a breath of life remains within me I mean to expend it in defending, guarding, and serving you. My faith in the power of my love amounts to superstition; I feel that so long as I care for you, nothing irretrievably bad can happen to you. This is neither pride nor fatuousness on my part; it is a sort of intuition that comes to me I think from Heaven above.

JULIETTE.

Oscar Wilde to Lord Alfred Douglas

Born in 1854, Oscar Fingal O'Flahertie Wills Wilde was the son of Sir William Wilde, an Irish surgeon, and Jane Francesca Elgee, a writer and literary hostess who wrote under the name "Speranza." He studied classics at Trinity College, Dublin, then at Magdalen College, Oxford, and early impressed his teachers and peers with the dazzling wit and incisive brilliance that continues to fascinate readers today.

In 1884 Wilde married Constance Mary Lloyd: "I am going to be married to a beautiful girl called Constance Lloyd, a grave, slight, violet-eyed little Artemis, with great coils of heavy brown hair which make her flower-like head drop like a blossom, and wonderful ivory hands which draw music from the piano so sweet that the birds stop singing to listen to her."

Love faded quickly, partly because Constance had two pregnancies soon after they were married, both of which kept her in bed with morning sickness (which Wilde found disgusting), and in quick succession bore two sons (when he hoped for a girl). He became a popular writer and epigrammist, the most famous literary celebrity of his day. Then, sometime in 1892, he fell in love with Lord Alfred Douglas. Biographer Richard Ellmann summarizes: "Wilde wanted a consuming passion; he got it and was consumed by it."

Early on someone tried to blackmail Wilde for love letters he wrote to Douglas and that Douglas, with characteristic carelessness, left in the pocket of a suit of clothes that he gave away. Theirs was, to quote Wilde's famous line, "the love that dare not speak its name," yet Douglas could be indiscreet and even boastful about his affair with the writer.

For Wilde the consequences were disastrous. Seeking to blame Wilde for his son's manifest imperfections, Lord Alfred's father, John Sholto Douglas, ninth Marquess of Queensberry, publicly insulted Wilde. Wilde took umbrage and, at Lord Alfred's instigation, sued him for criminal libel, a foolhardy move since by English law a defendant in a libel suit must enter a formal plea of justification. Queensberry used his plea of justification as an opportunity to accuse Wilde of twelve counts of sodomy; he also charged him with immorality in works such as *The Picture of Dorian Gray* (1891).

"In your war of hate with your father," Wilde wrote to Douglas from prison after losing both the libel suit and the following criminal prosecution for sodomy, "I was at once shield and weapon to each of you." From beginning to end, Douglas proved to be vain and selfish, reckless and cowardly, yet Wilde was too much in love to pay attention. "What a silly thing love is!" Wilde once wrote. "It is not half as useful as logic, for it does not prove anything and it is always telling one things that are not going to happen, and making one believe things that are not true."

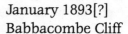

January 1893[?]
Babbacombe Cliff

My Own Boy,

Your sonnet is quite lovely, and it is a marvel that those red rose-leaf lips of yours should have been made no less for music of song than for madness of kisses. Your slim gilt soul walks between passion and poetry. I know Hyacinthus, whom Apollo loved so madly, was you in Greek days.

Why are you alone in London, and when do you go to Salisbury? Do go there to cool your hands in the grey twilight of Gothic things, and come here whenever you like. It is a lovely place—it only lacks you; but go to Salisbury first. Always, with undying love, yours

OSCAR

Rosa Luxemburg to Leo Jogiches

In 1899, when Marxist political activist, theorist, and writer Rosa Luxemburg celebrated her twenty-eighth birthday, she received a flood of presents. None pleased her more than an edition of the works of German economist Rodbertus, a present from Leo Jogiches. Her thank-you note to Jogiches, reprinted here, was far more personal than the gift itself had been. From German economy she moved rapidly to thoughts of an apartment, a more permanent relationship, a child, a life together. The letter is especially touching, for it reminds us that a single-minded revolutionary can be tender and loving as well.

A German Jew, Luxemburg had differences with leading communists of her day (including Lenin) but nonetheless subscribed to the basic Marxist ideal of equitable distribution of property. Her relationship with the émigré revolutionary Leo Jogiches was often difficult, since he was every bit as bold, forceful, and strong-willed as she. A typical incident occurred when Rosa accepted the editorship of the *Sächische Arbeiterzeitung.* She wrote to him immediately; he telegrammed her to "decline unconditionally"; she went right ahead with her decision; he acquiesced—but only after considerable discussion.

Although their relationship ended in 1906, the two remained comrades, committed to the same political cause, until their macabre political executions in 1919. Both were members of *Spartakus,* a German collective deemed responsible for a popular Marxist uprising in Germany in 1919. The fascistic German *Freikorps* (forerunners of the Nazis) moved swiftly and brutally to put down the Marxists, murdering hundreds of workers and arresting Rosa Luxemburg along with other well-known figures in the *Spartakus* movement. Instead of a trial, Luxemburg was led from a hotel, smashed in the head with a rifle butt, and dragged into a waiting car. The officer in charge then shot her and had her corpse thrown off a bridge into the Landwehr Canal. In the several months before her body was found, popular myths arose that she had escaped, had gone underground, and was waiting for the right time to rise again. For some, the idea was frightening, for others a ray of hope in a grim and violent time.

After her death, Leo Jogiches sent an official telegram to Lenin. Luxemburg, he wrote, had "carried out [her] ultimate revolutionary duty." Although he was given an opportunity to escape from Germany, Jogiches decided to remain behind to work on her papers and to try to solve her murder. "Somebody," he said, "has to stay, at least to write all our epitaphs." He spoke too soon. A few weeks later he, too, was taken into police custody and shot in cold blood by a detective.

March 6, 1899

I kiss you a thousand times for your dearest letter and present, though I have not yet received it. . . . You simply cannot imagine how pleased I am with your choice. Why, Rodbertus is simply my favourite economist and I can read him a hundred times for sheer intellectual pleasure. . . . My dear, how you delighted me with your letter. I have read it six times from beginning to end. So, you are really pleased with me. You write that perhaps I only know inside me that somewhere there is a man who belongs to me! Don't you know that everything I do is always done with you in mind; when I write an article my first thought is — this will cause you pleasure — and when I have days when I doubt my own strength, and cannot work, my only fear is what effect this will have on you, that it might disappoint you. When I have proof of success, like a letter from Kautsky, this is simply my homage to you. I give you my word, as I loved my mother, that I am personally quite indifferent to what Kautsky writes. I was only pleased with it because I wrote it with your eyes and felt how much pleasure it would give you.

   . . . Only one thing nags at my contentment: the outward arrangements of your life and of our relationship. I feel that I will soon have such an established position here (morally) that we will be able to live together quite calmly, openly, as husband and wife. I am sure you understand this yourself. I am happy that the problem of your citizenship is at last coming to an end and that you are working energetically at your doctorate. I can feel from your recent letters that you are in a very good mood to work. . . . Do you think that I do not feel your value, that whenever the call to arms is sounded you always stand by me with help and encourage me to work — forgetting all the rows and all my neglect! . . . You have no idea with what joy and desire I wait for every letter from you because each one brings me so much strength and happiness and encourages me to live.

   I was happiest of all with that part of your letter where you write that we are both young and can still arrange our personal life. Oh darling, how I long that you may fulfil your promise. . . . Our own little room, our own furniture, a library of our own, quiet and regular work, walks together, an opera from time to time, a small—very small—circle of intimate friends who can sometimes be asked to dinner, every year a summer departure to the country for a month but definitely free from work! . . . And perhaps even a little, a very little, baby? Will this never be permitted? Never? Darling, do you know what accosted me yesterday during a walk in the park— and without any exaggeration? A little child, three or four years old, in a beautiful dress with blond hair; it stared at me and suddenly I felt an overpowering urge to kidnap the child and dash off home with him. Oh darling, will I never have my own baby?

And at home we will never argue again, will we? It must be quiet and peaceful as it is with everyone else. Only you know what worries me, I feel already so old and am not in the least attractive. You will not have an attractive wife when you walk hand in hand with her through the park—we will keep well away from the Germans. . . . Darling, if you will first settle the question of your citizenship, secondly your doctorate and thirdly live with me openly in our own room and work together with me, then we can want for nothing more! No couple on earth has so many facilities for happiness as you and I and if there is only some goodwill on our part we will be, must be, happy.

Jack London to Anna Strunsky

Born into poverty in San Francisco in 1876, Jack London became one of America's most popular writers as well as a kind of folk hero. He could include on his résumé seaman, coal shoveler, vagrant, labor organizer, jute-mill worker, hobo, Klondike adventurer, social activist, world traveler, international war correspondent, rancher, mayoral candidate, self-made millionaire, and author of such perennial favorites as "To Build a Fire," *The Call of the Wild*, *White Fang*, and *The Sea-Wolf*. London had an opinion about everything—and everyone had an opinion about him. President Teddy Roosevelt once denounced him as a "nature faker." Even London's death, at the age of forty, caused a scandal. Four physicians diagnosed natural causes, but a rumor persisted that he had taken a drug overdose. His death on November 22, 1916, received more attention in the American press than the death on the previous night of Emperor Franz Josef of Austria.

London's love life was in keeping with his impetuous and impassioned life. In 1900 he decided it was time to settle down, marrying Bessie Mae Maddern even as he insisted that he did not believe in love, but only in the procreation of strong, Anglo-Saxon offspring. Both before and after marriage, however, London wrote to the vivacious, dark-eyed Anna Strunsky, a writer and intellectual. The two collaborated on a treatise about love in the form of a fictitious correspondence, *The Kempton-Wace Letters* (1903), in which he took the materialist position of espousing marriage purely for mating purposes, while she played the idealist, insisting that love was life's essential requirement. Anna won the argument on two counts: she had the last word in the book, and perhaps predictably, London fell in love with her.

Although she was named the correspondent in London's separation from Bessie in 1904, Strunsky never played the traditional part of the "other woman." Apparently she never permitted a sexual consummation of their affair and insisted on calling off the romance altogether when she discovered that Bessie was pregnant for a second time. Yet, in a pattern that was typical for London, the two continued to be friends after their romance ended. She went on to marry someone else, but after London's death, delivered a touching tribute: "He was youth, adventure, romance. He was a poet and a social revolutionist. He had a genius for friendship. He loved greatly and was greatly beloved."

April 3/01.
Oakland

Dear Anna:—
Did I say that the human might be filed in categories? Well, and if I did, let me qualify—not all humans. You elude me. I

cannot place you, cannot grasp you. I may boast that of nine out of ten, under given circumstances, I can forecast their action; that of nine out of ten, by their word or action, I may feel the pulse of their hearts. But of the tenth I despair. It is beyond me. You are that tenth.

Were ever two souls, with dumb lips, more incongruously matched! We may feel in common—surely, we ofttimes do—and when we do not feel in common, yet do we understand; and yet we have no common tongue. Spoken words do not come to us. We are unintelligible. God must laugh at the mummery.

The one gleam of sanity through it all is that we are both large temperamentally, large enough to often understand. True, we often understand but in vague glimmering ways, by dim perceptions, like ghosts, which, while we doubt, haunt us with their truth. And still, I, for one, dare not believe; for you are that tenth which I may not forecast.

Am I unintelligible now? I do not know. I imagine so. I cannot find the common tongue.

Large temperamentally—that is it. It is the one thing that brings us at all in touch. We have, flashed through us, you and I, each a bit of the universal, and so we draw together. And yet we are so different.

I smile at you when you grow enthusiastic? It is a forgivable smile—nay, almost an envious smile. I have lived twenty-five years of repression. I learned not to be enthusiastic. It is a hard lesson to forget. I begin to forget, but it is so little. At the best, before I die, I cannot hope to forget all or most. I can exult, now that I am learning, in little things, in other things; but of my things, and secret things doubly mine, I cannot, I cannot. Do I make myself intelligible? Do you hear my voice? I fear not. There are poseurs. I am the most successful of them all.

Jack.

Edith Wharton to W. Morton Fullerton

W. Morton Fullerton, Harvard man and son of a minister, came to England to work for the London *Times* but was later transferred to the Paris bureau because of his excellent French. In France, he was every bit as popular as he was in England, where he was well known for the elegance with which he seduced both men and women.

When she met Morton in 1907, Edith was unhappily married to Edward Robbins ("Teddy") Wharton. The marriage had been a disaster from the start. Like many upper-class young women of the time, she came to her marriage not only as a virgin but innocent of the mechanics of sex. Teddy did nothing to ease her anxieties. She regarded their wedding night almost as a rape, and insisted on separate bedrooms thereafter. He engaged in numerous affairs, and was seemingly determined to make them as public and humiliating for his wife as possible.

Enter Morton Fullerton. Sensuous, romantic, tender, and charming, Fullerton took pride in his skills as a lover and a gentleman. Wharton fell head-over-heels in love with this expert and in her mid-forties was able to explore the full range of her sexuality for the first time.

This charming letter to Fullerton was written early in their relationship. Already Wharton is suffering from moments of despair, intimations that Fullerton does not love her with the same constancy and devotion with which she loves him. But most of it is rapturous. She deliciously and mischievously describes the other patrons at a restaurant where she dines alone; she wittily describes some recent reading in biology books: "I can't help seeing all these funny creatures with faces & gestures—the biophors, for instance, small & anxious to please."

Everything—the "cucumber-faced" lady at lunch, "monstrous" heterozygotes—is part of love's narrative. Few have ever told the story with more zest and imagination than Edith Wharton.

The Mount
Monday, June 8, 1908

Just now, as the last course of luncheon was being served
with due solemnity, I had a sudden vision of our first luncheon
at Duval's, with the kindly prognathous lady-in-waiting, & the
moist hippopotamus American with his cucumber-faced
female—do you remember? And then the second day, when
the old gentleman in the corner kept us so long in suspense, &
finally softened just as we despaired?

And how kind people were wherever we went—our friends
in the train at Creil, our waiter at Montmorency, that dearest
of concierges in the *jardin de* Mme Turquet—*yes,* even the
Sneezing Man in the dining-room of the Grand Cerf, who
drove us out under the lilacs in the court!

—Admire the ingenuity of woman! I vowed I wouldn't write
you again until I had overcome my black mood—& thereupon
set to work to overcome it, *in order to write you.* Can you
match that outside of Liguori?—I really am better today, but
yesterday, in my despair, I very nearly cabled you the one
word: *Inconsolable.* Luckily I bethought me in time that you
might feel impelled to answer, & as our telegrams are all
telephoned from the village—*si figuri!!*

I am ashamed to write so often, because, with this life I lead
here, there's absolutely nothing to tell. I have finished three
more chapters of my novel (this reminds me of: *"J'ai tué six
loups"*), & I've read Lock's "Heredity & Variation," & begun
Déperet's "Transformations du Monde Animal," which seems
to be another of the admirable popular exposition books in
the red series.—That reminds me—do you know "L'Hérédité"
by Delage, which Kellogg constantly speaks of as the best on
the subject? And if you do, could I understand it, even in bits?
I must confess to being always a little *ahurie* [bewildered]
when I meet with biophors and determinants—though they
seem like old friends after the allelomorphs & heterozygotes
in Lock's "simple" exposition of Mendelism.—My biological
reading is always embarrassed by the fact that I can't help
seeing all these funny creatures with faces & gestures—the

biophors, for instance, small & anxious to please, the determinants loud and domineering, with eye-glasses; so that I am burdened with a hideous new fauna, to which that monstrous animal the heterozygote, has just added another & peculiarly complicated silhouette—

Oh, dear—what nonsense to send three thousand miles! —Shall we talk of you instead? Do you want to know some of the things I like you for? (you've never told *me*!)—Well—one is that kind of time-keeping, comparing mind you have—that led you, for instance, in your last letter, to speak of "the camaraderie we invented, *or, it being predestined, we discovered*"—How I laughed over that revision, I who revise, who "edit" every sentence as I utter it, & to whom, in the most rushing moments, words keep their sharp edges of difference!

Et puis—I like the way in which you instantly discriminate between the essential & the superfluous, in people & things— & your feeling as I do about the "green worms" of life—caring about the waitress's losing her tip if we moved our table, & being worried lest the taxi-man you sent back to me at the R. des Deux Mondes should have waited & missed a fare—if you knew how every little thing like that *sank in!*

And then—most of all, perhaps—for the quality I least know how to define—unless one calls it a "radiant reasonableness." Because you & I (I think I have it too, you see!) are almost the only people I know who feel the "natural magic," *au-delà* [the other side], dream-side of things, & yet need the *netteté* [the clearness], the line—in thinking, in conduct—yes! in feeling too—And I've always felt about that poor dear maligned Goddess of Reason as somebody in Comus does about Philosophy—

> How charming is divine philosophy!
> Not harsh and crabbèd, as dull fools suppose,
> But musical as is Apollo's lute. . . .

June 10th. I said:—"This letter shall not be as long as the last—I shall keep it over till the next steamer. One must make one's self wanted, waited for, &c, &c—" & then everything in me cried out—

No! The basest thing about the state of "caring" is the tendency to bargain and calculate, as if it were a game of skill played between antagonistics. (We know it is—*soit!* Just as we know—or were supposed to till lately—that we hadn't any "free-will"; nevertheless:—) Pascal's terrible "*il faut de l'adresse pour aimer*" ["one needs skill in order to love"] has a noble side if it means the exercise of tact, insight, sympathy, self-effacement; but it is the most sordid of counsels if it appeals to the instinct to dole out, dissemble, keep in suspense, in order to prolong a little a feeling that hasn't enough vitality to survive without such aids.—There would have been the making of an accomplished flirt in me, because my lucidity shows me each move of the game—but that, in the same instant, a reaction of contempt makes me sweep all the counters off the board & cry out:—"Take them all—I don't want to win—I want to lose everything to you!"—But I pause, remembering you once told me that, on this topic, I serve up the stalest of platitudes with an air of triumphant discovery!—

June 11th. Such a happy thing has happened.—Two or three days ago, in the garden, I heard a cuckoo-call from the woods.—I never heard it before in America, & actually believed we had no American cuckoo—at least no New England variety. I set it down to a cuckoo clock somewhere in the servants' quarters; but this morning it came again, sweeter, more insistent, the very voice of Montmorency.—This time I knew it was no clock, & my bird books informed me that there is a cuckoo who "ranges" as far north as this; but he must be rare, for our coachman, who is a savant ornithologist, told me he *thought he had heard the note once, in his seven years here, but was not even sure of that!*—

I said I would write only to *answer* you; but the papers tell me that the Kronprinz is due this morning & so I am answering the letter that she (or he?) may be bringing—*is* bringing, I am going to believe!— If you knew how I long for the moment when it will be *your* turn to answer, when I shall no longer feel that my letters are being cast into the void. But that will not be for another week. . . .

I meant to tell you in Paris how glad I should be of a chance to see your sister. Is there any possibility of her coming our way before she goes to Europe? If yes, I wish you would give her my messages, & ask her to let me know—in spite of the cruel things I suspect her of saying—so justly—as to my inability to do justice to the tender sentiment in fiction! She should remember that mine is the low and photographic order of talent *a qui a besoin de se documenter* [that needs to gather together historical and social facts]—& consequently. . . .

How I hate to stop talking to you! Goodbye—

Wallace Stevens to Elsie Moll

On July 26, 1900, Wallace Stevens, at the age of twenty-one, solemnly confided to his journal that he would never marry. Four years later, back home in Reading, Pennsylvania, a friend introduced him to Elsie Viola Moll, and soon he realized that he had fallen in love. A shy, beautiful young woman, Elsie Moll left high school in her first year to take a job to help support her struggling family. She spent her days playing piano at a department store and giving piano lessons at home. At the time of their meeting, Stevens had degrees from Harvard and New York University Law School, had just passed his bar exam, and was beginning a solid business career.

Yet secretly he burned to be a writer. When he met Elsie Moll, he discarded the journal in which he recorded his innermost thoughts and, instead, used their long courtship correspondence as an intimate chronicle of his emotional life and of his feelings for her. It was in 1908, four years after he met her, that he went back home to Reading and presented Elsie with a Tiffany engagement ring. Even after marriage, he continued to write her elaborate, elegant, and poetic letters. Although this one was written five months after their marriage and nearly five years after their first meeting, it reads like new love.

In one of his very first letters to Elsie Moll, Wallace Stevens wrote: "I should like to make a music of my own life, a literature of my own, and I should like to live my own life." He did precisely this but in his own fashion, working as a business executive for an insurance firm in Hartford, Connecticut, while writing poetry on the side. He began publishing his poetry when he was in his mid-thirties and did not publish his first book until he was forty-four. He wrote much of the poetry for which he remains famous after he turned fifty.

Stevens's poetry often recreates in verse the kind of poignant emotions recorded in his early letters to Elsie Moll. Often in the poetry of middle age there is a recreation of love that is delicate, nuanced, lyrical, beautiful, and new:

> Just as my fingers on these keys
> Make music, so the selfsame sounds
> On my spirit make a music, too.
>
> Music is feeling, then, not sound;
> And thus it is that what I feel,
> Here in this room, desiring you,
>
> Thinking of your blue-shadowed silk,
> Is music.

Monday evening
February 15, 1909
New York

My dearest Bo:—

—Your letters were the first light—and a balmy light.—Let us think only of each other. The thought has become a large part of us (at least of me) and the chief comfort. And only good thoughts—like lovers of goodness, as we must be, if we are wise.—Sometimes I am terribly jangled, full of clashing things. But, always, the first harmony comes from something I cannot just say to you at the moment—the touch of you organizing me again—to put it so.—I have such a hatred of complaining and quarrelling—and there has been such a deuce of a lot of it all around me—and I in the midst of it.

—Your voice comes out of an old world. That is not eloquence. It is the quickest way to express it. It is the only true world for me. An old world, and yet it is a world that has no existence except in you.—It is as if I were in the proverbial far country and never knew how much I had become estranged from the actual reality of the things that are the real things of my heart, until the actual reality found a voice—you are the voice.

—What I mean is that these hideous people here in the house (it is not polite to say so) and the intolerable people that come and go all day at the office—they make up the far country and occupy me so much that I forget that I am not one of them and *never* will be.

—What am I then? Something that but for you would be terribly unreal. A dreamy citizen of a native place—of which I am no citizen at all. Sometimes I am all memories. They would be *all* dream except that you make them otherwise. You are my—you know what I want to say—what in the fairy tales is called the genius—the thing that comes in smoke a-building marble palaces—thing for the mystery of it.—But that mood works itself out as I write of it.—Do you remember the verses in "Songs"—no: "Harps Hung Up in Babylon"—

> "Though palmer bound, I shall return
> ———
> From Eden beyond Syria"

Well, I feel as if I had been returning to-night—from very rough water to the only haven I have.—I cannot tell you how hard it has been at the office—the work staggers one. But pooh! I'll not think of it.

Your loving
Wallace

Zelda Sayre to
F. Scott Fitzgerald

The story of Scott and Zelda is among the most familiar in American literary history. He was a handsome young man from Minnesota, awed by the beautiful people he encountered at Princeton. She was from an old and genteel Southern family. They met, appropriately, at a country club dance near her home in Montgomery, Alabama. It was July, 1918, and he was a soldier stationed at nearby Camp Sheridan. She thought he looked wonderful in a uniform, and he thought her the golden girl of his dreams. They fell in love, and then Zelda began to hesitate about making their engagement formal. In June 1919, she abruptly called off the engagement, insisting it would be best for him, too, if they never married. But they did marry, and her premonition proved correct. They virtually destroyed one another with excessive love and excessive living.

Who was the more guilty party in the destruction of the Fitzgeralds has been the subject of many and contradictory biographies. Even this early letter of Zelda's indicates that the relationship was fraught with problems from the start. There is something both abject and aggressive about this love letter, as if Zelda is almost daring Scott to hurt her so that she can prove she loves him more than he loves her. The letter is also beautifully written, which proved to be another of the many problems that beset their marriage. He was inspired by her prose and sometimes included excerpts of it in his fiction. She exaggerated the extent of the borrowings and accused him of plagiarizing from her in virtually all of his work.

Unquestionably, each had squandered a talent, and each found it convenient to blame the other for the loss. They fell into a pattern of mutual recrimination. He blamed her for demanding too much, for being unfaithful, for tormenting him; she blamed him for demanding too much, for being unfaithful, for tormenting her. Both published heavily autobiographical fictions in which they presented their view of the marriage and worked hard at killing whatever love once existed between them.

Scott died of a heart attack in 1940, at the age of forty-four, in the apartment of his lover, Sheilah Graham. Eight years later Zelda died in a hospital fire. The tragedy of their marriage makes it hard to remember that she had once written to him, "You came—like Summer, just when I needed you most." They had, for a time, been young and promising together. "Old death is so beautiful—so very beautiful," Zelda wrote in spring of 1919. "We will die together—I know."

Spring 1919 or 1920

I look down the tracks and see you coming—and out of every haze & mist your darling rumpled trousers are hurrying to me—Without you, dearest dearest I couldn't see or hear or feel or think—or live—I love you so and I'm never in all our lives going to let us be apart another night. It's like begging for mercy of a storm or killing Beauty or growing old, without you. I want to kiss you so—and in the back where your dear hair starts and your chest—I love you—and I can't tell you how much—To think that I'll *die* without your knowing— Goofo, you've *got* to try [to] feel how much I do—how inanimate I am when you're gone—I can't even hate these damnable people—Nobodys got any right to live but us—and they're dirtying up our world and I can't hate them because I want you so—Come Quick—Come Quick to me—I could never do without you if you hated me and were covered with sores like a leper—if you ran away with another woman and starved me and beat me—I still would want you *I know*—

Lover, Lover, Darling—
Your Wife

Vita Sackville-West to Virginia Woolf

They met at a dinner party hosted by art critic Clive Bell in London in 1922. After only one more meeting, Vita Sackville-West wrote to her husband, Harold Nicolson: "I love Mrs. Woolf with a sick passion." For the next twenty years the passion continued, sometimes shading into longing, yearning, desire, jealousy, later settling into a precious friendship of two women passionate about life and literature.

Each one was a prominent literary figure in her own right. Vita wrote over forty books. She was a poet, novelist, biographer, historian, translator, travel writer, and, without a doubt, one of the finest letter writers of all time. Mainly a traditionalist in her choice of literary forms, she was more bold than Virginia about her love for other women, less bold in her feminism. But certainly she was aware that women were legally and socially discriminated against. The daughter of Victoria and the third Baron Sackville, Vita was prevented from inheriting the palace that Queen Elizabeth I had given to her ancestor in 1566 because of "technical fault" (i.e., she was a woman).

Vita's marriage was an unusual one, both in the freedom and the contentment it granted each partner. Bisexual since adolescence, Vita eloped with a childhood friend, Violet Trefusis, after she learned that her husband was homosexual. There was a "mad and irresponsible summer of moonlight nights, and infinite escapades and passionate letters." The two women went to Paris together. Vita dressed as a boy. And then, when complications arose, she returned home to Harold. Their marriage lasted some fifty years and succeeded, their son recalled, "beyond their dreams." Vita continued to love Violet into old age and maintained a series of discreet affairs with other women throughout her life.

Most notable of these was the affair with Virginia Woolf. One of the greatest writers and literary innovators of the twentieth century and, like Vita, a wonderful correspondent, Woolf was also a brilliant feminist whose *A Room of One's Own* (1929) remains a compelling articulation of what it means to be a writer and a woman. Vita and Virginia loved each other as women and as writers. Vita wrote *Seducers in Ecuador* (1924) for Virginia; Virginia wrote *Orlando* (1928) for Vita.

In her diary, Vita recorded one of her early meetings with Virginia. "Dined with Virginia at Richmond. She is as delicious as ever," Vita wrote on February 22, 1923. "How right she is when she says that love makes everyone a bore. . . . But perhaps she feels this because she . . . has had no *grande passion* in her life." As suggested by the opening sentence of the letter reprinted below, it was a lack that Vita intended to remedy.

Milan
Thursday 21st (January 1926)

I am reduced to a thing that wants Virginia. I composed a beautiful letter to you in the sleepless nightmare hours of the night, and it has all gone: I just miss you, in a quite simple desperate human way. You, with all your undumb letters, would never write so elementary a phrase as that; perhaps you wouldn't even feel it. And yet I believe you'll be sensible of a little gap. But you'd clothe it in so exquisite a phrase that it would lose a little of its reality. Whereas with me it is quite stark: I miss you even more than I could have believed; and I was prepared to miss you a good deal. So this letter is just really a squeal of pain. It is incredible how essential to me you have become. I suppose you are accustomed to people saying these things. Damn you, spoilt creature; I shan't make you love me any the more by giving myself away like this—But oh my dear, I *can't* be clever and stand-offish with you: I love you too much for that. Too truly. You have no idea how stand-offish I can be with people I don't love. I have brought it to a fine art. But you have broken down my defences. And I don't really resent it.

However I won't bore you with any more.

We have re-started, and the train is shaky again. I shall have to write at the stations—which are fortunately many across the Lombard plain.

Venice.

The stations were many, but I didn't bargain for the Orient Express not stopping at them. And here we are at Venice for ten minutes only,—a wretched time in which to try and write.

No time to buy an Italian stamp even, so this will have to go from Trieste.

The waterfalls in Switzerland were frozen into solid iridescent curtains of ice, hanging over the rock; so lovely. And Italy all blanketed in snow.

We're going to start again. I shall have to wait till Trieste tomorrow morning. Please forgive me for writing such a miserable letter.

V.

Ogden Nash to Frances Leonard Nash

In 1965, when Ogden and Frances Nash were approached about selling personal letters dating back to November of 1928 to the University of Texas, Frances Nash agreed on one condition: she would give up the letters from her husband that she had so carefully preserved and cherished for almost forty years if he would destroy all of hers. He was a public figure, one of America's most popular and prolific writers of humorous verse. She was an intensely private person, a shy woman who could see no literary value in this invasion of her privacy. Yet, Linell Nash Smith, the couple's daughter and the editor of the family letters, notes that it is a shame her mother's letters were destroyed. Ogden's to Frances are so alive, witty, and loving that one longs for a glimpse of the woman who inspired, received, and responded to them. Reading only one side of a correspondence, their daughter notes, "is like watching someone play tennis against a backboard."

Ogden Nash took enormous pride in his role as a conventional, unexciting, happily married family man. When an interviewer once pressed him for some juicy anecdotes of his private life, he demurred: "I have no private life and no personality." Another reporter was determined to dig up some dirt on the humorist but gave up: "There's no money in *this* stuff—it reads like something for *Reader's Digest*."

Compared to the colorful life led by many writers, his might, in- deed, seem dull. Born in 1902, to a well-traveled and successful father who was a partner in a naval-stores firm and a mother who was a college-educated feminist, he had an uncommonly happy childhood. When his father lost his fortune, Ogden dropped out of college and came home to help support the family, financially and emotionally. For a while he taught French at a private school, where, he said, he "lost his entire nervous system carving lamb for a table of fourteen- year-olds." He tried working in stocks, drifted into editing. Then on November 13, 1928, he saw Frances Leonard across a crowded room, and his whole life changed. It was at a dinner dance in Baltimore, and he surreptitiously switched the place cards so that he could sit next to her at dinner. He was witty and charming; he paid her dis- creet compliments. "My aim was then, as it is now," he said in ret- rospect, "to persuade her to stay beside me for the rest of my life."

In 1966, Nash wrote a poem called "The Non-Biography of a No- body." Yet despite Nash's disclaimers about the ordinariness of his life, he actually achieved something truly rare: a love that lasts. He and Frances enjoyed a rich and often wondrous relationship. His final words before his death in 1971 were, simply and perfectly, "I love you, Frances."

Sunday night
August 25, 1929

Frances darling,

Have you heard that I love you? I'm not sure that I made it clear to you, and I don't want to have any misunderstanding. It's such a young love yet—just nine and a half months old, born November 13th 1928 at about nine o'clock in the evening. But it's big for its age, and seems much older. I do hope you're going to like it, I'm sending you some now for you to try; but if it's not satisfactory, don't ever let me know.

This is a peculiarly gifted and intelligent pen. Look what it's writing now: I love you. That's a phrase I can't get out of my head—but I don't want to. I've wanted to try it out for a long time; I like the look of it and the sound of it and the meaning of it.

It's past one now and I've got to have some sleep before I face Nelson Doubleday tomorrow. But tell me something before I leave. I was told tonight on what seemed to me the best authority that you are fond of me. Can you confirm this rumor?

Then there's another problem. As long as I'm thinking about you I can't go to sleep; and I'd rather think about you than go to sleep; how am I to sleep?

Oh Frances, do tell me that everything really happened, that it wasn't just something that I wanted so much that it crystalized in my imagination.

Good night. I've just sent St. Joseph off to watch you on the train; he has promised that he will do his duty like an honest saint.

> *I do love you.*
> Ogden

Margery Latimer to Carl Rakosi about Jean Toomer

Margery Latimer, a well-known feminist essayist and novelist, met Jean Toomer, one of the most prominent authors of the Harlem Renaissance, at a group session he was conducting as a member of the mystic-communitarian Gurdjieff movement. Writing to a friend, Margery described the meeting: "Then Toomer came and sat beside me on the couch and when I didn't look at him I could feel myself changing inside, growing quieter, all merging inside, all turning to cool moving water, all my elements." The two fell in love, with his playing Pygmalion to her blossoming Galatea, encouraging her to discover a new confidence, beauty, and grace within herself. As she wrote in another letter, "I got what I have longed for in men—rebirth." Jean, too, believed in the mystical powers of love but knew, from experience, that love could be transitory:

I have loved;
Yes, and forgotten those I felt I would forever love—
To love again.

The prominent and handsome couple married in 1931. When reporters asked Toomer for a statement, he declared that their interracial marriage symbolized "the birth of a new order, a new vision, a new ideal of man" that would replace the "outworn" categories of "white, black, brown, red." Although Toomer carefully went on to delineate his views on race, the press was interested only in sensational headlines: "NEGRO WHO WED WHITE WRITER SEES NEW RACE," one banner headline taunted; "AMERICA, THE RACIAL MELTING POT," ran another. Hate mail followed. The newlyweds were followed everywhere by reporters and were eventually hounded from their small seaside home in Carmel, California. They moved back to the relative anonymity of Chicago.

The honeymoon was clearly over, but a new joy followed when Margery prepared to have a baby: "I have a child inside me. . . . I love my husband. I love the world. Thank you, God." But once more happiness proved to be short-lived. Within hours after the birth of a daughter, Margery started to hemorrhage and then fell into a coma. Ten months after the marriage that seemed to portend so much hope and promise, Margery Latimer Toomer was dead.

October 1931

I don't know where to find you. Where are you? I've been doing things and I couldn't write before. I am going to marry Jean Toomer in November! I haven't told Kenneth or hardly anyone. My mother is in love with him too and we are having a splendid time together. I wish you were here. We simply must see each other soon. I wish you could be here for my wedding. I do want you very much. You asked about Jean's family. He was brought up by his grandparents in Washington. His grandfather was governor of Louisiana during the reconstruction and boasted of having negro blood to get the negro vote. He was a politician. Pinchback was his name. Jean's mother eloped, lived with her husband a year, and then came back to her parents and they made her get a divorce.

People in [my hometown of] Portage think Jean is an East

Indian. He looks very much like one, that color—beautiful rich skin, gold shade, very fine features, and bones, very tall and slender, beautiful mouth, very sleek hair and fine hands. My mother knew about the racial thing and for a time felt quite agitated. Then when she saw that he really is the right person for me she jumped the hurdle and now we are enormously happy. He has lived his life almost entirely with white people and I don't think he has been spoiled by white women, although most women fall in love with him. I feel that if negro blood could produce him then let's have more of it in the world! But most people won't believe that he has any negro blood. Personally I like it.

. . . You don't know how marvelously happy I am and my stomach seems leaping with golden children, millions of them, and my head is all purged of darkness and struggle and misery. A kiss for you and love from Margery.

Henry Miller to
Anaïs Nin

You have silenced me," the prolific Henry Miller wrote to the equally prolific Anaïs Nin—then went on (and on) to describe just how she had silenced him, why, to what effect, what it meant, would mean, or might mean. Theirs was as sexy and as literary an affair as any, with each of them fleeing from the other's arms in order to write about it—he copying passages from her letters and his own into semiautobiographical novels such as *Tropic of Cancer* (1934, France; 1961, U.S.); she making copies of her letters for inclusion in her monumental lifelong literary project, her diaries, in which she recorded her amorous exploits and emotions with both candor and bravado.

Both were sexual pioneers—in their love affair and in the ways in which they wrote about it in their fiction. *Tropic of Cancer*, for which Nin wrote a preface, was a banned book in many countries and for many years (and remains on the "banned" list of many town libraries in America today). Nin's diaries were so explicit about her extramarital affairs that she felt she could not publish them until after her husband's death. Since Ian Hugo (Hugh P. Guiler) outlived his wife, Nin's diaries were published posthumously, except for one slim volume that she heavily edited.

Sexuality was the core of Nin's and Miller's writing. One of Miller's most famous and notorious books, *Tropic of Capricorn*, was published in France in 1939 but could not be published in the U.S. until 1962. But there were at least a dozen other novels as well as travel accounts, essay and story collections, and plays. In her lifetime, Nin published literary criticism, novels, short stories, and, of course, the multivolumed diary, some portions of which remain unpublished. They led busy lives as lovers and as writers, and both agreed with Miller's dictum that "more obscene than anything is inertia."

Hotel Central, Paris
March 10, 1932
1:30 A.M.

Anaïs:

I was stunned when I got your note this morning. Nothing I can ever say will match these words. To you the victory—you have silenced me—I mean so far as expressing these things in writing goes. You don't know how I marvel at your ability to absorb quickly and then turn about, rain down the spears, nail it, penetrate it, envelop it with your intellect. The experience dumbed me. I felt a singular exaltation, a surge of vitality, then of lassitude, of blankness, of wonder, of incredulity . . . everything, everything. Coming home I kept remarking about the Spring wind—everything had grown soft and balmy, the air licked my face, I couldn't gulp down enough of it. And until I got your note I was in a panic . . . I was afraid you would disavow everything. But as I read—I read very slowly because each word was a revelation to me—I thought back to your smiling face, to your sort of innocent gaiety, something I had always sought for in you but never quite realized. There were times you began this way—at Louveciennes—and then the mind crashed through and I would see the grave, round eyes and the set purse of your lips, which used almost to frighten me, or, at any rate, always intimidated me.

You make me tremendously happy to hold me undivided— to let me be the artist, as it were, and yet not forgo the man, the animal, the hungry, insatiable lover. No woman has ever granted me all the privileges I need—and you, why you sing out so blithely, so boldly, with a laugh even—yes, you invite me to go ahead, be myself, venture anything. I adore you for that. That is where you are truly regal, a woman extraordinary. What a woman you are! I laugh to myself now when I think of you. I have no fear of your femaleness. And that you burned— I want that—I would not have it otherwise. You see, in spite of all my intimations, I was not quite prepared for the tempest you invoked. That moment in the room when, standing and swaying, you clung to me with your very womb, it seemed, that blinded me. And then do you know what happened later—you will forgive me, I hope—the blood on your face kept reminding me of the garden scene in *L'Age d'Or* and I was growing frantic and hysterical. Then I remember vividly your dress, the color and the texture of it, the voluptuous airy spaciousness of it—precisely what I would have begged you to wear had I been able to anticipate the moment. I was aware, too, of all that you hint at but tremendously relieved that you treated these things (I am about to say brazenly)—but no, it was nonchalantly.

And today, in the most precious good health, I had very languorous, pleasurable sensations of aches in my arms— from holding you so tightly. It dawned on me very very slowly. I wish I could retain it.

Anaïs, I am sending you this note to the other address. In my crude way I have a certain feeling of delicacy which prevents me from sending such things to Louveciennes. You will understand, I hope. I am enclosing more of Fred's manuscript, and some more of mine, too. Note how you were anticipating what I wrote today—I refer to your words about "caricature . . . hate etc." I will call around noon tomorrow, and if I don't succeed in getting you I *may* phone you again in the evening. I am timid about that sort of thing, or is it false delicacy? I don't know. When I phone I shall be able to say if it is possible to meet tomorrow—you see I am not yet straightened out with the police about my working card—the red tape is endless.

Henry

John Steinbeck to Elaine Scott

Thisletter was written from the small house in Pacific Grove, California, where Steinbeck went to live alone after the separation from his second wife, Gwyndolyn. It was a "wild and violent heart-broken time," Steinbeck wrote in retrospect, "which stays with me like the memory of a nightmare." Then one day his friend, actress Ann Sothern, came up to visit from Los Angeles and brought Elaine Scott, a Texan who had run a theatrical agency with her husband in New York and had recently moved to Hollywood. Steinbeck took the two lovely women on a tour of Cannery Row and other places that he had written about. Gossip columnist Louella Parsons got wind of the visit and wrote about it in her infamous column for the Hearst newspapers. Steinbeck made light of this public exposé when he wrote his first letter to Elaine, less than a week after they met. But the main purpose of the letter was to seduce. It is trademark Steinbeck—witty, charming, disarming. And it worked. Within a few weeks the couple was engaged in a passionate affair. They married a year later, just as soon as her divorce was final.

It was a good marriage. They traveled together, lived together, worked together. Sometimes they took joint assignments, he writing about and she photographing the places to which they traveled. She encouraged his political work, including that with the Kennedy administration, and she was with him when he won the Nobel Prize for literature in 1962. About their love, Steinbeck wrote: "If one finds it— there is no need for words."

But, in fact, there *was* need for words. Elaine inspired much of his late work. His usual procedure was to write six or seven letters each morning as a warm-up for writing. His letters to her often went directly into his books. On one trip Steinbeck took across America with his dog, he wrote to Elaine daily. She called them his "diary-letters," and in one of their telephone conversations she told him she thought of these diary-letters as his "Travels with Charley." He replied, "You've just given me my title."

June 6, 1949

Dear Miss West Forty-seventh Street
between Eighth and Ninth:

Am a widower with 10,000 acres in Arizona and seven cows so if you can milk I will be glad to have you give up that tinsel life of debauchery and sin and come out to God's country where we got purple sage. P.S. Can you bring a little sin and debauchery along? You can get too much purple sage but you can only get just enough sin.

I am really glad that you got some rest and that you feel somewhat restored. I guess it is that purple sage. I think I will try to bottle it.

Annie Rooney [Ann Sothern] called to say that the skirts had arrived. I would like one too but I ain't pretty enough. This has been my tragedy—with the soul to wear a scarlet-lined opera cape and small sword I have the physical misfortune always to be handed a hod. I have never quite got over this sadness. Let me know whether you want me to get another. I have been tempted to buy the whole stock because there will never be any more. The new regime is not going to approve of them I guess and they are unique as far as I know.

I was sad when you two bugs went away. Now I haven't even a half-assed reason for not working.

I am told that darling Louella [Parsons, gossip columnist] tagged Annie and me last night. This will henceforth be known as The Seven Days That Shook the Pine Inn. Running naked through the woods with flowers in your hair is against the law and I told you both but you wouldn't listen.

Sometime during the summer I will drift down your way.

Neale [Steinbeck's valet] is flying a twin engine Cessna to

New York on the 15th. He'll have a little vacation and bring back my kids on the 1st.

Love to you and Annie.

J.

Pablo Neruda to Matilde Urrutia

Born in southern Chile in 1904, Pablo Neruda (Neftalí Ricardo Reyes Bosoalto) was one of the most important and prolific of Latin America's poets, with over thirty books to his credit. A diplomat as well as a poet, Neruda represented Chile from 1926 to 1938 in various parts of the Far East and in Spain, where he witnessed the Spanish Civil War firsthand. He was outspoken in his criticism of General Franco and eventually, during World War II, joined the Communist Party, an act that forced him into exile from Chile.

With the election of Salvador Allende to the Presidency in 1970, Neruda was named ambassador to France, a post he held until shortly before his death in September of 1973, just twelve days after the CIA-instigated military coup in which the socialist Allende was assassinated and Chile fell under the rule of the ruthless Augusto Pinochet, a right-wing military dictator whose troops ransacked and vandalized the poet's house.

Neruda didn't separate politics from poetry. As suggested in interviews following his winning of the 1971 Nobel Prize for literature, Neruda believed strongly that the fully committed poet also has a responsibility to act in the world. Yet side by side with his public and political verse Neruda also produced a large body of intensely private, even intimate, poems. Love was a constant yet changing theme in the private poems, beginning with his 1924 volume *Twenty Love Poems and One Song of Despair* and in many ways culminating in *One Hundred Love Sonnets* (1959), a tribute to Matilde Urrutia Neruda, with whom he began living in 1955. The love expressed in these latter poems is passionate, profound, never naïve:

Death is the stone into which our oblivion hardens. I love you.
I kiss happiness into your lips. Let us gather up sticks for a
fire. Let us kindle a fire on the mountains.

My beloved wife, I suffered while I was writing these
misnamed "sonnets"; they hurt me and caused me grief, but
the happiness I feel in offering them to you is vast as a
savanna. When I set this task for myself, I knew very well that
down the right sides of sonnets, with elegant discriminating
taste, poets of all times have arranged rhymes that sound like
silver, or crystal, or cannonfire. But—with great humility—I
made these sonnets out of wood; I gave them the sound of
that opaque pure substance, and that is how they should
reach your ears. Walking in forests or on beaches, along
hidden lakes, in latitudes sprinkled with ashes, you and I have
picked up pieces of pure bark, pieces of wood subject to the
comings and goings of water and the weather. Out of such
softened relics, then, with *hatchet* and *machete* and *pocketknife*,
I built up these lumber piles of love, and with fourteen boards
each I built little houses, so that your eyes, which I adore and
sing to, might live in them. Now that I have declared the
foundations of my love, I surrender this century to you:
wooden sonnets that rise only because you gave them life.

October 1959

~

Matilde: the name of a plant, or a rock, or a wine,
of things that begin in the earth, and last:
word in whose growth the dawn first opens,
in whose summer the light of the lemons bursts.

Wooden ships sail through that name,
and the fire-blue waves surround them:
its letters are the waters of a river
that pours through my parched heart.

O name that lies uncovered among tangling vines
like the door to a secret tunnel
toward the fragrance of the world!

Invade me with your hot mouth; interrogate me
with your night-eyes, if you want—only let me
steer like a ship through your name; let me rest there.

John Cheever to ———

In John Cheever's short stories of modern suburban life, the wife personifies emotional aridity. It is impossible not to draw the parallel to John's long and not very happy marriage to Mary, a woman who believed in the high virtue of proper appearances. Yet one gains sympathy for this wife—fictional and real—after reading Cheever's letters with their detailed accounts of infidelities with various women and men.

An alcoholic, Cheever was prone to violent mood swings. His family frequently experienced his harsh temper, although he greeted the larger world with a demeanor of steady geniality. His savage portraits of hypocritical, controlling women may well have been projections of his own self-hatred. Among the papers on his desk when he died was a fragment of an autobiographical narrative in which he discussed his fear of being a homosexual and his sense that "the only homosexuals I knew corresponded in no way to what I hoped to make of myself." For Cheever, there was too great a variance between sexual desire and his ideal of a respectable suburban life. The result was a doubled and contradictory world: flagrant adulteries yet public praise for monogamy as the best way of life; homosexual love affairs offset by rabidly homophobic pronouncements.

For all the contradictions, there also seems to have been joy in Cheever's life. His family and friends remember his zest for living, which is evident in his letters. And as the following letter to one of his (anonymous) male lovers makes clear, he knew how to love tenderly, passionately, and fully.

John Cheever ranks among the finest of modern letter writers. He wrote between ten and thirty letters a week but kept no carbons, never attempted to publish them, and urged friends and family to destroy any they received from him. After his death, his son Benjamin edited and published his correspondence, but he also remembered his father's cautionary advice. "Saving a letter," Cheever had insisted, "is like trying to preserve a kiss."

Cedar Lane
March 31, 1977

Dear _____ ,

To scrutinize and examine my feeling for you is idle but there is nothing much else I can do with you in _____ . All of my speculations may be no more than the thinking of a lecherous old man who hankers after the skin of someone younger but I will throw this out. Any dizzy analyst would declare that you are the ghost of my dead brother come back from the grave to solace the ghost of my long-gone youth. He would also declare that I am the spectre of your father, gotten richer and more literary. I think this [is] shit. All I seem to know is that on that morning at _____ when we waited for _____ , you seemed to lift from my shoulders, an aloneness that I was happy to lose. I can't imagine what your feeling was. My happiness continued through the plane trip and made Palo Alto seem charming. I wanted only that you be there; that if I woke in the night and asked for you I would hear your voice. That it may be my destiny to carry this aloness [sic] forever is a possibility and it is surely not your destiny, as a young man to carry my bags.

That is about it for this morning. The singular heat goes on and the botanicals, having no memory-bank, are all coming into bloom. We have all the flowers of spring. The old wander around, lamenting the fact that the hyacinths will soon be withered and buried in snow but they overlook the fact that the hyacinths are very resilient. So are you and I.

Love,
John

2

LOVE'S INFINITE VARIETY

LOVE IS TENDER

Marcus Aurelius to Fronto

Written in 144–45 A.D., Marcus Aurelius's letter to Fronto (Marcus Cornelius) is a remarkably vivid account of everyday life in ancient, imperial Rome—sleeping late, catching a cold, gargling with honey water, attending a sacrifice. It is also a tender expression of a twenty-four-year-old's love for his forty-year-old teacher. Not discovered until 1815, the letter is charming in its candor. Marcus Aurelius notes how he and his mum sit casually on his bed, chatting together about their love lives. "What do you think my Fronto is now doing?" he asks. "And what do you think my Gratia is doing?" she responds. They wonder who loves more, an argument without conclusion that Marcus Aurelius dutifully reports in his letter to Fronto.

The letter is all the more charming in that it was written by a future Emperor of Rome (161–80) to Fronto, the most famous orator of the day, a man who had been a devoted teacher but who, at the time of this writing, was dispirited by illness and isolation. The letter is unself-conscious in its declaration of love precisely because the imperial prince had no reason to hide his homosexuality. Although the Romans tended to deride the Greek idealization of homosexual love, homosexuality was nonetheless widely practiced and accepted in ancient Rome.

"Farewell, my Fronto," Marcus Aurelius closes his letter, "most honey-sweet, my love, my delight." But Fronto was more than just an older lover. Fronto was also a teacher—and he taught his star pupil well. Marcus Aurelius would go on to be regarded as a brilliant and benevolent ruler who would help his people through famine, pestilence, and the constant threat of invasion. Although a political leader, he was also a Stoic philosopher and the author of twelve books of

69

"Meditations," another indication of the difference between the ancient world and our own.

Hail, my sweetest of masters.

We are well. I slept somewhat late owing to my slight cold, which seems now to have subsided. So from five A.M. till 9, I spent the time partly in reading some of Cato's *Agriculture*, partly in writing not quite such wretched stuff, by heavens, as yesterday. Then, after paying my respects to my father, I relieved my throat, I will not say by gargling—though the word *gargarisso* is, I believe, found in Novius and elsewhere—but by swallowing honey water as far as the gullet and ejecting it again. After easing my throat I went off to my father and attended him at a sacrifice. Then we went to luncheon. What do you think I ate? A wee bit of bread, though I saw others devouring beans, onions, and herrings full of roe. We then worked hard at grape-gathering, and had a good sweat, and were merry and, as the poet says, "still left some clusters hanging high as gleanings of the vintage." After six o'clock we came home.

I did but little work and that to no purpose. Then I had a long chat with my little mother as she sat on the bed. My talk was this: "What do you think my Fronto is now doing?" Then she: "And what do you think my Gratia is doing?" Then I: "And what do you think our little sparrow, the wee Gratia, is doing?" Whilst we were chattering in this way and disputing which of us two loved the one or other of you two the better, the gong sounded, an intimation that my father had gone to his bath. So we had supper after we had bathed in the oil-press room; I do not mean bathed in the oil-press room, but when we had bathed, had supper there, and we enjoyed hearing the yokels chaffing one another. After coming back, before I turn over and snore, I get my task done and give my dearest of masters an account of the day's doings, and if I could miss him more, I would not grudge wasting away a little

more. Farewell, my Fronto, wherever you are, most honey-
sweet, my love, my delight. How is it between you and me? I
love you and you are away.

Harriet Beecher Stowe to Calvin Stowe

Written eleven years after their marriage, this letter from Harriet
to her husband Calvin is both a tender avowal of love and an implicit
renegotiation of the marriage contract. The terms sound quite modern. As other of her letters make clear, Stowe was exhausted by domesticity, the tending of a large house, seven children, and a husband
who was often demanding of her attentions. Although she believed
strongly in the importance of her maternal role, she also felt inspired
to write partly because the income would allow her to pay for additional servants to help with cooking, cleaning, and occasional child
care. A prolific writer, Harriet confided to her friend Georgiana May:
"If you see my name coming out everywhere—you may be sure of
one thing. That I do it for *the pay.*"

Calvin was supportive of his wife's efforts. In one letter he informed her that she "must be a *literary woman.*" Yet, like many working women past and present, Harriet Beecher Stowe often had to jug-
gle conflicting demands. When she wrote, she worried about her
possible shortcomings as a mother and wife; when she confined herself to domesticity, she longed to write. Sometimes, she confided to
her husband, she felt "as if anxious thought [had] become a disease
with me from which I could not be free."

Despite such anxieties, she would become the single most important political novelist of the nineteenth century. *Uncle Tom's Cabin*
(1852) galvanized the abolitionist movement. She was a national figure almost overnight and was later invited to the White House by
Abraham Lincoln, who reportedly called her "the little lady who
started the great war." Already forty years old when she published
Uncle Tom's Cabin, Stowe went on to publish eight more novels and
over one hundred tales. And she insisted that her great abolitionist
novel came partly from her own experience: "I wrote what I did be-

cause as a woman, as a mother, I was oppressed and heartbroken, with the sorrows and injustice I saw."

January 1, 1847

My Dearest Husband

. . . I was at that date of marriage a very different being from what I am now and stood in relation to my Heavenly Father in a very different attitude. My whole desire was to live in love, absorbing passionate devotion to one person. Our separation was my first trial—but then came a note of comfort in the hope of being a mother. No creature ever so longed to see the face of a little one or had such a heart full of love to bestow. Here came in trial again sickness, pain, perplexity, constant discouragement—wearing wasting days and nights—a cross, deceitful, unprincipled nurse—husband gone . . . When you came back you came only to increasing perplexities.

Ah, how little comfort I had in being a mother—how was all that I proposed met and crossed and my way ever hedged up! . . . In short, God would teach me that I should make no family be my chief good and portion and bitter as the lesson has been I thank Him for it from my very soul. One might naturally infer that from the union of two both morbidly sensitive and acute, yet in many respects exact opposites— one hasty and impulsive—the other sensitive and brooding— one the very personification of exactness and routine and the other to whom everything of the kind was an irksome effort— from all this what should one infer but some painful friction.

But all this would not after all have done so very much had not Providence as if intent to try us throws upon the heaviest external pressure . . . but still where you have failed your faults have been to me those of one beloved—of the man who after all would be the choice of my heart still were I to choose—for were I now free I should again love just as I did and again feel that I could give up all to and for you—and if I do not love never can love again with the blind and unwise love with which I married I love quite as truly tho far more wisely. . . .

In reflecting upon our future union—our marriage—the past obstacles to our happiness—it seems to me that they are of two or three kinds. 1st those from physical causes both in you and in me—such on your part as hypocondriac morbid instability for which the only remedy is physical care and attention to the laws of health—and on my part an excess of sensitiveness and of confusion and want of control of mind and memory. This always increases on my part in proportion as I blamed and found fault with and I hope will decrease with returning health. I hope that we shall both be impressed with a most solemn sense of the importance of a wise and constant attention to the laws of health.

Then in the second place the want of any definite plan of mutual watchfulness, with regard to each other's improvement, of a definite time and place for doing it with a firm determination to improve and be improved by each other—to confess our faults one to another and pray one for another that we may be healed. . . .

Yours with much love
H.

Samuel Clemens to Olivia Langdon Clemens

Samuel Clemens (Mark Twain) liked to say that he fell in love with an ivory miniature. A young man named Charles Langdon, whom Clemens met on a steamship bound for the Holy Land, showed him a small portrait of his sister, "Livy" Langdon. Upon his return to America, Clemens made a point of meeting its original. Livy was a retiring young woman, almost an invalid, but intelligent, sensitive, and cultured, the kind of woman Clemens had envisioned for a wife who would also be a lifelong companion. Her genteel family disapproved, however, of the flamboyant writer who had achieved fame through humor and a rough-and-tumble Western style. Clemens thereupon strove to woo Livy and win her family's approval through the one weapon he had: words. In several dozen courtship letters to Livy, Clemens represented himself as a reprobate begging to be reformed, a sensitive and socially responsible writer who would achieve moral perfection under the tutelage of Livy and her religious, philanthropic, civic-minded family. He wooed her long and extravagantly and, finally, she reciprocated his affections.

"I have *read* those absurd fairy tales in my time, but I never, never, never expected to be the hero of a romance in real life as unlooked for and unexpected as the wildest of them," Twain wrote in a newspaper article (" 'Mark Twain' Married and Settled") on Valentine's Day, 1870.

Many a lover has felt this way. But, for Sam and Livy, the feeling continued. "She poured out her prodigal affections in kisses and caresses, and in a vocabulary of endearments whose profusion was always an astonishment to me."

Throughout their long marriage, Livy provided companionship, friendship, and literary counsel. He seems, despite long absences and a good deal of female admiration, to have remained a faithful and devoted husband. Together they faced many problems—financial woes, sickness, the tragic deaths of children—but his letters to her remained tender and touching up until her death in 1904.

To Mrs. Clemens on her Thirtieth Birthday:

Hartford, November 27, 1875.

Livy darling, six years have gone by since I made my first great success in life and won you, and thirty years have passed since Providence made preparation for that happy success by sending you into the world. Every day we live together adds to the security of my confidence that we can never any more wish to be separated than that we can ever imagine a regret that we were ever joined. You are dearer to me to-day, my child, than you were upon the last anniversary of this birth-day; you were dearer then than you were a year before—you have grown more and more dear from the first of those anniversaries, and I do not doubt that this precious progression will continue on to the end.

Let us look forward to the coming anniversaries, with their age and their gray hairs without fear and without depression, trusting and believing that the love we bear each other will be sufficient to make them blessed.

So, with abounding affection for you and our babies, I hail this day that brings you the matronly grace and dignity of three decades!

Always Yours
S. L. C.

Anton Chekhov to Olga Knipper

Anton Chekhov (1860–1904) first laid eyes on Olga Leonardovna Knipper on September 14, 1898, when he attended a rehearsal of Aleksey Tolstoy's verse drama, *Tsar Fyodor Ioannovich,* in which she played Irina, the wife of the czar. "Her voice, her nobility, her sincerity," Chekhov wrote to one of his friends, "it's all so fine it brings a spasm to your throat. . . . Were I to stay in Moscow, I would fall in love with this Irina." There were one or two other meetings. He watched her act in his own play, *The Seagull.* By the fall of 1899 the writer was madly in love with the actress, and she with him; two years later, they married.

Among the greatest of modern dramatists and short story writers, Chekhov had a somber and even sardonic view of life and human relationships. Yet when an early biographer dubbed him "the voice of twilight Russia," he was furious, and when his wife expressed concern over what she perceived to be the sadness of his work, he corrected her. "But, darling, that is utter nonsense!" he responded. "There is no sadness in me, there never was; most of the time life is bearable and when you are with me, things are really fine."

The relationship seems to have been a good one. Biographers argue about how many women Chekhov loved before and after his marriage to Knipper. But all agree that the couple loved one another both passionately and tenderly. Their separations while she was acting were hard on him, but he also admired his wife's talent and was unusually supportive of her stage career. Their separations also provided them both with the opportunity to write witty, touching, and candid love letters populated by a remarkable menagerie of pet names for one another: pony, pup, sweet dog, crocodile, cockroach, dogman, goldfish, river perch.

Olga was with Anton in Germany on the morning of 1904 when his pulse became weak, his breathing uneasy. She called a doctor, who ordered a bottle of champagne to help revive him. "I'm dying," Chekhov said, picking up the glass, smiling, and then toasting his wife. "It's a long while since I have drunk champagne." He drank the champagne, lay down, and died. His body was returned to Russia in a refrigerated rail car marked "For Oysters." Death amid oysters and champagne: a Chekhovian ending if ever there was one!

Yalta,
March 6, 1904

You ought to be ashamed of yourself writing with such awful ink, my little baby cachalot, my darling. You may not believe it, but I give you my word, I had to peel the envelope away from the letter, as if they'd been glued together on purpose. Masha has sent me the same sort of sticky letter. It's downright revolting. Not only are the letters sticky, but you use them to frighten me with your premonitions: "There's something horrible hanging over my head," etc. Our vile cold weather makes me feel bad enough as it is. There's snow in the mountains and a thin layer of snow on the roofs, and the air is colder than in Moscow.

Go ahead and take the apartment on Leontyev Lane, it's a good location, close to everything. I'll come two or three days before your arrival from Petersburg. Got it? I received a letter from Vishnevsky. He writes about the splendid full houses you've been having in Petersburg, praises the apartment on Leontyev Lane, and so on. Mikhailovsky [the novelist Nikolai Garin] came to see me. He's going to the Far East and says that your brother Kostya is also planning to go—for an enormous salary, of course. And you can't deny that when a woman never stops talking about ovaries, kidneys and bladders, and when she talks of nothing else, it makes you want to throw yourself out the window. Lyova [Olga's nephew] will recover, barring any unforeseen developments, of course.

What a revolting dream I had! I dreamed I was sleeping in bed with someone other than you; with some lady, very repulsive, a bragging brunette, and the dream went on for more than an hour. Now what do you make of that!

I want to see you, my darling. I want to talk with my wife, with my only woman. There's nothing new. All anyone talks about is the Japanese.

Well, may the Lord bless you and keep you; don't mope, don't overwork and be cheerful. Where did you get the idea that I had caught cold on the way from Tsaritsyno to Moscow? Please excuse my crudity, but what utter nonsense! It's only in Yalta that people catch colds. What I have is the most abominable case of sniffles.

I embrace my little cockroach and send her a million kisses.

A.

LOVE IS PASSIONATE

Emily Dickinson to Susan Gilbert

There is no way of knowing what went on behind the closed chamber door at Emily Dickinson's house in Amherst. Some would say she spent every day and night writing poetry or lowering down cookies in a basket for the neighborhood children. Others postulate that she might have had love affairs with both men and women.

Whether either of these scenarios is true, Dickinson certainly wrote eloquently about the power of love. In one poem, for example, she uses breathless verse to mimic the erotic joys of sending and receiving a love letter: "Going to Him! Happy Letter!" she writes exuberantly. "Tell Him just how the fingers hurried—/ Then—how they waded—slow—slow—"

Interestingly, the same year (1862), she revised this poem, substituting female pronouns (and slower rhythms) throughout:

> Going—to—Her!
> Happy—Letter! Tell Her—
> Tell Her—the page I never wrote!
> Tell Her, I only said—the Syntax—
> And left the Verb and the Pronoun—out!
> Tell Her just how the fingers—hurried—
> Then—how they—stammered—slow—slow—
> And then—you wished you had eyes—in your pages—
> So you could see—what moved—them—so—

We don't know if there was a particular woman who was the object of this poem. But we do know that some of Dickinson's most ardent writing was addressed to Susan Gilbert, the woman who would become her sister-in-law.

"How vain it seems to *write*, when one knows how to feel," the poet expressed her longing for Sue. "How much more near and dear to sit beside you, talk with you, hear the tones of your voice."

27 June 1852

Susie, will you indeed come home next Saturday, and be my own again, and kiss me as you used to? Shall I indeed behold you, not "darkly, but face to face" or am I *fancying* so, and dreaming blessed dreams from which the day will wake me? I hope for you so much, and feel so eager for you, feel that I *cannot* wait, feel that *now* I must have you—that the expectation once more to see your face again, makes me feel hot and feverish, and my heart beats so fast—I go to sleep at night, and the first thing I know, I am sitting there wide awake, and clasping my hands tightly, and thinking of next Saturday, and "never a bit" of you.

. . . Be patient then, my Sister, for the hours will haste away, and Oh *so* soon! Susie, I write most hastily, and very carelessly too, for it is time for me to get the supper, and my mother is

gone and besides, my darling, so near I seem to you, that I
disdain this pen, and wait for a *warmer* language. . . .

Your Emilie—

Emma Goldman to Ben Reitman

Here's the public Emma Goldman, anarchist, activist, lecturer,
editor, writer, publisher, the Emma Goldman that emerges from her
autobiography: She lived from 1869 to 1940. In 1885, the increasing
anti-Semitism in her native Lithuania prompted her emigration to
the United States. Her love affair with anarchist Alexander Berkman
gained a good deal of publicity and helped to militate against her in
1893 when she was tried for "inciting a riot." In prison, she took up
nursing; went to Vienna after her release to study midwifery; and, for
the rest of her life, supported both workers' and women's causes. On
her 1897 U.S. lecture tour, enormous audiences turned out to hear
her, but then she had to go underground when a Polish immigrant
claimed he was acting on her behalf when he assassinated President
McKinley. In 1906 she founded *Mother Earth*, an anarchist journal,
and the Mother Earth Publishing Association, which published writers such as Mary Wollstonecraft, Henrik Ibsen, and Oscar Wilde, as
well as books on sex and birth control. Throughout all of these activities, Goldman continued to write her own books and articles, including an appreciative study of the political importance of modern
drama. A lifelong feminist, she valued motherhood as highly as ca-
reerism. As an activist, she was arrested and sentenced for cam-
paigning on behalf of birth control; she was arrested and deported to
Russia for speaking against conscription in World War I. She later
lived in England, France, and Canada, where she died.

But of course the public person is never the whole story. Alongside
the powerful political convictions that motivated her life, Emma
Goldman had equally compelling personal needs, chief among them
the need for love. In the hundreds of letters that she wrote to Dr. Ben
Reitman, a married man whom she met in Chicago in 1908 and with

whom she continued to have an affair until 1917, Goldman exposed her soul. To the public, she presented a strident pose; in private, there was anguish, insecurity, yearning. An acquaintance noted how Reitman, a freewheeling doctor who liked to work and live among street people, had come into Goldman's life "with the sweep of a cyclone, only to take [himself] out with the same force." Indeed, their whole relationship could be characterized by this cyclone metaphor—no stability, no predictability, the whole thing threatening to blow away at any moment. "If ever our correspondence should be published," Goldman wrote to him, "the world would stand aghast that I, Emma Goldman, the strong revolutionist, the daredevil, the one who has defied laws and convention, should have been as helpless as a shipwrecked crew on a foaming ocean."

September 27, 1908

You have opened up the prison gates of my womanhood. And all the passion that was unsatisfied in me for so many years, leaped into a wild reckless storm boundless as the sea. . . . Can you then imagine that I could stay away from you? What is love, family ties, the power of association to the wanderer in the desert. His mind is bent on the spring that will quench his thirst. . . . Yet, if I were asked to choose between a world of understanding and the spring that fills my body with fire, I should have to choose the spring. It is life, sunshine, music, untold ecstasy. The Spring, oh ye Gods, that have tortured my body all these years, I will give you my soul only let me drink, drink from the Spring of my master lover. . . . There. You have the confession of a starved tortured being, my Ben.

Jean Cocteau to Valentine Gross

They seemed the perfect couple. He was a brilliant young poet, already involved in every aspect of the bustling Parisian artistic scene that would later be labeled "Modernism." She was a successful artist whose paintings and drawings of Diaghilev's dancers were exhibited at the opening of the Théâtre des Champs-Elysées in 1913. He called her his "swan" because of her lovely long neck and stately carriage. They were young and beautiful and renowned together; they met Stravinsky and chatted with Picasso. More than one Parisian match-maker agreed with Madame Cocteau that Jean and Valentine were destined to marry. At a party in which Valentine, always an exotic dresser, appeared in a long white veil, Cocteau grandly exclaimed that this was their engagement party. Sent away to the front with the out-break of World War I, he wrote her exquisite letters. "How can I thank you?" he wrote from his tent. "Stupid to thank a rose for its fragrance and the sky for its stars. You were born marvelous, as others are born ugly or bad. I inhale you and feel better."

But neither monogamy nor garden-variety heterosexuality held any appeal for Cocteau. His passion for Valentine was strongest on paper, as he wrote to her amid the bombs and flares of war. After his return from the war, their friendship endured for several years but was pla-tonic. She married someone else. The list of the men he loved is al-most as long as the list of his artistic talents: poet, novelist, dramatist, artist (painter, sculptor, potter, weaver, jeweler), choreographer, ac-tor, director. Unfortunately, almost none of Cocteau's letters to these lovers survive, including letters to Jean Marais, the handsome young actor who starred in his film *Beauty and the Beast*, and with whom he enjoyed a long and happy relationship.

In his youth, Cocteau possessed a spirit that struck more than one observer as the personification of life and love. After meeting him at the home of a friend, Edith Wharton wrote probably the best descrip-tion of Cocteau's electric appeal: "The first time I went, I met a young man of nineteen or twenty, who at that time vibrated with all the youth of the world. This was Jean Cocteau, then a passionately imag-inative youth to whom every great line of poetry was a sunrise, every sunset the foundation of the Heavenly City. . . . I have known no other young man who so recalled Wordsworth's 'Bliss was it in that dawn to be alive.' "

May 28, 1916
5 h.

Ma chère Valentine,
Dune dune dune cave cave cave cano cano canon
　Ratodromes
　Your letter—miraculous. You should come yourself, like the true angel you are, long-throated, great-winged, flying to me among the Tauben and the seraphim of the '75's. You *are* my angel, my good angel, watching over me, stimulating me. I am wandering bewildered on a planet of iconoclasts, where nothing, no one but you, ever speaks of *building*—everyone is destroying, smashing, wasting—sowing bile and death.

7 h.

　Back from dinner at the battery. Watched Boches through telescope—sea H. Heine—phosphorescent waves—purring searchlights—stars—secret machines—Terrific beauty— horrible but irresistible, like gypsies. Impossible to live anywhere else. I kiss your hands. . . .
　P.S. I long to follow a coastal trench that would come out at Boulogne in your house—hold your hands, tell you how grateful I am. I picture you in your long hall—sirens—wax in your ears like Ulysses, bound to the mast. May Satie have the same idea!

Céline (Louis Destouches) to Elizabeth Craig

He was a French doctor working with the League of Nations in Switzerland, she an American ballet student when they met in 1926, outside a bookstore in Geneva. When Louis went to Paris to try to find a producer for a new play, she stayed in Switzerland where she practiced with Alexandre Volinine, a star in the Diaghilev company, and eagerly awaited Céline's passionate letters. Later, they moved to France, living first in Clichy, an impoverished suburb of Paris where Céline treated patients without charge, and then in Montmartre, where Céline did most of the work on *Journey to the End of the Night* (1932). The poverty around him inspired some of the content of this novel, but it was from Elizabeth's dancing, he said, that he learned the rhythms of his prose. She was his muse, his "Molière in drag," yet the bleak depressions that he fell into when writing his novel prompted Elizabeth to return, alone, to America in 1933. "I loved him tremendously," she said sadly, in retrospect. "But you couldn't live like he did day after day and also digest your food."

Louis came to Los Angeles with the intention of bringing her back to France but discovered her engaged to someone else. When he returned alone to France, he denounced her to his friends, insisting that she was caught in the grips of alcohol, drugs, and gangsters. A decade later, he tried to find her but failed.

A Stanford professor, Alphonse Juilland, finally located Elizabeth in 1988. She was a widow, eighty-six years of age. When Professor Juilland gave her an English translation of *Journey to the End of the Night*, Elizabeth learned for the first time that Louis had dedicated his masterpiece to her. She told the professor that she had long ago burned Louis's letters because she "didn't want to be the kind of woman who reads love letters from another man for the rest of her life."

Yet three days before her death at the age of eight-seven, Elizabeth Craig Tankel called her nephew into her room and made a confession. From a jewelry box inscribed "Elizabeth," a gift from Louis, she produced five love letters that she could never bring herself to destroy. These date from the earliest days of her romance with Louis.

The letters reveal another side of a writer who repeatedly denounced love (he called it an "*obscénité*"), a writer whose sexuality has been much discussed by biographers. Since Elizabeth did not know French, Louis had to woo her in English. His rudimentary vocabulary, poor spelling, broken grammar, and hesitant diction are poignant precisely because they come from the pen of "Céline," one of the most admired prose stylists of modern France.

1927

Dear little *écureuil,*
I hope you are having a nice time. Here it is rather monotoneous. I am allmost afraid of the appartement. You must *not smoke or drink* little one. Dont abuse of your freedom. I am sure you are very busy but do not loose your object of sight. It might be more easy to start in the same time as the theatre a sort of theatrical hotel annexed to it which would pay anyhow the expense of the theatre—a sort of block composed of the hotel and the theatre.? Dont you think—?—

   It is here motionless, they say there is a Council going on. What about it? Keep in mind that we want to go to Paris, sooner or later—you must find something to keep you excited about and I do want excitment too. my God! supply your old boy with excitement—not especially sex—but just tricks that are after all much more fun. How is Volinine? How are the pupils—Is he making a fortune? I am all prepared to hear all kinds of funny combinations—

Yours very vy sincerely—
Love *Louis.*

TRIANGLES

Jane Welsh to Thomas Carlyle

T he flirtation alluded to in the following letter characterized Jane Welsh's aspirations toward learning. The precocious only child of a Scottish physician, Jane yearned to be appreciated for her mind and found herself attracted to her tutor, Edward Irving. But this was never a serious relationship. Instead, it was Irving's less suitable friend, Thomas Carlyle, the son of a stonemason, who won the young girl's heart by flattering her intellect. In this early courtship letter, Jane confesses her earlier passion for Edward but makes it clear that it is Thomas she really loves.

Thomas was crude, difficult, penniless, and unknown but also undeniably brilliant when he began the six-year epistolary courtship with talented, bright-eyed Jane. Although she repeatedly discouraged his amorous attentions, she found his intellectual interest irresistible. During the first years of their correspondence he set her various intellectual challenges (at one point he directed her to write a tragedy based on the life of Queen Boadicea) to which she responded with sometimes remorseful and sometimes witty letters explaining how her social life as an eligible Edinburgh heiress prevented her from indulging the life of the mind. Thomas offered her a way out of affluent, middle-class Edinburgh—a world of tea parties and shuttlecocks—and she took it. Too proud to have the world think he had married Jane for her money, he insisted that Jane will over her entire inheritance to her mother.

Poverty was the condition of their marriage, the life of the mind its center and *raison d'être;* but with one major shift in focus. It was now the wife's responsibility to do whatever was required to foster her husband's genius. Thomas wrote. Jane strove heroically against grime, noisy workmen, and even neighborhood roosters to provide him with the comfort and the absolute silence he required for inspiration. She even endured through Thomas's infatuation with a rich, brilliant bluestocking who seemed to him to possess all the refinement that his wife had, inexplicably, lost.

Thomas thought it a good marriage. Only after Jane's sudden death in 1866 did the husband read the wife's diaries and discover how difficult her life had been. Wracked by remorse, he devoted the last years of his life to editing her diaries and voluminous correspondence (but, it should be added, co-opting her voice). "How pungent is remorse," Carlyle exclaimed, "when it turns upon the loved dead, who cannot pardon us, cannot hear us now!"

Templand, Sunday, 24 July, 1825.

My Dearest,

I thought to write to you from this place with joy; I write with shame and tears. The enclosed Letter, which I found lying for me, has distracted my thoughts from the prospect of our meeting, the brightest in my mind for many months, and forced them on a part of my own conduct which makes me unworthy ever to see you again, or to be clasped to your true heart again. I cannot come to you, cannot be at peace with myself, till I have made the confession which Mrs. Montagu so impressively shows me the need of.

Let me tell it then at once. I have deceived you, — *I* whose truth and frankness you have so often praised, have deceived my bosom friend! I told you that I did not care for Edward Irving; took pains to make you believe this. It was false: I loved him — must I say it — *once* passionately loved him. Would to Heaven that this were all! it might not perhaps lower me so much in your opinion; for he is no unworthy man. And if I showed weakness in loving one whom I knew to be engaged to another, I made amends in persuading him to marry that other and preserve his honour from reproach. But I have concealed and disguised the truth; and for this I have no excuse; none, at least, that would bear a moment's scrutiny.

Woe to me then, if your reason be my judge and not your love! I cannot even plead the merit of a *voluntary* disclosure as a claim to your forgiveness. I make it because I *must*, because this extraordinary woman has moved me to honesty whether I would or no. Read her Letter, and judge if it was possible for me to resist it.

Write, I beseech you, instantly and let me know my fate. This suspense is worse to endure than any certainty. Say, if you *can*, that I may come to you, that you will take me to your heart after all as your own, your trusted Jane, and I will arrange it as soon as ever I am able; say no, that you no longer wish to see me, that my image is defaced in your soul, and I will think you *not unjust*. Oh that I had your answer! Never were you so dear as at this moment when I am in danger of losing your affection, or what is still more precious to me, your respect.

JANE B. WELSH

Geraldine Jewsbury to Jane Welsh Carlyle

Thomas Carlyle may have had little consideration for his wife's intellect or emotions, but her friend, writer Geraldine Jewsbury, valued Jane Welsh Carlyle above all others. "I love you more than anything else in the world," she wrote in 1842. "It may do you no good now, but it may be a comfort some time, it will always be there for you." Her letters to Jane are far more passionate than anything Thomas bothered to pen. "O *Carissima mia*," Geraldine writes. "You are never out of either my head or my heart. After you left on Tuesday I felt so horribly wretched, too miserable even to cry, and what could be done?"

As Lillian Faderman has shown, many nineteenth-century women enjoyed close-knit relationships that were frequently more open and intimate than those they had with their husbands. For Jane, this was certainly the case. Her life was narrowly circumscribed by her husband's demands and her husband's contempt. She envied her friend's financial and personal independence, her career as a successful novelist; she was racked by jealousy whenever Geraldine engaged in heterosexual relationships, even though Geraldine insisted that these romances were insignificant. "You are of infinitely more worth and importance in my eyes," Geraldine protested to Jane. "You come nearer to me."

Although they had fantasies of going off together, nineteenth-century divorce laws kept this but a fantasy. They loved one another for more than twenty-five years, until Jane's death in 1866, but never were able to live together. Instead, they dreamed of a time when women's ideas would be valued as much as men's and when women would be free to lead their own lives, wherever those lives might lead.

1849

I believe we are touching on better days, when women will have a genuine, normal life of their own to lead. There, perhaps, will not be so many marriages, and women will be taught not to feel their destiny *manqué* if they remain single. They will be able to be friends and companions in a way they cannot be now.

. . . I do not feel that either you or I are to be called failures. We are indications of a development of womanhood which as yet is not recognized. It has, so far, no ready made channels to run in, but still we have looked, and tried, and found that the present rules for women will not hold us—that something better and stronger is needed.

. . . There are women to come after us, who will approach nearer the fulness of the measure of the stature of a woman's nature. I regard myself as a mere faint indication, a rudiment of the idea, of certain higher qualities and possibilities that lie in women, and all the eccentricities and mistakes and desires and absurdities I have made are only the consequences of an imperfect formation, an immature growth . . . I can see there is a precious mine of a species of womanhood yet undreamed of by the professors and essayists on female education, and I believe also that we belong to it.

Edgar Allan Poe to Sarah Helen Whitman

Life of my life—soul of my soul," Poe writes to Helen (Sarah Helen Whitman) on November 14, 1848. Two days later he writes an even more impassioned letter: "Ah, Annie Annie! *my* Annie!" Poe was consistent in his purple epistolary prose—even if he addressed it to different women.

His love life was various, if nothing else. In 1835 he obtained a license to marry his cousin, Virginia Clemm, aged thirteen, and then, after their marriage, moved with her and her mother first to Richmond, Virginia, and then to New York City. Lacking any kind of regular employment and making money only sporadically from his writing, Poe, his wife, and her mother nearly starved to death, and Virginia's health declined precipitously. Poe blamed himself for her death from tuberculosis during the winter of 1847. An alcoholic who was prone to profound depressions, Poe sought solace from his guilt over his wife's death in the company of the two women addressed in the letters reprinted here. Mrs. Sarah Helen Whitman was a poet from Providence, Rhode Island, whom he had met on one of his lecture tours. A widow, she might have been able to provide Poe with some degree of emotional and financial support, but he found himself desperately attracted to Mrs. Annie Richmond. She, however, already had a husband and was unwilling to leave him in order to marry Poe. Unable to make up his mind between the two, Poe took an ounce of laudanum in a suicide attempt, but succeeded only in falling desperately ill. The brush with death scared him enough that he resolved to get his life in order. He returned to Richmond, and there became engaged to another woman, Mrs. Shelton, with whom he had had an affair many years before. On his way north to get Mrs. Clemm to bring her to the wedding, he was found wandering delirious near a saloon in Baltimore. Four days later he was dead.

Steamboat, New York
Nov 14 1848

My own dearest Helen, *so* kind so true, so generous—so
unmoved by all that would have moved one who had been less
than angel:—beloved of my heart of my imagination of my
intellect—life of my life—soul of my soul—dear, dearest Helen,
how shall I ever thank you as I ought.

I am calm & tranquil & but for a strange shadow of coming
evil which haunts me I should be happy. That I am not
supremely happy, even when I feel your dear love at my heart,
terrifies me. What can this mean?

Perhaps however it is only the necessary reaction after such
terrible excitements.

It is 5 o'clock & the boat is just being made fast to the
wharf. I shall start in the train that leaves New York at 7 for
Fordham. I write this to show you that I have not *dared* to
break my promise to you. And now dear *dearest* Helen be true
to me—

Edgar Allan Poe to Annie L. Richmond

Fordham Nov. 16th 1848—

Ah, Annie Annie! *my* Annie! What cruel thoughts about
your Eddy must have been torturing your heart during the last
terrible fortnight, in which you have heard *nothing* from me—
not even one little word to say that I still lived & loved you.
But Annie I know that you *felt* too deeply the nature of my love
for you, to doubt *that*, even for one moment, & this thought
has comforted me in my bitter sorrow—I could bear that you

should imagine *every other evil except that one*—that my soul had been untrue to yours.

Why am I not *with* you now *darling* that I might sit by your side, press your dear hand in mine, & look deep down into the clear Heaven of your eyes—so that the words which I now can only *write*, might sink into your heart, and make you comprehend what it is that I would say—And yet Annie, *all* that I wish to say—all that my soul pines to express at this instant, is included in the one word, *love*—To be with you now—so that I might whisper in your ear the divine emotion[s], which agitate me—I would willingly—oh *joyfully* abandon this world with all my hopes of another:—but you *believe* this, Annie—you do believe it, & will always believe it— So long as I think that you *know* I love you, as no man ever loved woman—so long as I think you comprehend in some measure, the fervor with which I adore you, *so* long, no worldly trouble can ever render me absolutely wretched.

Oh, *my darling, my* Annie, my own sweet *sister* Annie, my *pure* beautiful angel—*wife* of my soul . . .

forever your own

Eddy—

Maud Gonne to William Butler Yeats

Maud Gonne shared William Butler Yeats's fascination with the occult and supernatural. She was less fascinated by the poet and playwright himself. An Irish revolutionary, she wanted to be in the thick of the politics of the time. He was an Irish nationalist as much by romantic inclination as by activist conviction, and he entertained a fantasy of mystical union in which she would retire with him to his rural retreat in the west of Ireland where he would write and she would serve as his muse. From their initial meeting in 1889, he knew in his heart this woman wouldn't be happy in Sligo.

Yeats's love for Maud Gonne amounted almost to an obsession. Longing for her inspired his early poems, his plays, his dreams, and, of course, his love letters. Even after it was obvious that they had no future together, he continued to love her deeply. His letters to others obsessively recount his meetings with Maud Gonne, what she said or didn't say to him, what her words meant, really meant, or might have meant. She did not discourage his attentions but also put them in perspective. She is reported to have said she was just the hatrack upon which Willie hung his poetry.

The two continued to be friends and correspondents for years. He finally consoled himself that, although she wouldn't have him, she was far too dedicated to the Irish cause ever to marry another. Then, in 1903, Gonne wrote Yeats that she had just married Major John MacBride in Paris. "The ears being deafened, the sight of the eyes blind/ With lightning," is how Yeats described his emotions upon reading the news. He was thirty-seven years old, disillusioned with Ireland, and bereft of the woman of his dreams. He reeled. And, as always, he wrote about it, in his poetry but also, indirectly, in a correspondence with Gonne that continued after her marriage.

This letter about her astral union with Yeats was written while she was married to MacBride. After MacBride died, Yeats, still floundering, came to Paris to offer Gonne a proposition: If she gave up politics, he'd marry her. She stalled him for a while, then, predictably, refused his offer. On the rebound, he married Georgie Hyde-Lees and finally found the end of his lifelong spiritualist search. Georgie, too, was intrigued by the occult. On their honeymoon she tried automatic writing for the first time and was surprised to find herself suddenly seized by a higher power. Willie and Georgie looked down with amazement upon the paper that all at once seemed to make lucid the complicated, mythological systems that Yeats had tried to understand for most of his adult life. Inspired by her automatic writing and steady in his new marriage, Yeats, over fifty years of age, went on to write some of his most beautiful and most lyrical poetry.

Paris
26 July 1908

Willie,

It is not in a week but in a day that I am writing to you. I had such a wonderful experience last night that I must know at once if it affected you & how? for above all I don't want to do any thing which will take you from your work, or make working more arduous. — That play is going to be a wonderful thing & must come first — nothing must interfere with it —

Last night all my household had retired at a quarter to 11 and I thought I would go to you astrally. It was not working hours for you & I thought by going to you I might even be able to leave with you some of my vitality & energy which would make working less of a toil next day — I had seen the day before when waking from sleep a curious some what Egyptian form floating over me (like in the picture of Blake the soul leaving the body) — It was dressed in mothlike garments & had curious wings edged with gold in which it could fold itself up — I had thought it was myself, a body in which I could go out into the astral — at a quarter to 11 last night I put on this body & thought strongly of you & desired to go to you. We went some where in space I dont know where — I was conscious of starlight & of hearing the sea below us. You had taken the form I think of a great serpent, but I am not quite sure. I only saw your face distinctly & as I looked into your eyes (as I did the day in Paris you asked me what I was thinking of) & your lips touched mine. We melted into one another till we formed only *one being, a being greater than ourselves* who felt all & knew all with double intensity — the clock striking 11 broke the spell & as we separated it felt as if life was being drawn away from me through my chest with almost physical pain. I went again twice, each time it was the same — each time I was brought back by some slight noise in the house. Then I went upstairs to bed & I dreamed of you confused dreams of ordinary life. We were in Italy together (I think this was from some word in your letter which I had read again before sleeping). We were quite happy, & we talked of this wonderful spiritual vision I have described—you said it would tend to increase physical desire—This troubles me a little—for there was nothing physical in that union—Material union is but a pale shadow compared to it—write to me quickly & tell me if you know anything of this & what you think of it—& if I may come to you again like this. I shall not until I hear from you. My thought with you always

MAUD GONNE

D. H. Lawrence to Ernest Weekley

In April of 1912, D. H. Lawrence decided to call on one of his old professors from Nottingham University College, Ernest Weekley, to gain advice on procuring a lectureship in Germany. He left Weekley's house without the lectureship but having sparked the interest of the professor's wife, Frieda, a German aristocrat with sophisticated tastes, a frank manner, and flashing jade and amber eyes. Lawrence couldn't keep his eyes off her. A few days after meeting her, he dropped her a note: "You are the most wonderful woman in all England." She responded by asking if he really knew all the others.

Lawrence found Frieda's tough-mindedness appealing, just as she was attracted to his impulsiveness. When Lawrence visited Frieda a short time later, she informed him that her husband was out of town and asked him, bluntly, to stay the night. He, as bluntly, refused, but insisted that she should leave her husband and run away with him. She was shocked. She was the mother of three children. Her husband had no reason to suspect anything was wrong in their marriage. When she agreed to run away with Lawrence and told her husband, Ernest collapsed into what he later described as a form of temporary insanity. Nonetheless, Frieda steeled herself, deposited her children with in-laws, and went off to meet Lawrence. "I hope you've got some money for yourself," Lawrence said in his last note before their elopement. "I can muster only eleven pounds."

Theirs was not a relationship based on practicality. They spent most of their days on the move, perpetually short of funds, always arguing. But the turbulent and nomadic life did provide Lawrence with ample material for four very personal travel books as well as for his fiction. For Frieda it was a life far more exciting than her previous one as a mother and the wife of a middle-aged professor.

Lawrence wrote the letter that is reprinted here in May of 1912, barely a month after meeting Frieda. They were staying in a small hotel in Metz, Germany. He was alone a good deal while she visited her family, trying to break the news gently that she had abandoned her children and eloped with a coal miner's son. Meanwhile, Ernest was sending her family frantic telegrams from England, trying to present his side of the story. Partly in retaliation, Lawrence wrote this letter to his old professor. It is surely one of the stranger justifications for adultery ever penned. Sounding a note familiar to any reader of *Sons and Lovers* (1913) or *Women in Love* (1920), Lawrence insisted that it was for Frieda, really, that both he and Ernest had to make sacrifices. For after all, the writer insisted, "women in their natures are like giantesses. They will break through everything and go on with their own lives."

May 7, 1912
Hotel Deutscher Hof, Metz

You will know by now the extent of the trouble. Don't curse my impudence in writing to you. In this hour we are only simple men, and Mrs. Weekley will have told you everything, but you do not suffer alone. It is really torture to me in this position. There are three of us, though I do not compare my sufferings with what yours must be, and I am here as a distant friend, and you can imagine the thousand baffling lies it all entails. Mrs. Weekley hates it, but it has had to be. I love your wife and she loves me. I am not frivolous or impertinent. Mrs. Weekley is afraid of being stunted and not allowed to grow, and so she must live her own life. All women in their natures are like giantesses. They will break through everything and go on with their own lives. The position is one of torture for us all. Do not think I am a student of your class—a young cripple. In this matter are we not simple men? However you think of me, the situation still remains. I almost burst my heart in trying to think what will be best. At any rate we ought to be fair to ourselves. Mrs. Weekley must live largely and abundantly. It is her nature. To me it means the future. I feel as if my effort of life was all for her. Cannot we all forgive something? It is not too much to ask. Certainly if there is any real wrong being done I am doing it, but I think there is not.

D. H. LAWRENCE

Delmira Agustini to Manuel Ugarte

One of Latin America's greatest poets, Delmira Agustini was introduced to the public as a child prodigy in 1902 when her first poems were published as if she were a "girl of twelve years." In reality she was sixteen. She kept up the pretense of being an ingenue all her life and continued to be known as "la Nena," the Little Girl. The youngest child and only daughter of overprotective parents, she was educated at home and always carefully chaperoned. Even in letters to her future husband, Enrique Job Reyes, she often wrote in a sexless baby talk: "I behaves well vewy much: I say to you vewy much 'Nighty night, my old man.' " She called him "Daddy" and signed her letters, "Your Little Girl."

However, behind the pose of sweet "la Nena" lurked a passionate poet and lover. At the same time that she was writing infantile letters to Reyes that were probably scrutinized by her mother, she also wrote him secretly in more direct and erotic language. Possibly these letters were never sent. But the split personality also explains how she could publish highly erotic verse under a guise of virginal innocence as well as how she could carry on a double romantic life. She fell madly in love with a well-known Argentine writer and womanizer, Manuel Ugarte, yet went on with her planned marriage to Reyes.

Predictably, the marriage was a disaster. As suggested in the letter reprinted here, her honeymoon with Reyes was filled with fantasy-thoughts of Ugarte. Accusing her husband of "vulgarity," she began divorce proceedings weeks after their wedding. Yet even while she was filing for a divorce, she continued to secretly meet and have a sexual relationship with her husband. By contrast, the great love of her life, with Ugarte, was never consummated.

Her duplicitous life ended tragically. One night, shortly before their divorce was finalized, Reyes walked in on his wife and supposedly surprised her in bed with another man—not Ugarte but a notorious, local Don Juan. Or so it was reported in the Uruguayan newspapers. What is definite is that on July 6, 1914, Agustini was found dead, half undressed, with two bullets in her head. Her husband lay dying beside her.

This letter of Delmira Agustini's was written shortly after her marriage. It is in response to one from Manuel Ugarte accusing her of writing him a "literary arabesque" instead of a frank avowal of her love: "Let us imagine that I have not received your letters," he demands. "Write to me for the first time, will you? And let not the ink serve as a mask."

1914

Your letter has done me almost more harm than your silence. I had believed that you interpreted me better. I am sure that I did not say in my *literary arabesque* one thing that was not true, and that did not, indeed, pale to the truth. And strangest in this case is that I protest your words, and, deep down, perhaps I think you are right.

It is true. I have not been absolutely sincere with you. But think, there are sincerities which are difficult. That light artistic veil was almost necessary. . . . Think that everything I have said to you and I say to you could be condensed in two words [*Te amo:* I love you]. In two words that can be the most sweet, the most simple, or the most difficult and painful. . . . Think that those two words that *I could have in good conscience* said to you the day after meeting you, have had to drown on my lips if not in my soul.

To be absolutely sincere I had to say them. I had to say that you are responsible for the torment of my wedding night and of my absurd honeymoon. . . . What might have been a long humorous novel became a tragedy.

What I suffered that night I will never be able to tell you. I entered the room as though I entered a sepulchre without more consolation than to think that I would see you. While they dressed me I asked I know not how many times if you had arrived. I could recount every one of my gestures that night. . . . The only conscious look I had, the only *inopportune* greeting I initiated were for you. I had a lightning bolt of happiness. It seemed to me for a moment that you watched me and understood me. That your spirit was very close to mine in midst of all those troublesome people. Later, between kisses and greetings, the only thing I hoped for was your hand. The only thing I desired was to have you close for a moment. The moment of the portrait. . . . And afterwards, suffer until I bid you goodnight. And afterwards suffer more, suffer the unspeakable . . .

Without knowing it you shook up my life. I could have told you that all this was in me new, terrible and delicious. I did not expect anything, I could not expect anything except bitterness from this feeling, and the greatest voluptuousness of my life has been to sink myself in it. I knew that you came to leave me the sadness of the memory and nothing more. And I preferred that, and I prefer the dream of *what could have been* to all the realities in which you do not vibrate.

I have to tell you all this, and more, to be absolutely sincere. But, among other things, I have been afraid of discovering myself to be deep *deep down*, one of those poor weak souls completely surrendered to love. Just imagine that misery before your ironic smile of a powerful man. . . . And I, I have known how to smile as ironically as you. . . .

It has been said. If after all this you again accuse me of being deceitful and subtle, I will accuse you simply of being a bad interpreter of sentimental matters. I would never accuse you of anything worse. Nor would I wait for the spring breeze to bring me perfumes from over there to write to you without knowing why.

And know that I feel intimately wounded.

Delmira

Anaïs Nin to June Miller

Anaïs Nin began her famous diary in 1914, at the age of eleven, and wrote in it almost daily until her death in 1977, candidly recording her philosophical, emotional, physical, and sexual life. Although she also wrote fiction, she felt that her diary was her purest and most authentic form of expression, since only in the diary was she free from the demands of readers or the requirements of censors.

Published posthumously, *Henry and June: From the Unexpurgated Diary of Anaïs Nin* begins when Nin meets novelist Henry Miller in Paris in 1931. He wanted a conventional affair, spiced with lots of letters about it. His forcefulness and crudeness frightened her, and she balked at the affair. "We talk, fencingly," is how Nin described the titillating verbal and sexual tug-of-war she was engaged in with Miller.

It was only when Henry's wife June joined him in Paris that Nin fell in love—with June. "Henry faded. [June] was color, brilliance, strangeness." Nin thought June "the most beautiful woman on earth."

For the next four weeks Nin bought June perfume and clothing, they exchanged jewelry, they held hands, they kissed. But they stopped short of a full, sexual relationship, both fearful of their attraction. After June returned to New York, Henry and Anaïs finally became lovers. Periodically, each partner accused the other of thinking of June. The triangle continued. Nin's unexpurgated diary of her time with Henry and June ends, "So Henry is coming this afternoon, and tomorrow I am going out with June."

February 1932

I cannot believe that you will not come again towards me from the darkness of the garden. I wait sometimes where we used to meet, expecting to feel again the joy of seeing you walk towards me out of a crowd—you, so distinct and unique.

After you went away the house suffocated me. I wanted to be alone with my image of you. . . .

I have taken a studio in Paris, a small, shaky place, and attempt to run away only for a few hours a day, at least. But what is this other life I want to lead without you? I have to imagine that you are there, June, sometimes. I have a feeling that I want to be you. I have never wanted to be anyone but myself before. Now I want to melt into you, to be so terribly close to you that my own self disappears. I am happiest in my black velvet dress because it is old and is torn at the elbows.

When I look at your face, I want to let go and share your madness, which I carry inside of me like a secret and cannot conceal any more. I am full of an acute, awesome joy. It is the joy one feels when one has accepted death and disintegration, a joy more terrible and more profound than the joy of living, of creating.

DECEMBER LOVE

George Eliot (Marian Evans) to John Cross

At the age of thirty-seven, Marian Evans stunned her peers by eloping to Germany with George Henry Lewes, a writer who considered himself released from his own marital obligations by his wife's adulterous relationship with another man. Widely respected as a formidable intellect, editor, journalist, and translator of the Continental philosophers, Evans soon suffered the hostility of literary society, like any Victorian woman who dared to cause a scandal. Ousted from her elite intellectual world, Evans switched to writing fiction under the *nom de plume* "George Eliot" and became one of the most famous novelists of her century.

Lewes's writing career was also transformed by love. He progressed from minor journalism to biography and philosophy much esteemed for its intellectual vigor and vitality. Theirs was a rare partnership. But since the two were hardly ever apart, no love letters survive to tell that part of their story.

Lewes died in 1878, shortly after George Eliot finished her last novel, *Daniel Deronda*. In her bereavement, she edited and completed Lewes's last book, *Problems of Life and Mind*. Throughout this period of her widowhood she received one friend, John Cross, a man twenty years her junior, who was in mourning from the recent death of a beloved mother. The two comforted one another. When Eliot announced their engagement, she again rocked the Victorian literary world.

On their honeymoon in Venice, Cross threw himself from their hotel window and had to be fished out of the Grand Canal by gondoliers. Gossips whispered of a suicide attempt, but he insisted he had been temporarily deranged by fever from the fetid Venetian atmosphere. Despite such an unpromising beginning and her declining health, the brief marriage was apparently quite congenial. "I am left alone in the new house we meant to be so happy in," Cross lamented after his wife's death.

In this early letter to Cross, the sixty-year-old novelist is again in love. Aware of his self-consciousness about the disparity in their age as well as in their intellectual stature, she tries to reassure him. Who cares, she says, that he can't elucidate the theories of Kepler? Is he jealous of an article about Lewes that had recently appeared? The article was "very well done," she says in her most professional and dismissive tone. The past is past, and only he can make her feel like Beatrice, the lovely young woman whom Dante celebrated in his *Vita Nuova* and *Divine Comedy*. Brilliantly, poetically, she minimizes his self-consciousness by reversing the disparities between them, all with the single, perfect literary allusion to Dante and his muse.

The Heights, Witley, Nr. Godalming.
October 16, 1897, Thursday.

Best loved and loving one—the sun it shines so cold, so cold, when there are no eyes to look love on me. I cannot bear to sadden one moment when we are together, but *wenn Du bist nicht da* [when you are not there] I have often a bad time. It *is* a solemn time, dearest. And why should I complain if it is a painful time? What I call my pain is almost a joy seen in the wide array of the world's cruel suffering. Thou seest I am grumbling today—got a chill yesterday and have a headache.

All which, as a wise doctor would say, is not of the least consequence, my dear Madam.

Through everything else, dear tender one, there is the blessing of trusting in thy goodness. Thou dost not know anything of verbs in Hiphil and Hophal or the history of metaphysics or the position of Kepler in science, but thou knowest best things of another sort, such as belong to the manly heart—secrets of lovingness and rectitude. O I am flattering. Consider what thou wast a little time ago in pantaloons and black hair.

Triumph over me. After all, I have *not* the second copy of the deed. What I took for it was only Foster's original draft and my copy of it. The article [on George Henry Lewes] by Sully in the *New Quarterly* is very well done.

I shall think of thee this afternoon getting health at Lawn Tennis, and I shall reckon on having a letter by tomorrow's post.

Why should I compliment myself at the end of my letter and say that I am faithful, loving, more anxious for thy life than mine? I will run no risks of being 'inexact'—so I will only say *'varium et mutabile semper'* [woman is ever fickle and changeable] but at this particular moment thy tender

Beatrice.

Emma Goldman to Arthur Swenson

Emma Goldman's tempestuous love affair with Ben Reitman ended stormily in 1917, but it did not end definitively. In 1927, at the height of her depression over the execution of fellow anarchists Sacco and Vanzetti, Goldman realized that Reitman was trying to revive their love affair of a decade past. She was indignant. She wanted to remain friends; he wanted to make love to her again.

Emma got her way. They remained friends, if at a distance, for the rest of their lives. When Emma was silenced by a stroke three months before her death in 1940, Reitman wrote her an encouraging letter: "You have lived your 'three score and ten.' I hope you will have many more healthy, happy, useful years." He then added, "Keep sweet."

Reitman may have been the great love of her life, but he was not her only love. In her mid-fifties, she had an affair with a young Swedish anarchist, Arthur Swenson. She met him after she was deported from the United States for protesting conscription during World War I. She had left Russia and was living in Europe, moving from place to place as one visa after another expired. Swenson tried to help her but was not terribly practical. They tried to stow away together on a boat to Denmark, but a policeman found them entangled together under a blanket and made them return to shore.

As this letter makes clear, Goldman was convinced, from the very beginning of their relationship, that Swenson would leave her for a younger woman. Twenty-four years was too great a difference in their ages. Once, when he was preparing to leave for Germany, she predicted that he would fall in love with a girl in Berlin. "You tell me of all the young attractive girls in Berlin," he wrote, trying to assure her. "Ah, there are lots of them here too, but my love belongs to you and only you . . . My Emma is the youngest and most attractive of them all. And by God, I love her!"

December 8, 1922

Dear, dear Arthur

When one's life depends upon a surgical operation it is folly to postpone the painful process. One's condition only grows worse and brings one near to death.

For months I have seen with absolute clarity that my peace of mind and soul and my very life depend upon our *separation*. But I have gone on postponing the painful operation until I can bear it no longer. . . .

Don't for one minute think I am blaming you, my Arthur. My brain sees, even if my heart refuses to submit to the verdict of my mind. You are thirty and I am fifty-two. From the ordinary point of view it is natural that your love for me should have died. It is a wonder it should ever have been born. How, then, can it be your fault? Traditions of centuries have created the cruel injustice which grants the man the right to ask and receive love from one much younger than himself and does not grant the same right to the woman. Every day one sees decrepit men of more than 52 with girls of twenty, nor is it true that these girls are with such men only for money. I have known several cases where girls of twenty were passionately devoted to men of sixty. No one saw anything unusual in that. Yet even the most advanced people cannot reconcile themselves to the love of a man of thirty for one much older than he. You certainly could not. . . .

I want to retain the memory of three glorious months, so full of beauty and warmth—

I am your friend whom you can always call upon, I will never fail you.

> Always devotedly,
> Emma

H. L. Mencken to Sara Haardt

F ew people even remember that H. L. Mencken, the acerbic journalist and man of letters, was married. Although he had many women friends and aided talented writers (female as well as male), he is remembered as the misogynist who once defined "love" as "the delusion that one woman differs from another." Yet when lecturing at Goucher College, he met Sara Haardt, a promising, articulate twenty-four-year-old teacher and fiction writer eighteen years his junior, and he was captivated. Convinced of her talent, he originally advised her *not* to marry him, since he believed marriage prevented women from fulfilling their potential. Sara, as brilliant as she was beautiful, agreed, feeling that any woman who gave up her career for marriage made a terrible sacrifice that she would later regret. For several years they maintained separate lives and careers, but wrote one another almost daily. Their correspondence reveals the intensity of their intellectual and emotional lives. Mencken's letters are reserved. He was not a man to put passion into print. Yet when Sara, more voluble, does not respond on a given day, Mencken urges her to write more, and more often. Seven years and seven hundred letters later, the couple finally overcame their philosophical opposition to matrimony. By all reports, it was an unusually happy union.

March 4th, 1925
Baltimore, Maryland

Dear Sara:—

Good news, indeed! It was, I take it, a bout with the flu. The damned disease is still epidemic. I escape it only by violating Art. XVIII. The medical journals are now full of reports on the hiccough pest I had three months ago. The symptoms were very curious and amusing: hiccoughs for three days and a fearful itching of the scalp. God has many tricks up his sleeve. I admire such humors.

I gave out no statement regarding the *Mercury*. Nathan very foolishly did so, with the result that he is now in an embarrassing position. But I can't do anything to help it. My announcement will be made in the July number, in three lines. We are still very far from a settlement. It may come to rough stuff yet. Knopf, unfortunately, is an innocent bystander, and his interests must be thought of.

In the Borglum affair I sympathize with the disciples of Jeff Davis. Borglum is a hog for money, and generally disreputable. During the war he made a great deal of money out of dubious airship contracts.

Twenty seven! You are just beginning to get your growth. A woman is at her most charming after 30, especially a brunette. You will be very handsome when you begin to oxidize. As for me, I begin to feel, at 44½, that the morticians have their eye on me. By the time you are that age I shall be 62. Think of it!

The article on the Southern lady is very good stuff. Some polishing, perhaps, wouldn't hurt it, but I think it is saleable as it stands. Try it on the magazines I mentioned in my last. They all pay excellent honoraria. If they don't buy it, let me see it again. I think, with a few small changes, I can use it. But we are still paying less than the *Century, Harper's,* etc. We closed our first year $2,200 ahead, but with no salaries paid to editors. What a world!

Isaac Goldberg now proposes to write a book about me, with illustrations. Inasmuch as he knows no more about me than Coolidge, I must dig up the materials myself. It turns out to be a frightful job. I have spent two whole days trying to discover and arrange the history of the Menckenii. When that is finished I must go through all my early newspaper stuff, and make selections from it. Then I must try to remember the details of my spiritual history—how I became a Christian, etc. If I had plenty of time it would be amusing, but I have very little. Goldberg will give a show, but he'll not make a book. That job is reserved for you. Title: "An American Patriot." I authorize you to publish it ten years after my lamentable exitus from these scenes.

Friend Sary, I miss you like hell. I have, in fact, transferred my eating from the Marconi to Max's place in Park Avenue. If you were at hand I should probably risk your yells by trying to neck you. I have been practicing on a fat woman. When we meet you will see some technique. So beware again!

Ich kuss die Hand!

Yours,
HLM

Brenda Venus to Henry Miller

In 1976 an unknown actress with the improbable name of Brenda Venus wrote a letter to the ailing, eighty-four-year-old Henry Miller, a writer who in his younger years had been known for his sexual libertinism and groundbreaking fictional portrayals of male sexuality. Venus expressed her desire to meet him and enclosed a number of photographs. Never one to pass up an opportunity to spend time with a beautiful woman, Miller responded enthusiastically, writing two letters on June 9, 1976, which were reciprocated by more letters from Venus. This was the beginning of a four-thousand-page exchange that lasted until Miller's death in 1980.

Miller's letters to Brenda Venus display a remarkable vitality, especially considering that his health was in serious decline. In the relationship, he assumed alternate roles as father, mentor, and classic dirty old man, roles that must have been both flattering and unthreatening to Venus, who was trying to make her way in the brutal world of the would-be Hollywood starlet. Commenting on a letter she wrote to commemorate Miller's eighty-sixth birthday, Venus noted that he "had taken me down a path of trust, faith, and love, and I was happy that I had followed." She was proud to play the role of final muse to one of America's lustiest (some would say pornographic) writers. For his part, Miller felt immeasurable love and gratitude to the young woman. Except for her, he would have "been forced to drowse away his last years with the needle and the knockout drops for company."

Jan. 22, 1980

My Forever Henry,

You teach me so-o much. You help me understand Life. You are as close to perfection as a rose. Your will, your spirit, your strength is astounding. I am always in awe of you. You as a man. The most special human being in the whole world. I feel like all the nice happenings in my life are attributed to you. You are firmly cemented in my heart, in my mind, in my soul.

The rose that never dies, the light that never goes out.

Now, because of you, I can just let things be as they are. That is really a step up the ladder for me, yes?

Because of you, I deal with the moment, with today. I don't worry about tomorrow, I know it'll be here soon enough. Each day is very precious, especially when I see your face, hold your hands, look in your eyes.

Tony and Val love you very much. I watched Tony look at you yesterday and I could see the love he has for you. I know it is difficult for children and their parents, because there is always a difference of opinion on attitude. It's amusing that the very thing parents dislike in their children is usually a characteristic they dislike in themselves and vice-versa. Tony is leaving soon, have you told him you love him lately? It's not so difficult to say . . . I love you, I love you, I love you. It makes me feel wonderful when I say it to the one I love. I wonder if it does the same for others.

Since Paris, I feel different. I can't really explain the reason, except to say that all the years seemed to come together in my mind. Everything became crystal clear. Especially the importance of just being, being oneself to the fullest.

You make me laugh, you make me cry, you make me fight for what I believe and not question the things I cannot change, but accept them for what they are, people, especially.

I hope the doctor has a good report on your health. And I hope you eat a lot of my chicken soup. I know if you eat well, you will be feeling great in a few days. I know!

This letter is too long for your eyes right now. So, I'll close.

Your watercolors are better than ever, but I'm your greatest fan—

> All my love now and forever—
> BRENDA

Henry Miller to Brenda Venus

September 29, 1980

And now, a man of 87, madly in love with a young woman who writes me the most extraordinary letters, who loves me to death, who keeps me alive and in love (a perfect love for the first time), who writes me such profound and touching thoughts that I am joyous and confused as only a teenager could be. But more than that—grateful, thankful, lucky. Do I really deserve all the beautiful praises you heap on me? You cause me to wonder exactly who I am, do I really know who and what I am? You leave me swimming in mystery. For that I love you all the more. I get down on my knees, I pray for you, I bless you with what little sainthood is in me. May you fare well, dearest Brenda, and never regret this romance in the midst of your young life. We have been both blessed. We are not of this world. We are of the stars and the universe beyond.

Long live Brenda Venus!

God give her joy and fulfillment and love eternal!

HENRY

EPISTOLARY LOVE

Charles Baudelaire to Apollonie Sabatier

Baudelaire's tormented, off-and-on relationship with Jeanne Duval had come to an unsatisfactory and inconclusive end sometime around 1852. A beautiful woman of mixed Caucasian and African ancestry, it was Duval's image that recurred in many of the love poems in Baudelaire's most famous collection, *The Flowers of Evil* (1857). They had spent fourteen obsessive years together, intoxicated by passion and opium. Although he realized that the relationship had been a destructive one, Baudelaire could hardly imagine existence without her. "Whenever I see a beautiful object, a lovely painting of a country scene, anything pleasant at all," he lamented, "I find myself thinking: why isn't she at my side to admire this with me, to buy that with me?"

Heartbroken and wary from the end of the relationship, Baudelaire kept his next great romance epistolary. It was his way of energizing his poetry without jeopardizing his ego or making a commitment. The object of his new affections was Apollonie Sabatier, a beautiful courtesan at the center of the Parisian art world. He began writing to her anonymously at the end of 1852 and continued until the spring of 1855. His letters to her are formal, stylized, idolizing; many contain worshipful poems. It was the perfect relationship for a poet of love who was afraid to love again.

Then, disaster. Sabatier discovered the identity of her correspondent and fell passionately in love with him. Baudelaire backed off. She wrote to him: "Look, my dear, do you want me to tell you my thoughts on the matter, thoughts that are very cruel and cause me much suffering? I think you don't love me. That's what's causing your fears, your hesitations at embarking on an affair which, in those conditions, would become a source of boredom for you and a constant torment for me."

Monday, May 9, 1853

Really, Madame, I ask your pardon a thousand times for this stupid, anonymous doggerel which smacks horribly of childishness; but what can I do about it? I am as egoistic as a child or as an invalid. I think of persons I love when I suffer. Usually I think of you in verse and when the verse are finished, I cannot resist the desire to have them read by the person who inspired them.—At the same time, I hide myself like someone who is terribly afraid of appearing ridiculous.—Isn't there something essentially comic in love?—especially for those who are not involved.

But I swear to you that this is really the last time I shall expose myself to ridicule; and if my ardent friendship for you lasts as long as it had lasted before I said a word to you about it, we shall both be old.

However absurd all this may seem to you, remember there is a heart which it would be cruelty to mock and in which your image is always alive.

~

Once, only once, beloved and gentle lady,
Upon my arms you leaned your arm of snow,
And on my spirit's background, dim and shady,
That memory flashes now.

The hour was late, and like a medal gleaming
The full moon showed her face,
And the night's splendour over Paris streaming
Filled every silent place.

Along the houses, in the doorways hiding,
Cats passed with stealthy tread
And listening ear, or followed, slowly gliding,
Like ghosts of dear ones dead.

Sudden, amid our frank and free relation,
Born of that limpid light,
From you, rich instrument, whose sole vibration
Was radiancy and light—

From you, joyous as bugle-call resounding
    Across the woods at morn,
With sharp and faltering accent strangely
sounding,
    Escape one note forlorn.

Like some misshapen infant, dark, neglected,
    Its kindred blush to own,
And long have hidden, by no eye detected,
    In some dim cave unknown.

Your clashing note cried clear, poor, prisoned spirit,
    That nothing in the world is sure or fast,
And that man's selfishness, though decked as merit,
    Betrays itself at last.

That hard the lot to be the queen of beauty,
    And all is fruitless, like the treadmill toil
Of some paid dancer, fainting at her duty,
    Still with her vacant smile.

That if one build on hearts, ill shall befall it,
    That all things crack, and love and beauty flee,
Until oblivion flings them in his wallet,
    Spoil of eternity.

Oft have I called to mind that night enchanted,
    The silence and the languor over all,
And that wild confidence, thus harshly chanted,
    At the heart's confessional.

James Whitcomb Riley to Elizabeth Kahle

*T*he *Love Letters of the Bachelor Poet, James Whitcomb Riley* chronicles one of the stranger love affairs in literary history. Although the letters run the gamut of love's emotions, they were exchanged between a man and woman who took three years to meet, were disappointed when they saw one another face-to-face, and so parted in order that they might resume their correspondence. Only after she wed someone else did Elizabeth put an end to the most intimate (if literary) relationship of her life.

The letters began in 1879 when Elizabeth, describing herself as a "romantic girl," wrote Riley to say that she was moved by his verse and included a few poems of her own. He answered with a personal history that amounted to a disclaimer of his most romantic poetry as well as the persona projected in his poems: "I believe it a duty that I owe both to you and to myself at this juncture," he wrote, "to assure you of the fact that I am a young man and unmarried. I write sentimental verses occasionally, simply because I don't believe in love and am anxious to convince myself of my error, possibly—I don't know why else. I have many friends, but more enemies—and can scarcely tell which I most enjoy—for I really enjoy being hated by some people." Elizabeth was not frightened off by this dismal response, and for the next five years, the two freely and candidly confided in one another. At the same time, he rose from impoverished obscurity to become one of the most financially successful of all American poets, chiefly with homey, cheerful verses written in Hoosier dialect—"When the Frost Is on the Punkin," "Knee-deep in June," or "Old Sweetheart of Mine." Elizabeth witnessed the turmoil and depression of the man himself. "The sun shines," he wrote her at the height of his fame, "but *I* don't." The letters clearly provided each of them with a rare emotional outlet. For Riley, it was one of the most important relationships of his life.

And of his afterlife. Following his death in 1916, Elizabeth Kahle attended a séance in which she asked a medium to contact him. Riley responded, characteristically, by letter. In fact, Elizabeth swore that for over two years Riley continued to reach out to her from beyond the grave. A love poem from him even appeared on the slate of a psychic in Cincinnati, accompanied by Riley's request that his posthumous epistle be forwarded to Elizabeth in Pittsburgh:

> There are memories embalmed in the love of the heart
>   Which live on while existence doth run;
> In the fondest of these hath my whole love been part
>   Of the life of Elizabeth Brunn.

Greenfield, August 23, 1879

My dear friend: —

Your letter is so kind—so very kind and good, that I must write at once to thank you for it and *grab* your two warm hands close in my own and wring them fervently. Only you mustn't be concerned about my health or welfare—anything— 'cause I don't deserve such interest from anyone so good as you. I *do* smile, though, when you say, "I want to ask, like I do of *children* when they cry, what *is* the matter? Tell me."

Surely if you feel like that, then indeed you comprehend me *just as I am,*—a little helpless child—who would thank God with all his boyish heart if you just could—now this minute— put your hands over my eyes and say, "Now you must sleep;" only—only—I want to be strong enough to bear my burden, and your dear words make me weak. You don't know—you *can't* know—what a weight it is, and how heavier it grows each weary step I take.

Forgive me, but you *mustn't* be so good to me, because *I want you to be happy*—not like me, who cannot even lift my empty hands at time, and ask God's help. You make me want to call you "little girl." You make me want to come to you creeping on my face and hands, to hide away from all the world and rest—rest! But this is Fate's hand clutching mine, and dragging me from pleasant ways through tangled labyrinths and steep defiles, and over stony paths where no flowers bloom, and no bird ever sings, and *no one* (should I not thank God for that?) to—*Sit down in the darkness and weep with me on the edge of the world—so love lies dead."* Yet, I wish that I might *talk* with you a little for *I am good* and you must *know that always.* You are like me in many things, and in one thing in particular, you are inclined to *tire* of it all (I mean this thing of *living on* and *on*—for—what?)—and ever yearning for some indefinable good that is ever kept from you. Am I not right? Well, I do not know *your* strength, but I will pray that it, too, is like my own; that you can say with me,— "It all *means something,* since God wills it, and may He give me strength and patience to abide." And it *does* mean something since God wills it, and He *will* give us strength and patience to abide. And I smile now as I fancy our two souls are kneeling here together side by side, praying in one voice, and God will hear it.

> *"Now* another *new moon* is here."

The poems you send are both good. The moon-poem especially—only it is so passionately hopeless. It is like the sound of my own voice,—or Yours—Ours! God bless us yet a little more than this!

And you are not to *cry* now, 'cause I'm almost well, and will be *quite* when your next letter comes,—that will cure me. And I do promise you not to work quite so hard as I have been doing. *And I have heard you call to me, and I have answered* saying—"God bless you, little girl, you rest me so!"

There,—

J. W. R.

George Bernard Shaw to Ellen Terry

Playwright, music critic, and lecturer, George Bernard Shaw was also a freethinker, an advocate for women's rights, an opponent of private property, and a proponent of the radical redistribution of wealth so that all would be economically comfortable and equal. He even wanted to reform the idiosyncracies of English spelling and punctuation so the language would be accessible to all. He was a strict vegetarian who refrained from alcohol, coffee, and tea. He married Charlotte Payne-Townshend in 1898 and they stayed contentedly married until her death in 1943 in what biographers like to refer to as a "marriage of companionship" (presumably a platonic relationship). An abstemious man, writing was his passion. Awarded the Nobel Prize for literature in 1925, he died in 1950 at the age of ninety-four years, and left behind over fifty plays and thousands of letters, including extraordinary love letters to the actress Ellen Terry.

Shaw and Terry wrote to one another for a year before they met. She was then in the midst of a long-standing relationship with a man Shaw disliked, the handsome young director, Henry Irving. But the real reason for her expressed reluctance to meet Shaw "in the flesh" was insecurity. She was nine years older than him and felt old. She insisted that she was a fine enough actress to make an audience believe she was "so nice, and so young and so happy, and always-in-the-air, light, and bodyless" but felt that offstage she was plain and tired, and feared that her unattractiveness would spoil the intimacy they experienced in their correspondence. Shaw responded that he understood what she meant, because in person he was "a disagreeably cruel looking middle aged Irishman with a red beard." He watched her from the other side of the footlights; they dreamed of touching one another and wrote to each other about what those dreams felt like.

Biographer Michael Holroyd has suggested that "they *acted* love." Shaw wrote plays for her and she acted them brilliantly. He tried to figure out why he had declined a sexual relationship with her in favor of "a lot of things to say." Ellen was bemused by the younger men in her life: Irving was afraid of emotional commitment, while Shaw shied away from sex. Both men were so jealous of one another that she wondered if she were the conduit for *their* feelings.

Yet she also realized that she and Shaw shared a rare and precious kind of love. "You are a fully self-possessed woman and therefore not really the slave of love," he praised her in his highest terms. "You," she wrote, even more tellingly, "have become a habit with me."

2 July 1897

No, I'm not altogether sorry you are ill, for when you are well you dont care for anybody (that's the glory of health—its iron-heartedness) but when you are ill, you become foolish, and love me. Heaven send you continual bad health, my dearest Ellen, so that you may be home writing to me, instead of making love to Napoleon and that limpid Lyceum audience.

Dont trouble about *The Man of Destiny*. All plays are thrown away on the stage: do you think even *that* piece would not be as much a secret between you and me as it is now if it were

played for a thousand nights at the Lyceum or the Théâtre
Français? It might have forced my Strange Lady to be no
longer strange to me if it had been rehearsed; but then that
plan was baffled. The matter concerned me no further. Words
cannot express my indifference to all this external business at
Croydon. If I could stay away tomorrow without seeming to
slight the company, it would not occur to me to go. As to H. I.
(of *him* you are thinking I know), serve him right. If all this
theatre business mattered I should say that he had thrown *you*
away, a blacker crime than the throwing of 50,000,000,000,000
Men of Destiny. But you also cannot be thrown away. A few
people know, though none of them know as well as I do.
Dearest love: send me one throb of your heart whilst it is still
tender with illness. It will be hard again on Monday; so be
quick, quick, quick.

FRIENDSHIP

Charlotte Brontë to Ellen Nussey

Friendship needs to be negotiated with every bit as much care and
tact as love, as this letter from novelist Charlotte Brontë to her friend
Ellen Nussey attests. All of the aspects of love—passion, tenderness,
separation, anxiety, anger, disillusionment, even triangles and unrequited affections—emerge in friendship, and never more so than in
the nineteenth century.

As social historians have shown, by the time of the Industrial Revolution, marriage was supposed to be based on mutual affection, not
arranged by families for political or commercial reasons. Yet the prevailing gender ideology of the time emphasized the "separate
spheres" of men's and women's lives. Industrialization meant that

men went away from the home to work, while women (even those who worked away from home) were responsible for the household and child-rearing. Many women felt isolated, and they turned to their friends for comfort, support, and emotional sustenance.

Charlotte Brontë met Ellen Nussey in 1831 at Miss Wooler's school at Roe Head where they were both students. Many of the girls she encountered at Miss Wooler's school would appear in her novel *Shirley* (1849), and two of the girls, Ellen Nussey and Mary Taylor, remained her lifelong friends. After Charlotte's death, Ellen published the story of how she met the author of *Jane Eyre* (1847) in a charming article, "Reminiscences of Charlotte Brontë," for *Scribner's Magazine*: "Arriving at school about a week after the general assembly of the pupils . . . I was led into the schoolroom, and quietly left to make my observations," she wrote of that meeting forty years earlier. "I became aware for the first time that I was not alone; there was a silent, weeping dark little figure in the large bay-window. . . . I was touched and troubled at once to see her so sad and so tearful." Charlotte confessed to Ellen that she was "homesick." Ellen confessed that she was homesick too. "A faint quivering smile then lighted her face; the teardrops fell; we silently took each other's hands, and at once we felt that genuine sympathy which always consoles, even though it be unexpressed."

Roe Head,
May 10th, 1836.

My Dearest Ellen,

Just now I am not at all comfortable; for if you are thinking of me at all at this moment I know you are thinking of me as an ungrateful and indifferent being. You imagine I do not appreciate the kind, constant heart whose feelings were revealed in your last letter; but I *do*.

Why then did I not answer it? you will say. Because I was waiting to receive a letter from Miss Wooler that I might know whether or not I should have time enough to give you an invitation to Haworth, before the School reopened, but Miss Wooler's letter, when it came, summoned me immediately away, and I had no time to write. Do you forgive me? I know you do; you could not persevere in anger against me long; if you would, I defy you.

You seemed kindly apprehensive about my health; I am perfectly well now, and never was very ill. I was struck with the note you sent me with the umbrella; it showed a degree of interest about my concerns, which I have no right to expect from any earthly creature. I won't play the hypocrite, I won't answer your kind, gentle, friendly questions in the way you wish me to. Don't deceive yourself by imagining that I have a bit of real goodness about me.

My Darling, if I were like you, I should have to face Zionward, though prejudice and error might occasionally fling a mist over the glorious vision before me, for with all your single-hearted sincerity you have your faults, but I am *not like you*. If you knew my thoughts; the dreams that absorb me; and the fiery imagination that at times eats me up and makes me feel society, as it *is*, wretchedly insipid, you would pity me and I dare say despise me.

But, Ellen, I know the treasures of the Bible, and love and adore them. I can *see* the Well of Life in all its clearness and brightness; but when I stoop down to drink of the pure waters, they fly from my lips as if I was Tantalus. I have written like a fool. Remember me to your mother and sisters. Good-bye.

CHARLOTTE

Come and see me soon; don't think me mad. This is a silly letter.

Herman Melville to Nathaniel Hawthorne

Perhaps no letters have ever better dramatized the relationship between literature and love or the fusion of friendship and passion than Herman Melville's famous missives to Nathaniel Hawthorne. Fifteen years younger than the author of *The Scarlet Letter* (1850), Melville viewed Hawthorne as friend and mentor and the one man on earth who might truly understand his great, metaphysical novel *Moby Dick* (1851), the one person on earth who would see clear to the depths of his soul.

Melville had already earned a reputation as a popular novelist with *Typee* and *Omoo*, tales loosely based on his experiences as a sailor marooned in the South Seas. But some critics had objected to the sexual content in the books as well as to the bitter remarks about the local missionaries. When *Moby Dick* appeared, many thought the former sailor had quite simply gone mad.

But Hawthorne admired the "wicked book," and that's what mattered. The letter reprinted here is an ecstatic expression of gratitude to a mentor who has read a writer's new work and complimented it. Even more, it is a lonely man's passionate declaration of love to a friend. Although Hawthorne and Melville were not lovers in a sexual sense of the word, this letter is the quintessential love letter, right down to the metaphysical conjoining of spirits and Melville's imagery of piercing the Godhead.

Hawthorne, for his part, was flattered to receive this letter—and frightened. Although Hawthorne's response has not survived, Melville's more guarded tone in subsequent letters suggests that there was a clear backing off. As has happened to many another who has impetuously or prematurely confessed a passion, Melville tried to recast his expression of love into a more moderate friendship. He even wrote jovial letters to Hawthorne's wife and to his son. The relationship between the two writers cooled. The far more timid Hawthorne continued to regard Melville with suspicion and made sure there was some distance between them. Never again would Melville feel himself, like a lover, losing his identity in the person of his Beloved: "Whence come you, Hawthorne?" Melville writes in the letter below. "By what right do you drink from my flagon of life? And when I put it to my lips, lo, they are yours and not mine."

November 17, 1851
Pittsfield, Monday afternoon.

My Dear Hawthorne,

   People think that if a man has undergone any hardship, he should have a reward; but for my part, if I have done the hardest possible day's work, and then come to sit down in a corner and eat my supper comfortably—why, then I don't think I deserve any reward for my hard day's work—for am I not now at peace? Is not my supper good? My peace and my supper are my reward, my dear Hawthorne. So your joy-giving and exultation-breeding letter is not my reward for my ditcher's work with that book, but is the good goddess's bonus over and above what was stipulated for—for not one man in five cycles, who is wise, will expect appreciative recognition from his fellows, or any one of them. Appreciation! Recognition! Is love appreciated? Why, ever since Adam, who has got to the meaning of this great allegory—the world? Then we pygmies must be content to have our paper allegories but ill comprehended. I say your appreciation is my glorious gratuity. In my proud, humble way,— a shepherd-king,—I was lord of a little vale in the solitary Crimea; but you have now given me the crown of India. But on trying it on my head, I found it fell down on my ears, notwithstanding their asinine length—for it's only such ears that sustain such crowns.

   Your letter was handed me last night on the road going to Mr. Morewood's, and I read it there. Had I been at home, I would have sat down at once and answered it. In me divine magnanimities are spontaneous and instantaneous—catch them while you can. The world goes round, and the other side comes up. So now I can't write what I felt. But I felt pantheistic then—your heart beat in my ribs and mine in yours, and both in God's. A sense of unspeakable security is in me this moment, on account of your having understood the book. I have written a wicked book, and feel spotless as the lamb. Ineffable socialities are in me. I would sit down and dine with you and all the gods in old Rome's Pantheon. It is a strange feeling—no hopefulness is in it, no despair. Content—

that is it; and irresponsibility; but without licentious inclination. I speak now of my profoundest sense of being, not of an incidental feeling.

Whence come you, Hawthorne? By what right do you drink from my flagon of life? And when I put it to my lips—lo, they are yours and not mine. I feel that the Godhead is broken up like the bread at the Supper, and that we are the pieces. Hence this infinite fraternity of feeling. Now, sympathizing with the paper, my angel turns over another page. You did not care a penny for the book. But, now and then as you read, you understood the pervading thought that impelled the book— and that you praised. Was it not so? You were archangel enough to despise the imperfect body, and embrace the soul. Once you hugged the ugly Socrates because you saw the flame in the mouth, and heard the rushing of the demon,—the familiar,—and recognized the sound; for you have heard it in your own solitudes.

My dear Hawthorne, the atmospheric skepticisms steal into me now, and make me doubtful of my sanity in writing you thus. But, believe me, I am not mad, most noble Festus! But truth is ever incoherent, and when the big hearts strike together, the concussion is a little stunning. Farewell. Don't write a word about the book. That would be robbing me of my miserly delight. I am heartily sorry I ever wrote anything about you—it was paltry. Lord, when shall we be done growing? As long as we have anything more to do, we have done nothing. So, now, let us add Moby Dick to our blessing, and step from that. Leviathan is not the biggest fish;—I have heard of Krakens.

This is a long letter, but you are not at all bound to answer it. Possibly, if you do answer it, and direct it to Herman Melville, you will missend it—for the very fingers that now guide this pen are not precisely the same that just took it up and put it on this paper. Lord, when shall we be done changing? Ah! it's a long stage, and no inn in sight, and night coming, and the body cold. But with you for a passenger, I am content and can be happy. I shall leave the world, I feel, with more satisfaction for having come to know you. Knowing you persuades me more than the Bible of our immortality.

What a pity, that, for your plain, bluff letter, you should get such gibberish! Mention me to Mrs. Hawthorne and to the children, and so, good-by to you, with my blessing.

Herman.

P.S. I can't stop yet. If the world was entirely made up of Magians, I'll tell you what I should do. I should have a papermill established at one end of the house, and so have an endless riband of foolscap rolling in upon my desk; and upon that endless riband I should write a thousand—a million—billion thoughts, all under the form of a letter to you. The divine magnet is on you, and my magnet responds. Which is the biggest? A foolish question—they are *One*.

P.P.S. Don't think that by writing me a letter, you shall always be bored with an immediate reply to it—and so keep both of us delving over a writing-desk eternally. No such thing! I sh'n't always answer your letters, and you may do just as you please.

Lydia Maria Child to Anne Whitney

Lydia Maria Child was among the most influential and popular novelists of her day. However, when she published an extensive anti-slavery tract, *Appeal in Favor of that Class of Americans Called Africans* (1833), she suffered social ostracism and financial ruin. Refusing to let this setback temper her convictions, she went on to write *History of the Condition of Women in Various Ages and Nations* (1835), a historical argument for women's equality, and *The Freedman's Books* (1865), which describes African-American heroes.

Not surprisingly, Anne Whitney, a sculptor and fellow abolitionist, wanted to add Child's bust to her collection of famous Americans.

Child declined the invitation to sit for Whitney, but the women began a friendship that lasted until Child died in 1880.

Although Child had had a difficult marriage—she was the main financial support of her family, and she had lived apart from her husband for a time—she here recounts a happy anecdote of her life with David Lee Child. She jokes that he had been "lover-like" right up to the end of his life and requested a photo of her "honest shoulders." She complied, posing in daring décolleté when she was in her early seventies.

It is also indicative of Child's personality that this letter moves effortlessly from girlish mischief to intellectual rigor. Near the end, she shrewdly discusses the ideas and the importance of the "Great Agnostic," Robert G. Ingersoll, whose piercing wit and unorthodox religious views were proving a bane to conservatives and liberals alike. In short, Lydia Maria Child—feminist, abolitionist, novelist—happens also to be a whole, vital, witty, sensual person who derives joy from the candor with which she can write a letter to a friend.

Wayland, May 22d, 1878.

Dear Anne,

Wind and weather permitting, I propose to go to Boston on Thursday, May 30'th. I shall have to go to the Bank, to Mr. Sewall's Office, to the Bookseller's, and several other places, on business. I shall dine *en route*, and hope to arrive at your house somewhere around 3 P.M. there to abide till Friday, when I propose to attend the Free Religious Meeting, for speaking. I propose to spend Friday night with my niece in Cambridge, and on Saturday return home to Wayland. We shall have Thursday afternoon and evening to settle the affairs of the universe; which will be abundant time for us to accomplish it; considering that one of us is so well posted up in all that relates to Matter, and the other so familiar with all that relates to Spirit.

If it should storm, all my plans will be frustrated.

I don't wonder you were surprised by the low dress in my photograph; especially, considering the age at which it was taken [in her early seventies]. The explanation is this: My dear old husband was as lover-like to the last year of his life, as he was during the days of courtship. He was often saying: "I fell in love with your *honest shoulders*; and I want you to have a photograph taken, on purpose for *me*, with the shoulders uncovered." So, at last, I humored the lover-like whim; and having no low dress, I folded a shawl about the bust.

Some years after it was taken, Mr. Prang [the lithographer] came here to look at photographs of me, with a view to make a picture of "Representative Women." Mr. Child showed him *his* photograph, and Mr. Prang thought it was the best that had been taken. I thought so, too; and I consented that he should copy merely *the head*. Contrary to my intention, the "honest shoulders" came to light; and I did not think it worth while to make any fuss about it. Head, shoulders, and all will be forgotten in a few years.

I am neither disgusted nor disturbed with Col. Ingersoll. I believe in *unlimited* freedom to express any amount of belief or unbelief. Because he is fighting *that* battle, I am willing to "hold up his hands till the going down of the sun." I have not arrived at his conclusions; and if I had, it would not be *my* way to state them thus. But it is *his* way. He is by nature full of fun. The prevailing theological ideas seem to him ridiculous, and he makes all manner of jokes at their expense. The ideas seem to *me* as ridiculous as they do to *him*; but I have so much pity for poor human-nature, wandering in the dark, that I have not the heart to joke about *anything* that furnishes any poor starving soul with consolation or support. Yet Ingersoll and I are, to a certain extent, doing the same work. He is *knocking* off fetters, and I am *melting* them off. Good riddance to fetters! say I. I want to see human souls stride about *freely* in search of truth. *You* are overturning superstition with the crow-bar of Science, *he* brings Fun in to give it a heave. By *all* our help, it will be rolled into the abyss of oblivion.

Tennessee Williams to Maria Britneva St. Just

After Tennessee Williams's death, his lifelong friend, Maria St. Just, published the letters he had written to her over the past thirty-five years. These reveal his inner life, his public opinions, his artistic processes, and, mostly, his abiding appreciation of their friendship.

Who is Maria St. Just? As director Elia Kazan notes, "most every author . . . has someone special that he or she looked to for a judgment-in-advance on his or her work. This might be a trusted editor but is less likely to be an intellectual than a person whose instinct the writer respects absolutely. In the case of Tennessee Williams, a man who would doubt praise when he thought it excessive and was equally able to shoulder off attacks and go on with his work, this one trusted person was Maria St. Just."

But Maria was more than just muse and editor to one of America's greatest playwrights. Born in Leningrad and raised in London, she studied ballet as a child and danced at Covent Garden in London. As an adult, she acted on the British stage, joining Sir John Gielgud's company and appearing with him and Dame Edith Evans in numerous productions. She played Blanche off-Broadway in Williams's *A Streetcar Named Desire* and was the model for the sexy, feisty Maggie in *Cat on a Hot Tin Roof.*

The two met on June 11, 1948, at a party hosted by Gielgud. "After a while, I noticed a little man sitting on a sofa. He was wearing a blue sock on one foot and a red one on the other. He looked unassuming and vulnerable, and nobody was talking to him. . . . I thought that he must be an understudy. I went up to him and asked him if he would like another drink. He seemed genuinely surprised at the interest I took." The shy man and the vivacious actress became instant friends. "Very occasionally one meets someone with whom one feels an immediate, deep rapport. I'd still no idea who he was. He told me that Chekhov was his favorite playwright. He'd never met a live Russian before."

For a brief time she thought she might be in love with him, but soon realized that he was sexually attracted only to men. Their relationship settled into a deep, steady platonic affection. "I just need someone to laugh with," he once said.

But they cried together, too, and turned to one another when it mattered. Even in his will, "Ten" named Maria his literary executor and entrusted her with the care of his beloved sister, Rose, the model for the fragile, dreamy Laura in *The Glass Menagerie*.

The meditation on friendship reprinted here was originally intended for his memoir. To his dismay, it was edited out of the American version. He sent her the typed copy because he wanted her to know what he had written about the special relationship they had shared.

June 22, 1976

T. W. for Maria

"Who is there to care beside yourself?" I exclaimed silently last night as I lay sleepless, turning over and over in my mind various unsatisfactory solutions to some very difficult problems which had to be resolved in the next few days.

What a flat-sounding word [friendship] is for what becomes, later on in life, the most important element of it! To me the French word for this deep relationship, probably all the deeper because it exists outside and beyond the physical kind of devotion, is much more appealing. It covers a broader spectrum and surely its depth is greater. The word is *l'amitié*.

That which we call and think of as "love" is often a promiscuous word in more senses than one. In all but the rarest cases in my experience I am afraid that it has depleted more than replenished the reservoir of my emotions, and in quite a number of cases it has also polluted and debased—and never mind if I come on as what I am, a man who is still a child in the shadow of a Protestant rectory.

L'amitié never involves a material transaction. You don't see it in a shop-window with a price tag attached to it or close beside it, and it requires no exertion of will to animate it with the breath of spirit. It is a consecrated thing and it is devoutly to be wished for, because, if it is real as opposed to artificial or trivial, it can endure until death, and Miss Elizabeth Barrett Browning was convinced that it lasted after. I think she is right to the extent that it lasts afterwards in the heart of the survivor.

. . . It is a delicate feeling, of course, and of course it is frangible and most certainly of all it must not be neglected. And yet it is long-suffering. It survives many unavoidable separations without disrepair, since it does not depend on physical presence as much as carnal attachment. Extended absences are a material element and this feeling that I call *l'amitié* has so little concern with material things.

I have been told and have no reason to doubt that *l'amitié* can exist between two men as well as between a man and a woman, but in my case it has occurred always with someone of the opposite gender.

I have had many close friendships with men which were without any sexual connotations, God knows. But I have found them less deeply satisfying than those I have had with a few women.

Of these women, the most important has been with [my dearest friend] Maria, as both Maria Britneva or as the Lady Maria St. Just.

PARENTS AND CHILDREN

George Sand to her mother, Madame Maurice Dupin

Biographers grow apologetic when they discuss Amandine-Aurore Lucille Dupin's decision to marry the Baron Casimir Dudevant. She was only eighteen years old when she left her mother's house to marry an old friend of her father's, a crude man many years her senior who was excessively fond of drink and young women.

Even after his marriage to Aurore, Dudevant flaunted his mistresses. The morning after the birth of their daughter, Aurore lay in bed, listening to her husband make love to one of the maids. As the marriage wore on, the Baron became both verbally and physically abusive.

What finally inspired Aurore to flee from such a humiliating relationship was discovering a letter that the elderly husband had written, sealed, and left in his desk for his wife to find after his death. Although her husband was still quite alive, she decided to read the letter anyway, expecting to find a tender and apologetic recap of their marriage that might help her through their remaining years together. She was amazed and disgusted to read a deliberately and cruelly insulting attack that blamed her for all that was rotten in their marriage.

It was the proverbial last straw. Aurore left him, went off to Paris, and almost overnight became "George Sand." Still in her twenties, she started writing fiction, hanging out with artists, wearing men's clothes, and having affairs. In quick succession, she wrote *Indiana* (1832), *Lélia* (1833), and *Jacques* (1834), novels about women who defy social convention. She continued to write fiction throughout a life that included passionate relationships with writer Alfred de Musset and composer Frédéric Chopin.

This letter catches the writer halfway between her old life as Aurore and her new life as "George Sand." Written in 1831, soon after George Sand left her husband, it is a classic in the "Mother, I have something to tell you" genre. Like many letters of this kind, it doesn't tell the whole story, but, by its insinuations and omissions, invites her mother to figure out just what's going on.

Nohant, May 31, 1831

You have been told that I wear the trousers; well, you have been deceived, as you would soon realize if you spent a day here. On the other hand, I do not want my husband to wear my skirts. Each to his dress, each to his freedom. I have failings, so has my husband his, and if I told you that ours is a model household, that there has never been the slightest cloud between us, you would not believe me. There is good and bad in my situation, as there is in everybody's.

In fact, my husband does what he wants—he has mistresses or not as he desires, he drinks muscatel or plain water according to his thirst, he accumulates or spends according to his taste, he builds, buys, changes, rules over his possessions and his house as he wishes. All this is no concern of mine and I find everything perfect, for I know that he is orderly, that he is thrifty rather than lavish, that he loves his children and in all his projects has only their interests in mind.

You see that I value and trust him, and since I have given him complete control over our wealth, I do not think that I can be suspected of wanting to dominate him. As for myself, I need very little. The same allowance, the same ease as you. A thousand crowns a year makes me wealthy enough, in view of the fact that I like writing and my pen already furnishes me a small income.

Besides, it is also just that the freedom my husband enjoys should be mutual. Otherwise he would be hateful and despicable to me and to all others, and this he does not want to be. Thus I am entirely independent. I go to bed when he rises, I go to La Châtre or Rome, I come home at midnight or six o'clock in the morning; it is entirely my business.

Elizabeth Ramsey to her daughter, Louisa Picquet

The eloquent writings and speeches of ex-slaves such as Frederick Douglass and Sojourner Truth reached an enormous audience in mid-nineteenth-century America. Their testimony to the endurance and determination of the human spirit contributed directly to President Abraham Lincoln's decision to sign the Emancipation Proclamation.

Yet slaves who wrote their letters, memoirs, plays, and stories did so against odds. It was illegal (and sometimes a capital offense) in most Southern states to teach a slave to read or write. Some slaves, such as Elizabeth Ramsey and her daughter Louisa Picquet, managed to communicate and to tell their story through literate blacks and sympathetic whites. Sometimes the transcribed narratives were published to support the abolitionist cause.

Louisa's memoir was popular partly because it so obviously refuted the pernicious pro-slavery ideology that African Americans were "animals" who had no human feelings and certainly no familial attachments. It was an ideology that allowed slave owners to perpetuate the worst kinds of abuse with a clear conscience. Children were torn from parents; mothers from families; wives from husbands; the elderly—no longer useful for childbearing or field work—were sometimes simply abandoned and left to die.

Elizabeth Ramsey experienced all of these horrors. A mulatto slave, she was only fifteen years old when she gave birth to Louisa. Louisa looked so much like her white half-sister that she became an embarrassment to the aristocratic family, and the slave mother and daughter were immediately sold away to a Georgia cotton planter. The planter hired them out to earn revenue; the mother was forced to bear more children for her new owner. When she was fourteen, the daughter, too, was pressed by the master to become one of his concubines. After he went bankrupt, the planter sold the girl to a man in New Orleans for the explicit purpose of becoming a mistress.

Elizabeth's heartbreaking letter to her daughter was transcribed by an unknown white person. It is in response to letters written by Louisa, who searched for her mother for twenty years, both in slavery and in freedom after she escaped to Ohio. Since she was uncertain of where her mother might be, she mailed copies of her letter to three different locations. Somehow, one got through, prompting this eloquent response.

After she finally located her mother, Louisa had to confront another problem. She had to raise money to buy the old woman out of slavery. She did this by publishing her story, as transcribed by the Reverend H. Mattison, an abolitionist in the American Methodist Episcopal Church.

Shortly before the outbreak of the Civil War, Louisa and her mother were finally reunited.

Wharton County, Texas, March 8, 1859

My Dear Daughter,

I a gane take my pen in hand to drop a few lines.

I have written to you twice, but I hav not yet received an answer from you I can not imagin why you do not writ. I feel very much troubel. I fear you hav not recived my letters or you would hav written; I sent to my little grand children a ring also a button in my first letter. I want you to writ to me on recept of this letter, whether you hav ever received the letters and presents or not. I said in my letter to you that Col. Horton would let you have me for 1000 dollars or a woman that could fill my place; I think you could get one cheaper [in St. Louis] that would fill my place than to pay him the money; I am anxios to hav you to make this trade.

You have no Idea, what my feelings are. I hav not spent one happy moment since I received your kind letter. It is true I was more than rejoyest to hear from you my Dear child; but my feelings on this subject are in Expressible. No one but a mother can tell my feelings. In regard to your Brother John Col. Hurton is willing for you to hav him for a boy a fifteen years old or fifteen hundred dollars. I think that 1000 dollars is too much for me. You must writ very kind to Col. Horton and try to Get me for less money. I think you can change his Price by writing Kindly to him aske him in a kind manner to let you hav me for less. I think you can soften his heart and he will let you hav me for less than he has offered me to you for.

You Brother John sends his love to you and 100 kisses to your little son; Kiss my Dear little children 100 times for me particuler Elizabeth. Say to her that she must writ to her grand mar ofton; I want you to hav your ambrotipe [photograph] taken also your children and send them to me. I would giv this world to see you and my sweet little children; may God bless you my Dear child and protect you is my prayer.

Your affectionate mother,
Elizabeth Ramsey

Samuel Clemens to the Rev. J. H. Twichell about Susy

In 1895, at the age of sixty, Samuel Clemens decided he could pay off the debts he had accrued on a series of disastrous investments by a lecture and reading tour that would take him, literally, around the globe. Although his creditors insisted that they would settle for a fifty percent repayment, both Mr. and Mrs. Clemens felt that honor demanded they pay back every cent they owed. They set out with daughter Clara, leaving behind two other daughters with family in Elmira, New York. They journeyed through Australia, New Zealand, India, Ceylon, and South Africa. Arriving in Europe, they were exhausted from the ardors of transcontinental ship and train travel yet happy to have recouped the money they needed to cancel their debt. Their joy was short-lived. In England, at the end of their tour, they received a cable informing them that their daughter Susy was seriously ill. Livy and Clara Clemens set off by steamer at once but arrived only in time for Susy's funeral. Samuel, still in England, bore the news alone.

The Reverend J. H. Twichell was one of the few people to whom Clemens could write about the magnitude of his grief. While the Clemenses were traveling, Twichell had twice come to spend time with Susy in her illness. "Susy was a rare creature," Clemens wrote to his friend, "and you knew it . . . She was my superior in fineness of mind, the delicacy and subtlety of her intellect." And certainly father and daughter had a very special relationship. At thirteen Susy set out to write his biography. For this project, she asked to see the courtship letters he had written to her mother because "I didn't know how I could write a Biography of him without his love letters." Her mother decided she was too young to read them but told her "they are the loveliest love letters that ever were written."

The letter that follows reveals Clemens's love for his daughter and his gratitude to the friend who visited her during her last illness. It also reveals how little the parents were able to cope with their daughter's death. For years after, they refused to celebrate any holidays. Writing several months after Susy's death, Clemens sensitively and lovingly describes his wife's bereavement. For the writer, only the pressure of two unfinished manuscripts serves as a partial escape from deadening guilt and loss.

London, January 19, 1897

Dear Joe,

Do I want you to write to me? Indeed I do. I do not want most people to write, but I do want you to do it. The others break my heart, but you will not. You have a something divine in you that is not in other men. You have the touch that heals, not lacerates. And you know the secret places of our hearts. You know our life—the outside of it—as the others do—and the inside of it—which they do not. You have seen our whole voyage. You have seen us go to sea, a cloud of sail, and the flag at the peak; and you see us now, chartless, adrift—derelicts; battered, water-logged, our sails a ruck of rags, our pride gone. For it is gone. And there is nothing in its place. The vanity of life was all we had, and there is no more vanity left in us. We are even ashamed of that we had; ashamed that we trusted the promises of life and builded high—to come to this!

I did know that Susy was part of us; I did *not* know that she could go away; I did not know that she could go away, and take our lives with her, yet leave our dull bodies behind. And I did not know what she was. To me she was but treasure in the bank; the amount known, the need to look at it daily, handle it, weight it, count it, *realize* it, not necessary; and now that I would do it, it is too late; they tell me it is not there, has vanished away in a night, the bank is broken, my fortune is gone, I am a pauper. How am I to comprehend this? How am I to *have* it? Why am I robbed, and who is benefited?

Ah, well, Susy died at *home*. She had that privilege. Her dying eyes rested upon nothing that was strange to them, but only upon things which they had known and loved always and which had made her young years glad; and she had you, and Sue, and Katy, and John, and Ellen. This was happy fortune—I am thankful that it was vouchsafed to her. If she had died in another house—well, I think I could not have borne that. To us, our house was not unsentient matter—it had a heart, and a soul, and eyes to see us with; and approvals, and solicitudes, and deep sympathies; it was of us, and we were in its confidence, and lived in its grace and in the peace of its benediction. We never came home from an absence that its face did not light up and speak out its eloquent welcome—and we could not enter it unmoved. And could we now, oh, now, in spirit we should enter it unshod.

I am trying to add to the "assets" which you estimate so generously. No, I am not. The thought is not in my mind. My purpose is other. I am working, but it is for the sake of the work—the "surcease of sorrow" that is found there. I work all the days, and trouble vanishes away when I use that magic. This book will not long stand between it and me, now; but that is no matter, I have many unwritten books to fly to for my preservation; the interval between the finishing of this one and the beginning of the next will not be more than an hour, at most. *Continuances,* I mean; for two of them are already well along—in fact have reached exactly the same stage in their journey: 19,000 words each. The present one will contain 180,000 words—130,000 are done. I am well protected; but Livy! She has nothing in the world to turn to; nothing but housekeeping, and doing things for the children and me. She does not see people, and cannot; books have lost their interest for her. She sits solitary; and all the day, and all the days, wonders how it all happened, and why. We others were always busy with our affairs, but Susy was her comrade—had to be driven from her loving persecutions—sometimes at 1 in the morning. To Livy the persecutions were welcome. It was heaven to her to be plagued like that. But it is ended now. Livy stands so in need of help; and none among us all could help her like you.

Some day you and I will walk again, Joe, and talk. I hope so. We could have *such* talks! We are all grateful to you and Harmony—*how* grateful it is not given to us to say in words. We pay as we can, in love; and in this coin practicing no economy. Good bye, dear old Joe!

Mark

F. Scott Fitzgerald to his daughter, Frances ("Pie") Fitzgerald

A dad writes to his daughter at camp. He talks about rewards for virtues, punishments for not fulfilling one's duties. He suggests she ask the camp director to find her Shakespeare's sonnet "Lilies that fester smell far worse than weeds." It is 1933, his alcoholism is out of control, his reputation in ruins. The fame from *The Great Gatsby* (1925), like the aura of the Golden Couple of the Jazz Age, has faded in the face of a grim national depression. His wife is on the verge of a third breakdown.

For the time, the daughter is safe, protected at a nice camp, surrounded by respectable girls, away from the craziness and violence of home. And F. Scott Fitzgerald is trying hard to muster himself into his role as a father. In places, there is an edge, a tone bordering on bitterness or sarcasm. But mostly this letter to "Pie" is heartbreaking, not so much for what it says to her, but for what it suggests about Fitzgerald's own sense of personal failure and about his hope—like any good parent's hope—that his child might enjoy a better life than his own.

La Paix, Rodger's Forge,
Towson, Maryland
August 8, 1933

Dear Pie:

I feel very strongly about you doing [your] duty. Would you give me a little more documentation about your reading in French? I am glad you are happy—but I never believe much in happiness. I never believe in misery either. Those are things you see on the stage or the screen or the printed page, they never really happen to you in life.

All I believe in in life is the rewards for virtue (according to your talents) and the *punishments* for not fulfilling your duties, which are doubly costly. If there is such a volume in the camp library, will you ask Mrs. Tyson to let you look up a sonnet of Shakespeare's in which the line occurs *"Lilies that fester smell far worse than weeds."*

Have had no thoughts today, life seems composed of getting up a *Saturday Evening Post* story. I think of you, and always pleasantly; but if you call me "Pappy" again I am going to take the White Cat out and beat his bottom *hard, six times for every time you are impertinent.* Do you react to that?

I will arrange the camp bill.

Half-wit, I will conclude.

Things to worry about:

    Worry about courage

    Worry about cleanliness

    Worry about efficiency

    Worry about horsemanship

    Worry about . . .

Things not to worry about:

    Don't worry about popular opinion

    Don't worry about dolls

    Don't worry about the past

    Don't worry about the future

    Don't worry about growing up

    Don't worry about anybody getting ahead of you

    Don't worry about triumph

    Don't worry about failure unless it comes through your own fault

    Don't worry about mosquitoes

    Don't worry about flies

    Don't worry about insects in general

    Don't worry about parents

    Don't worry about boys

    Don't worry about disappointments

    Don't worry about pleasures

    Don't worry about satisfactions

Things to think about:
    What am I really aiming at?
    How good am I really in comparison to my
      contemporaries in regard to:

      (a) Scholarship
             (b) Do I really understand about people
                  and am I able to get along with
                  them?
             (c) Am I trying to make my body a useful
                  instrument or am I neglecting it?

                                With dearest love,
                                [Daddy]

P.S. My come-back to your calling me Pappy is christening you by the word Egg, which implies that you belong to a very rudimentary state of life and that I could break you up and crack you open at my will and I think it would be a word that would hang on if I ever told it to your contemporaries. "Egg Fitzgerald." How would you like that to go through life with— "Eggie Fitzgerald" or "Bad Egg Fitzgerald" or any form that might occur to fertile minds? Try it once more and I swear to God I will hang it on you and it will be up to you to shake it off. Why borrow trouble?

                                Love anyhow.

Anne Sexton to
Linda Gray Sexton

Anne Sexton saved everything. There were her books, of course, but also unpublished poems, rough drafts, boxes of memorabilia, photographs, scrapbooks, invitations, dance cards, tapes of her psychiatric sessions, letters from friends, and carbons of the lengthy letters she wrote virtually every day of her life. She succumbed to the mad demon of suicidal depression but took pains to make sure that her work survived.

Sexton first attempted suicide in 1953 and was frequently hospitalized for depression during the late 1950s. She realized that eventually she would succeed in killing herself and prepared for the day by giving special mementos to her friends and even writing out by hand personal copies of favorite poems for them to have as keepsakes. In her Pulitzer prize–winning collection of poetry, *Live or Die* (1966), she carried on imaginary conversations with many who loved her—her children, her friends, her lover, even God. And three and a half years before her death on October 4, 1974, she wrote this letter to her daughter, a letter that anticipates the day the daughter turns forty and longs for a mother who is not there. Forty herself when she writes this letter, Sexton refers back to her own mother and looks ahead to her daughter's future. It is the letter of a mother who does not want her child to feel guilt over a mother's death, and it is the letter of a poet who hopes her daughter will find her, *talk* to her, by rereading her poems.

Anne Sexton spent the last day of her life lunching with her dear friend and fellow poet Maxine Kumin, and then reading galleys for *The Awful Rowing Toward God* (1975). The end was quiet and undramatic, as carbon monoxide always is. After the mother's death, the daughter became her literary executor, saw several books through publication, and spoke fearlessly and frankly of the tormented relationship she had with a mother who both loved and abused her. The daughter read the mother's letter well.

Anne Sexton's epitaph comes from a message inscribed on the side of an Irish barn, "Rats live on no evil star." The words read the same whether one starts at the beginning or the end. Sexton wanted the palindrome for her gravestone because, she said, it gave her hope.

April 1969

Dear Linda,

I am in the middle of a flight to St. Louis to give a reading. I was reading a *New Yorker* story that made me think of my mother and all alone in the seat I whispered to her 'I know, Mother, I know'. (Found a pen!) And I thought of you—someday flying somewhere all alone and me dead perhaps and you wishing to speak to me.

And I want to speak back. (Linda, maybe it won't be flying, maybe it will be at your *own* kitchen table drinking tea some afternoon when you are 40. *Anytime.*)—I want to say back

1st I love you.

2. You *never* let me down.

3. I know. I was there once. I *too*, was 40 and with a dead mother who I needed still.

This is my message to the 40-year-old Linda. No matter what happens you were always my bobolink, my special Linda Gray. Life is not easy. It is awfully lonely. *I* know that. Now you too know it—wherever you are, Linda, talking to me. But I've had a good life—I wrote unhappy—but I lived to the hilt. You too, Linda—Live to the HILT! To the top. I love you, 40-year-old Linda, and I love what you do, what you find, what you are!—Be your own woman. Belong to those you love. Talk to my poems, and talk to your heart—I'm in both: if you need me. I lied, Linda. I did love my mother and she loved me. She never held me but I miss her, so that I have to deny I ever loved her—or she me! Silly Anne! So there!

XOXOXO
Mom

3

ABSENCE

SEPARATION

Héloïse to Abelard

Born in 1079 into a minor noble family of Brittany, Peter Abelard gave up his claims to inheritance in order to become a philosopher and teacher. Handsome and arrogant, he made powerful enemies while also mesmerizing his students with disquisitions on logic, apparently a more passionate subject in Abelard's day than in ours. "I began to think myself the only philosopher in the world, with nothing to fear from anyone, and so I yielded to the lusts of the flesh," he wrote in his autobiographical work, *Story of His Misfortunes.*

The object of his lust was Héloïse, a stunning young student whose uncle Fulbert, a powerful priest, had educated her far beyond the standard for women of the time. So captivated was Abelard by Héloïse that he neglected virtually everything else in his life—his students, his professional obligations, all pretense of discretion or propriety. After she became pregnant, he disguised her as a nun and brought her home to Brittany, where she bore their son.

Héloïse knew that marriage would prevent Abelard from advancing in the priesthood, the only real road to success for a twelfth-century scholar. For this reason, she rejected the idea of matrimony, saying she preferred "love to wedlock and freedom to chains." Abelard felt obligated to marry Héloïse, but he, too, worried about jeopardizing his career. His compromise was a secret marriage, even though Héloïse feared that the sham ritual was likely to offend uncle Fulbert. Her hunch was correct. Enraged that Abelard had corrupted his niece and brought shame to his family name, Fulbert arranged for his servants to break into Abelard's room and castrate him.

The famous letters of Abelard and Héloïse were written after this horrible event, his from a monastery, hers from a convent. Their letters are filled with grief, misery, anguish, and, as in this letter, thoughts of death. Often Abelard counsels piety. Héloïse confesses that she took her vows not from love of God but for love of him. She worries that in their earlier life he was motivated more by lust than love. He admits she is right. Was hers the deeper, truer love? Or did he have to screen his letters for fear of detection and even further retribution? Both arguments have been advanced.

After Abelard died in April of 1142, Héloïse went on to become a powerful and learned abbess, much respected and admired. When she died in 1164, her body was buried next to his at the chapel of St. Denis.

To her only one after Christ, she who is his alone in Christ.
. . . We were greatly surprised when instead of bringing us the healing balm of comfort you increased our desolation and made the tears to flow which you should have dried. For which of us could remain dry-eyed on hearing the words you wrote towards the end of your letter: 'But if the Lord shall deliver me into the hands of my enemies so that they overcome and kill me . . .'? My dearest, how could you think such a thought? How could you give voice to it? Never may God be so forgetful of his humble handmaids as to let them outlive you; never may he grant us a life which would be harder to bear than any form of death.

The proper course would be for you to perform our funeral rites, for you to commend our souls to God, and to send ahead of you those whom you assembled for God's service—so that you need no longer be troubled by worries for us, and follow after us the more gladly because freed from concern for our salvation.

Spare us, I implore you, master, spare us words such as these which can only intensify our existing unhappiness; do not deny us, before death, the one thing by which we live. 'Each day has trouble enough of its own,' and that day, shrouded in bitterness, will bring with it distress enough to all it comes upon. 'Why is it necessary,' says Seneca, 'to summon evil' and to destroy life before death comes?

You ask us, my love, if you chance to die when absent from us, to have your body brought to our burial-ground so that you may reap a fuller harvest from the prayers we shall offer in constant memory of you. But how could you suppose that our memory of you could ever fade? Besides, what time will there be then which will be fitting for prayer, when extreme distress will allow us no peace, when the soul will lose its power of reason and the tongue its use of speech? Or when the frantic mind, far from being resigned, may even (if I may say so) rage against God himself, and provoke him with complaints instead of placating him with prayers?

In our misery then we shall have time only for tears and no power to pray; we shall be hurrying to follow, not to bury you, so that we may share your grave instead of laying you in it. If we lose our life in you, we shall not be able to go on living when you leave us.

I would not even have us live to see that day, for if the mere mention of your death is death for us, what will the reality be if it finds us still alive? God grant we may never live on to perform this duty, to render you the service which we look for from you alone; in this may we go before, not after you!

Wolfgang von Goethe to Christiane Vulpius

He was sure every woman he loved was the only woman he'd ever love. Of course, he was continually proving himself wrong. In the words of writer Thomas Mann, Goethe's "wooing was aimless, his loyalty perfidious, and his love a means to an end, a necessity for his work."

First came Charlotte Buff, who was engaged to another man when he met her. He loved her without hope of consummation and then milked his anguish in such youthful, sentimental fictions as the semi-autobiographical *The Sorrows of Young Werther* (1774). Later, the love of his life was Charlotte von Stein, a sophisticated woman who introduced him to the manners and mores of the Weimar court. "You . . . alone of all women have aroused love in my heart," he wrote to Charlotte, with whom he had an affair that lasted a decade.

Goethe left the brilliant Charlotte von Stein for Christiane Vulpius, a young woman with an unexceptional education and intellect whom he met in Rome in 1789. She seemed like an odd choice for one of the most brilliant and learned men of his generation, yet she remained Goethe's mistress until 1806, when she guarded his house against invading French troops, and, as a token of his appreciation, he married her.

Mann called Christiane Vulpius "a very pretty and thoroughly uneducated little flower girl." There were several other major and minor women in Goethe's life, before and after her, but Vulpius aroused the writer without threatening him. In short, she was the perfect muse for a man like Goethe and inspired the *Roman Elegies* (1795), a healthy and even robust account of sexual love rare in the Western lyric tradition. No angst, no guilt, no overblown expectation, no disappointment; the *Roman Elegies* describe two people delighting in one another and in their bodies: "Eyes that can feel like a hand, hands that can see like an eye."

September 10, 1792

I have written many letters to you and I don't know when they will reach you. I neglected to number the pages and now begin to do it. Again you will learn that I am well. You know that I love you dearly. If only you could be with me now! Everywhere here are large beds and you would not have to complain as you do sometimes at home. Ah! my darling! There is nothing better than being together. We shall always remind each other of it, when we are together again. Imagine! We are so near Champagne and can't find a good glass of wine. It shall be better on the Frauenplan, if only my sweetheart will take care of the kitchen and cellar.

Be a good *hausfrau* and prepare a nice home for me. Take care of the little boy and keep loving me.

Only keep loving me! because sometimes in my thoughts I am jealous and imagine that someone else could be more to your liking, since I find many men more handsome and agreeable than myself. But you must not see that, because you must think me the best one, because I love you terribly much and don't like anyone but you. I often dream about you, all kinds of confused things, but always that we love each other. And it shall remain like that.

I ordered two feather beds and pillows stuffed with feathers and different other good things through my mother. Only be sure that our little house will be nice, everything else will be taken care of. I'll find sundry things in Paris, another gift package will come from Frankfort. A basket with liqueur and sweets will be dispatched today. There should be always something added to the household. Keep on loving me and be a faithful child, everything else will take care of itself. As long as I did not possess your heart, what did anything else mean to me; now that I have it, I would like to keep it. In return I am yours too. Kiss the child, give my regards to Meyer, and love me.

Napoléon Bonaparte to Josephine

One of the most important social events in France in 1795 was an elegant Ball of the Victims attended by those who had lost relatives in the Terror, the bloody termination of the French Revolution. Instead of invitations, one gained admittance by presenting a relative's death certificate. One such hedonistic victim was Josephine Tascher de la Pagerie, Viscountess de Beauharnais, whose husband had been guillotined while she languished in Carmes prison. Newly released from jail, she was bent on making up for lost pleasures, which meant, above all, finding herself a husband who would pay off her mounting debts and support her in the manner to which she had been accustomed before the Revolution.

Enter Napoléon, the bourgeois republican from Corsica. He was captivated by her exotic Creole accent coupled with her good breeding and aristocratic pedigree. "That little puss-in-boots," she called him derisively—until he began sending expensive presents. Realizing a catch, Josephine lied about her age (she was thirty-two, not twenty-nine); fearing this sophisticated, "wealthy" woman would think him jejune, Napoléon lied about his (he was twenty-six, not twenty-eight). They were married on March 8, 1796, and two days later Napoléon set off on his military campaign to Italy, leaving little time for either to unravel the other's secrets.

As this letter makes clear, Napoléon was by far the more ardent correspondent. Despite many entreaties from Napoléon, Josephine postponed joining him at the front, preferring the amenities of Paris to life in an armed camp. Their separation was fortuitous for literary history since it inspired some of the wittiest and most passionate love letters ever written. Known for his excellent prose style, Napoléon performed best in his love letters, even though Josephine was too preoccupied with her own social life back in Paris to pay much attention to the letters that came twice daily. "A kiss on your heart," he promised her, steamily, by letter, "and then one a little lower down, much lower down."

Verona, November 13th, 1796

I don't love you, not at all; on the contrary, I detest you—You're a naughty, gawky, foolish Cinderella. You never write me; you don't love your husband; you know what pleasure your letters give him, and yet you haven't written him six lines, dashed off casually!

What do you do all day, Madam? What is the affair so important as to leave you no time to write to your devoted lover? What affection stifles and puts to one side the love, the tender and constant love you promised him? Of what sort can be that marvelous being, that new lover who absorbs every moment, tyrannizes over your days, and prevents your giving any attention to your husband? Josephine, take care! Some fine night, the doors will be broken open, and there I'll be.

Indeed, I am very uneasy, my love, at receiving no news of you; write me quickly four pages, pages full of agreeable things which shall fill my heart with the pleasantest feelings.

I hope before long to crush you in my arms and cover you with a million kisses burning as though beneath the equator.

Bonaparte.

Susan Chesnutt to Charles Chesnutt

The brief but touching letter reprinted here was written by Susan Perry Chesnutt to her husband, Charles Waddell Chesnutt, the late-nineteenth-century essayist, lecturer, social theorist, and novelist. Charles Chesnutt was born in Cleveland in 1858 to free black parents who had migrated from the South. The family returned to Fayette-ville, North Carolina, when Chesnutt was a child, and because of the poor quality of the education there, the young Charles was largely (and impressively) self-taught—in German, French, Latin, Greek, algebra, history, and music. By sixteen he was teaching school, and by twenty-five he was principal of a normal school for African-Americans where his wife, Susan, served as a teacher. After the couple moved north again, he passed his bar exam but, because of his color, was forced to take jobs as a stenographer.

Chesnutt turned to literature explicitly as a way to expose the horrors of racial discrimination. The eminent critic and novelist W. D. Howells pronounced his first fiction "new and fresh and strong" and said that "one of the places at the top is open to him." Although Chesnutt never found a popular audience, he became one of the most admired writers of his day.

This letter was written in 1883, when Chesnutt had moved to Cleveland and was trying to get established there before sending for his wife and children. Forty-five years later, the couple still seemed to be in love. In 1928, writing a thank-you note to a friend who had sent the couple a present for their fiftieth wedding anniversary, Chesnutt noted wryly but tenderly: "I can imagine marriages where fifty years would seem like an eternity, but except when I look at my children and see my gray hairs in the mirror, it doesn't seem any time at all, and Mrs. Chesnutt admits that she hasn't found it very tiresome; and we are both willing to hang on a while longer yet."

How I long to be with you once more. I don't believe I ever looked forward to the coming of warm weather so eagerly before. I have found out since you left what you were to me. You were a companion, and you knew me better even than my father or mother, or at least you were more in sympathy with me than anybody else, and my failings were overlooked. No one can tell, my dearest husband, how I miss that companionship. God grant that we may not be separated much longer, for I cannot stand it, I am afraid.

Natalie Barney to Liane de Pougy

F inishing school. A debutante ball. Dresses by Worth. Jewels by Cartier. Natalie Clifford Barney had all of these things. She was a beautiful American heiress, a true Golden Girl, and she wanted none of it. She escaped to Europe in 1899 and lived among the demimonde of Paris until her death in 1972. Poet, playwright, epigrammatist, and essayist, Barney, like Gertrude Stein, was also an accomplished *salonnière*. For over sixty years she kept an apartment at 20 rue Jacob in which she held her "Académie des Femmes," a salon at which she showcased writing by American and European women writers and intellectuals.

"Moonbeam," as she was called by the women who loved her, was perhaps the single most important muse for literature of the *belle époque*. She served as the model for Flossie in Colette's *Claudine* books, Evangeline Musset in Djuna Barnes's *Ladies Almanack*, Lurette in Lucie Delarue-Mardrus's *The Angel and the Depraved*, and Valerie Seymour in Radclyffe Hall's *The Well of Loneliness*. She was a woman of many talents and as many identities, some self-created. One of her own books was *New Reflections of the Amazon*, and, late in her life, she advised her friend Berthe Cleyrergue, "When I am no longer here, you will be asked about the Amazon. I want you to tell the truth."

The letter reprinted here was written in 1899, at the height of Barney's first passionate love affair. The letter is addressed to Liane de Pougy, one of Paris's most literary courtesans. Natalie was twenty-three, Liane thirty. Liane didn't even notice her at first, so Natalie sent her a spray of flowers with a message: "From a stranger who would like to cease being one to you." The two fell madly in love. "We'll dream, think, love," Liane wrote to Natalie. "Purify me with a great fire of divine love."

But there remained the problem of money. Natalie hated Liane's prostituting herself in order to afford luxuries, so Natalie concocted a plan where she would marry her rich fiancé back home, and they would live chastely together, with Liane as their "only child." Liane found it hard to believe any man would consent to such a marriage— and she was right. Natalie wrote this letter during one of many trips Liane took to be with one of the wealthy men who provided for her. "I received pearls," Liane wrote sadly to Natalie, "and I am weeping."

1899

My Liane,

Since you are spiritually happy and physically chaste, I must be that way too . . . To tire myself out (I know more agreeable, but less innocent, ways), I take long rides.

Yesterday I went twenty-eight kilometers looking for some beauty on which to feast my eyes, tired of the monotony of my surroundings. I saw pipes, piles of stones, old women and cows. I also saw some sheep: one of them refused to walk like or with the others . . . and they were beating him. A moral lesson which I certainly don't appreciate. Was I like that sheep? The voice of my reason sharply answers yes. Then there were villages where I felt I had to dismount to taste their cider and the patois of the region.

Two years ago I would have found these inns picturesque, but now they simply seem dirty. A sure sign of age, when uncleanliness no longer has any artistic appeal. Must I confess that I have never known the youthful madness of he who sang: "In a loft, how happy one is at twenty." I'm still only twenty-three, but I already think that one is better off "elsewhere." In your bed, for example.

In coming here, I was hoping that the Bretons would look something like you. Still another disillusionment. . . . But I do see you, my beloved, in the flowers of your country. These things that I respect are independent of time and are all over. They grow as easily in the immense garden of the Infinite as in the secret of your soul. While I kiss, nibble and inhale the ones around me, do you know what I'm thinking about?

It's time for me to take another ride on my horse. Good-bye. Your . . . and for always.

Natty

Henry James to Hendrik C. Andersen

Henry James was in his mid-fifties when he met Hendrik Andersen, a Norwegian-American sculptor traveling in Rome. Andersen was twenty-five, tall, handsome, idealistic, bursting with ambition, happy to be flattered by one of America's most renowned writers. In many ways, Andersen seemed the living embodiment of a character James had created some twenty years before, "Roderick Hudson," also a young American sculptor in Europe. James bought Andersen lunch, then dinner. Later he visited Andersen's studio and paid him $250 for a bust of a youthful Italian count, Alberto Bevilacqua. Back home alone at Lamb House in England, James took comfort in this amateurish statue. "Brave little Bevilacqua, and braver still Maestro Andersen," the famous novelist wrote to the obscure artist. "I've struck up a tremendous intimacy with dear little Conte Alberto. . . . He is the first object my eyes greet in the morning and the last at night."

Although they met only half a dozen times, James and Andersen carried on an epistolary relationship for some fifteen years, until shortly before James's death in 1916. James felt free to write to Andersen in a way that he could not to anyone else. In letters to Andersen, James's language is affectionate, passionate, tender, paternal, loving, physical, and, above all, tactile — as if the staid, reserved, even repressed older novelist craves nothing so much as touch.

Over the years, Andersen eluded James's grasp. In one poignant letter, James signs himself "your poor helpless far-off but all devoted H. J. who seems condemned almost and never to be near you, yet who, if he were, would lay upon you a pair of hands soothing, sustaining, positively *healing* in the quality of their pressure." In 1913, at the age of seventy and seriously ailing, James continued to reach out to this elusive younger man, hoping that perhaps they might somehow, somewhere "meet (and still embracingly) over the abyss of our difference in years and conditions."

105 Pall Mall S.W.
February 9th 1902

My dear, dear dearest Hendrik.

Your news [of your brother's death] fills me with horror and pity, and how can I express the tenderness with which it makes me think of you and the aching wish to be near you and put my arms around you? My heart fairly bleeds and breaks at the vision of you *alone*, in your wicked and indifferent old far-off Rome, with the haunting, blighting, unbearable sorrow.

The sense that I can't *help* you, see you, talk to you, touch you, hold you close and long, or do anything to make you rest on me, and feel my participation — this torments me, dearest boy, makes me ache for you, and for myself; makes me gnash my teeth and groan at the bitterness of things. I can only take refuge in hoping you are *not* utterly alone, that some human tenderness of *some* sort, some kindly voice and hand *are* near you that may make a little the difference.

What a dismal winter you must have had, with this staggering blow at the climax! I don't of course know *what* fragment of friendship there may be to draw near to you, and in my uncertainty my image of you is of the darkest, and my pity, as I say, feels so helpless. I wish I could go to Rome and put my hands on you (oh, how lovingly I should lay them!) but that, alas, is odiously impossible. (Not, moreover, that apart from *you*, I should so much as like to be there now.)

I find myself thrown back on anxiously and doubtless vainly, wondering if there may not, after a while, [be] some possibility of your coming to England, of the current of your trouble inevitably carrying you here—so that I might take consoling, soothing, infinitely close and tender and affectionately-healing *possession* of you. This is the one thought that relieves me about you a little—and I wish you might fix your eyes on it for the idea, just of the possibility.

I am in town for a few weeks but I return to Rye April 1st, and sooner or later to *have* you there and do for you, to put my arm round you and *make* you lean on me as on a brother and a lover, and keep you on and on, slowly comforted or at least relieved of the first bitterness of pain—this I try to imagine as thinkable, attainable, not wholly out of the question. There I am, at any rate, and there is my house and my garden and my table and my studio—such as it is!—and your room, and your welcome, and your place everywhere—and I press them upon you, oh so earnestly, dearest boy, if isolation and grief and the worries you are overdone with become intolerable to you. There they are, I say—to fall upon, to rest upon, to find whatever possible shade of oblivion in.

I will *nurse* you through your dark passage. I wish I could do something *more*—something straighter and nearer and more immediate but such as it is please let it sink into you. Let all my tenderness, dearest boy, do *that*. This is all now. I wired you three words an hour ago. I can't *think* of your sister-in-law—I brush her vision away and your history with your father, as I've feared it, has haunted me all winter. I embrace you with almost a passion of pity.

Henry James

F. O. Matthiessen to Russell Cheney

They met on the ocean liner *Paris* in 1924 and, from the start, knew they wanted to spend their lives together. F. O. Matthiessen was a promising Oxford graduate student who would go on to become a Harvard professor, literary scholar, and art critic. Russell Cheney, older and already established in his career as an artist, lived most of the year in France, partly for his art, partly for health reasons. The two spent part of each year together for over twenty years. When apart, they exchanged letters, more than three thousand letters (some 1,600,000 words), in which they detailed their ideas and aspirations and wrote, eloquently, of their continuing love. "On the back of your letter was a shopping list," Cheney ("Rat") wrote to "Devil" in 1929. "It sort of took my breath away it was so real."

But the relationship was not always easy. Cheney was from a large, blue-blooded Connecticut family in which he was much loved yet also held in some scorn both because of his artistic aspirations and his persistent attachment to Matthiessen. At one point, Cheney panicked when he learned that Matthiessen had told some friends about their relationship; he even wrote to Matthiessen advocating that they call off the physical part of the relationship and continue solely as friends. Matthiessen was realistic enough to see that this was impossible, but he was hardly free from the censorious mores of his time and place. Students and younger colleagues at Harvard reported his intense fear lest he be labeled a homosexual.

Subject to prolonged depressions throughout his life, Matthiessen committed suicide in 1950, leaving many to mourn his loss. Some attributed the death of the left-leaning author of the highly influential *American Renaissance: Art and Expression in the Age of Emerson and Whitman* (1941) to depression over the Cold War and its hints of the McCarthyism to come. But close friends also realized that Cheney's death in 1945 left a void in Matthiessen's life that no one and nothing else could fill. Just months before his death, Matthiessen wrote of the "problems of living alone for one who has known love and companionship."

The letter that follows was written when Matthiessen was still a student at Oxford. He spent an intense winter vacation with Cheney, traveling with him through Italy. Unable to tear himself away, Matthiessen broke a school rule and overstayed his vacation. In the letter he jokes that, in the best British public school tradition, he'll probably be spanked for this infraction (unable to sit, he'll be "eating off the mantelpiece"). He guesses at other possible punishments for his delinquency. From the tone of the letter it's obvious that he thought the precious days spent with Cheney were worth the risk.

Oxford, England
Wednesday
January 28, 1925

Dearest Rat,

It came this morning—your first letter—just as I had figured it would. I lay snuggled deliciously in bed while the chapel bells were ringing, saying to myself: I'll lie here until I know that by the time I'm up and dressed and down the postman will have been around and I will have a letter from Rat.

There were a few tears—inevitably—swift hot tears of supreme joy, no pain, no sorrow, only the sudden penetration of your complete tenderness and devotion and the desire to have my arms around you and hold you to me close.

It takes strong men—men, as Foster [a Yale classmate and close friend] would say, who are capable of shaping destiny to their own ends—to handle the situation of love and separation, and still maintain balance of life. We are complex—both of us—in that we are neither wholly man, woman, or child. We love each other, we have accepted each other, and now it requires great energy of creation to fashion our inner lives so that they can endure the many months that we are destined to be apart during the next fifty years.

Fortunately our work binds neither of us to any one place. Every summer when you are available I am free—to come and bring my books and writing. We can settle in France, or in America, or where you will for three month periods together. You say that I am building air castles? Well, what else do you suppose that I live by?

And in the meantime there is our sure antidote for loneliness: it is activity. These two days at Oxford have not been unhappy. I have plunged into new fields of reading, and my mind is sparking through new labyrinths. Hours slip by, slip into days, and I am energetic, keen, vigorous.

Of course, dear feller, it is harder for you: for you are the artist. Then, too, Cassis is more solitary than Oxford—for here I feel the undergraduate life pulsing on every side of me although I form no part of it. During your long quiet evenings you must either read and write, or be miserable and drink! How about a letter to Piccolo instead of that tenth cognac, Mr. Cheney?

I'm going out now to buy a frame for San Giorgio, and also to meet Mrs. Allcroft—you remember, the English lady I spent last Christmas with. I look forward to a long sympathetic talk, since I have not seen her since June.

Am I eating off the mantelpiece? Not yet, for the Fellows of the College are now busy electing a new Warden, and not until tomorrow will they have time for me. Popular opinion seems to point to the following alternatives:

(1) A fine of 5 to 10 pounds.
(2) "gated" for the rest of the term—which means that I wouldn't be allowed to go out after 7 o'clock any night!
(3) "Sent down," which means I would return to Cassis and lose my degree—not very likely.

Goody-bye, dear Heart—

Langston Hughes to Sylvia Chen

Poet, novelist, playwright, satirist, autobiographer, and literary critic, Langston Hughes was among the most versatile and gifted writers of the mid–twentieth century and one of the key figures in the Harlem Renaissance. Yet a full and rewarding literary career—over forty books and almost as many awards and prizes—could not cover the loneliness of his life. Biographer Arnold Rampersad has described Hughes's "years of nomadic loneliness and a furtive sexuality." He never married nor had children and blamed the emptiness of his emotional life on the unhappiness of his own childhood, spent among various relatives who did not love him enough.

Even when there were love affairs (probably with men as well as with women), they inevitably ended sadly or just trailed off into indifference. In his memoir, *The Big Sea* (1940), Hughes could write nostalgically of his affair with Anne Marie Coussey, whose wealthy father threatened to disinherit her if she continued her relationship with the penniless poet. "And we sat in my room on the wide stone window seat," Hughes writes of their final meeting, "dipping each berry into the cream and feeding each other, and sadly watching the sun set over Paris. And we felt . . . very young and helpless, because we could not do what we wanted to do—be happy together with no money and no fathers to worry about." What he does not mention in the memoir is that he could have seen her again, but declined.

He would decline other such opportunities with other lovers. The letter reprinted here is a classic example not just of Hughes's literary style but of his style as a lover. Sylvia Chen was a stunning Afro-Chinese dancer living in Moscow, "a delicate, flowerlike girl, beautiful in a reedy, golden-skinned sort of way." She made it clear that she would have considered marriage, and described him as the "first man I was ever intimate with." He flirted with other women and described Chen as "the girl I was in love with that winter." Thereafter followed a pattern of pursuit and neglect, until, suddenly, in the spring of 1934, he sent her an urgent telegram from the United States: "COME OVER HERE THIS IS SERIOUS I LOVE YOU." She almost bought it. Then she read the date: April Fool's Day.

Despite the cruelty of the tease, Hughes was serious enough about Chen to discuss her emigration status with the authorities. But he never informed her of this. Instead, he sent more desultory love letters, with lots of XXXX's and OOOO's. She read and answered them, but unknown to Langston, married someone else. "Yes I got tired of waiting on you to propose so got myself a consort," she wrote to Hughes a couple of years after her marriage. "Maybe you'd like to get on my waiting list for future consideration."

July 7, 1934

Darling Kid,

You know what would happen if you came over here? I would take you and keep you forever, that's what would happen. And even if you didn't come over here and I ever found you anywhere else in the world—I'd keep you, too. So you see, I love you!

Swell to have your letter. But listen—were you any more serious than I was? And how did I know I was so much going to *miss* the hell out of you after you went South to dance or I came half a world away from you? But I do miss you—lots more than you miss me, I guess,—and I want you, Sylvia baby, more than anyone else in the world, believe it or not. I love you.

But to change the subject. . . .

Please, dear kid, believe what I say about how much I like you. If you want me to say it over and *over* and more and *more,* just act like you don't believe it in the next letter you write me. . . .

> Two tons of love to you,
> Write soon,
> Langston

Wish I could kiss you! Do you?

John Melby to Lillian Hellman

In 1944, when World War II was winding down, Lillian Hellman was sent to Moscow by the U.S. government on a "cultural mission" to cement goodwill among wartime allies. At a U.S. Embassy dinner in

Moscow, she met John Melby, who was working there for the State Department. At first she didn't like him very much, since she assumed that like most U.S. officials in the U.S.S.R. he would be anti-Soviet. Nor was she looking for love. Her off-again, on-again relationship with novelist Dashiell Hammett was, for the moment, going smoothly, and as usual, Hammett was being exceptionally supportive of her work. On the other hand, Melby was very handsome, and she knew that Hammett's alcoholism and promiscuity could erupt at any time. When Melby and Hellman met again a few days later, there was electricity. As biographer Robert P. Newman has noted, "it was love at second sight."

They continued to write after Lillian returned to America. When John joined her in New York in the summer of 1945, he decided to divorce his wife and marry Lillian. Then in October, John got word that he was to report at once for State Department duty in China. Conditions there were difficult, colleagues unpleasant. Lillian's letters, when they finally managed to get through to him in China, revived his spirits and buoyed his love.

But all was not well. Lillian could feel the beginnings of Cold War anticommunist sentiment stirring. Her play *Another Part of the Forest* (1946) had attracted the suspicions of an anonymous FBI informant, who was certain that it was not really about a greedy Southern family at all but was part of "the Communist technique to play up the weak spots of American life." Meanwhile, John was writing from China, virulently attacking the ruling communist regime, but also forthrightly denouncing the idiocy of certain American bureaucrats, a candor that Hellman warned him was foolhardy.

By 1948, too much separation had put a strain on their relationship. They continued to write, but infrequently. Ironically, it was the State Department Loyalty-Security Board that brought them together again. In June of 1952, John Melby was charged with being a communist sympathizer. His hearing was chaired by Howard Donovan, a man whom John disliked and had once vetoed for an appointment as consul general in Singapore. Despite an unblemished record as an anticommunist, John was required to denounce all previous associations with accused communists, including Hellman. She came forward and testified on his behalf, insisting that he had never expressed communist sympathies. But when he broke his promise never to see her again, John was fired from his position and blacklisted. His security clearance was not reinstated until 1980.

Their love was passionate and enduring. A mutual sense that they were victims of McCarthy's henchmen revived their love, and they continued to write for over twenty years. Hellman's final two letters to Melby, written in 1978, had to be typed in capital letters because glaucoma had made her nearly blind. They exchanged telephone calls until her death, and she left him a small amount of money in her will. As John would say in 1983, a year before she died, "When we met, even after months of absence, we picked up right where we had left off."

San Francisco, May 25, 1945

Sweetheart, I don't think it is silly to make strange noises and gurgles in the springtime. In fact I think it is rather wonderful to be able to do so and I love you for it. There are times when your inarticulate sounds are quite as wonderful and meaningful as the articulate ones—no cracks, please—sometimes more so, and always exciting. I would give a great deal to hear some of them right now, instead of having to remember them. I can get very lonesome for them and for you and miss you both terribly. It is odd how lonely it is possible to be in the midst of so many people. Darling, I am very much in love with you.

Václav Havel to Olga Havel

On October 22 and 23, 1979, six members of the Committee to Defend the Unjustly Prosecuted, a group of pro-democracy activists, were tried in Prague, Czechoslovakia, for the crime of "subversion of the republic." Among the accused was the nation's foremost playwright, Václav Havel. For assembling, printing, and distributing materials critical of the Czech regime, he was sentenced to four and a half years at hard labor.

During his incarceration, Havel was not allowed to write anything except bland letters home about "family matters." Gradually, he discovered that he could move beyond the bounds established by the prison censors if he did so cagily and cautiously. "The more abstract and incomprehensible these meditative letters were, the greater their chance of being sent, since the censors did not permit any comments to be mailed that they could understand."

His 144 letters to his wife Olga, sent between June 4, 1979, and September 4, 1982, are thus written in a "complex, encoded fashion which was far more convoluted than I wanted and certainly more complicated than the way I normally write." Yet even with its abstract tone, the letter reprinted here is a stunning meditation on the meaning of separation.

During the fall of 1982, a few months after he wrote this wrenching letter, Havel was offered an early release from prison on the condition that he would write one sentence asking for pardon. He refused on principle and out of a sense of solidarity with his comrades.

His release came almost by accident. Stricken with a high fever, he had to be rushed to the hospital. On the brink of death, no longer concerned about prison censors, he wrote a letter to his wife, alerting her to his condition. Olga quickly conveyed the message to supporters outside the country, and there began interventions on his behalf from literary and political friends all over the world. One night prison officials came to his cell unannounced, and he was released immediately to a civilian hospital and freedom. After the collapse of the communist regime, he was elected President of the Republic of Czechoslovakia.

He published his *Letters to Olga* partly to reveal his thoughts during those long months in jail, but also as a tribute to his wife. "It's true that you won't find many heartfelt, personal passages addressed to my wife in my prison letters," he said. "Even so, I think that Olga is their main hero."

May 29, 1982

Dear Olga,

Several days ago, during the weather report (it precedes the news on television each day, so I see it regularly), something went wrong in the studio and the sound cut out, though the picture continued as usual (there was neither the announcement "Do not adjust your sets" nor landscape photographs, as there usually is in such cases). The employee of the Meteorological Institute who was explaining the forecast quickly grasped what had happened, but because she was not a professional announcer, she didn't know what to do.

At this point a strange thing happened: the mantle of routine fell away and before us there suddenly stood a confused, unhappy and terribly embarrassed woman: she stopped talking, looked in desperation at us, then somewhere off to the side, but there was no help from that direction. She could scarcely hold back her tears. Exposed to the view of millions, yet desperately alone, thrown into an unfamiliar, unexpected and unresolvable situation, incapable of conveying through mime that she was above it all (by shrugging her shoulders and smiling, for instance), drowning in embarrassment, she stood there in all the primordial nakedness of human helplessness, face-to-face with the big bad world and herself, with the absurdity of her position, and with the desperate question of what to do with herself, how to rescue her dignity, how to acquit herself, how to be.

Exaggerated as it may seem, I suddenly saw in that event an image of the primal situation of humanity: a situation of separation, of being cast into an alien world and standing there before the question of self. Moreover, I realized at once that with the woman, I was experiencing—briefly—an almost physical dread; with her, I was overwhelmed by a terrible sense of embarrassment; I blushed and felt her shame; I too felt like crying. Irrespective of my will, I was flooded with an absurdly powerful compassion for this stranger (a surprising thing here, of all places, where in spite of yourself you share the general tendency of the prisoners to see everything related to television as a part of the hostile world that locked them up): I felt miserable because I had no way of helping her, of taking her place, or at least of stroking her hair. . . .

> I kiss you,
> Vašek

THE FINAL SEPARATION

Voltaire to Madame Louise Denis, in memory of Madame Émilie, Marquise du Châtelet

W hen I add the sum total of my graces," Émilie, marquise du Châtelet, wrote to Frederick the Great of Prussia, "I confess that I am inferior to no one." She had a point. A scientist, mathematician, philosopher, and translator of ancient Greek and Latin classics, she had few equals among either sex in the late eighteenth century. Not even the talented, flirtatious transvestites that King Frederick kept at his court could equal her in appeal. "How fortunate," her lover Voltaire exclaimed, "to admire her whom I adore!"

Modern American marital standards are derived from nineteenth-century ideals of monogamy, affectional marriage, and the nuclear family. But the relationship between Émilie and Voltaire took place at a time when, according to an older aristocratic ideal, marriages were arranged and extramarital affairs were commonplace. "Love," noted the Countess of Champagne, "is for lovers, not for married couples." Émilie's arranged marriage was to Florent-Claude, the marquis du Châtelet, and she observed the custom of the day in that she was perfectly faithful to him when he was in town.

For his part, Voltaire was the most brilliant writer of the Enlightenment. Slim and elegant, a wonderful dancer and a witty dinner companion, he, too, had many lovers, mostly but not always female, and was the perfect match for Émilie. Even Émilie's husband dropped her a note to congratulate her on her conquest of Voltaire.

Nor did the lovers believe in monogamy outside of marriage. For at least part of their relationship, they enjoyed a complicated *ménage à quatre;* then, briefly, when Émilie took another lover, a *ménage à cinq.* "The most beautiful person in the world spends her life writing you in algebra," Voltaire began a letter of invitation to one of Émilie's lovers, "I write in prose to say I am your admirer, your friend." For both, however, their love for one another marked the intellectual and emotional high point of their lives.

The letter reprinted here was one of many tributes Voltaire penned as a memorial to Émilie, who died on September 1, 1749, at the age of forty-three, from complications following childbirth. Voltaire was so upset that he wept inconsolably, ran from the house, hit his head on a post, and fell down the stairs. "My death, too, lies at that door," he sobbed.

In this letter to his brilliant niece, Madame Louise Denis, he writes about putting his life in order again after the death of "a great man" (what he considered the highest tribute he could pay to Émilie). Masculinizing Émilie was also a way of expressing his sorrow without arousing his niece's jealousy, since, of course, she, too, was one of his lovers.

Cirey, 23 September [1749]

You comfort me, my dear, most touchingly. I admit that I am in great need of it. I spend all my days here in tears, arranging the papers which remind me of her. I am not mourning a mistress, far from it, I am mourning a friend and a great man, and my sorrow will certainly last as long as my life. You will make it happy, this life filled with so much sorrow. I dedicate it entirely to you.

I am staying here for another two days to finish putting everything into order. I will spend two more with one of Émilie's woman friends, and then return to Paris with my horses, by short stages. I cannot do otherwise because the post-chaise I lent to her son is smashed into a thousand pieces. I am experiencing all the difficulties one can meet with in a desolate countryside, far from all help. But I do not feel them. It is a pinprick to a wounded man. This Cirey, my dear, is the palace of Alcina. It all vanishes. It is nothing more than a horrible desert. But I still have you.

If you write again mark your letter to wait at St Dizier until I get there. I look forward to seeing your five acts in Paris. You may be sure that I am more interested in it than in *Catilina*. I do not think and cannot think of the occupations which were my delight, I cannot bear my work, but I will love yours as one loves one's grandchildren. Once again, darling, my heart, my life are yours, and you will do what you will with them.

V.

Sullivan Ballou to Sarah Ballou

More Americans died in the Civil War than in either World War I or II. Every aspect of American life was changed by it. Both the savagery of the war and its disruption of civilian life were recorded poignantly in the thousands and thousands of letters written between soldiers and their loved ones back home.

Sullivan Ballou, whose letter is reprinted here, was not a professional writer. Yet few have expressed so poignantly what it means to love in the face of death. A major in the 2nd Rhode Island Volunteers, Sullivan wrote home to his wife Sarah one week before the first Battle of Bull Run. He died in that bloody skirmish.

July 14, 1861
Camp Clark, Washington, D.C.

My very dear Sarah,

The indications are very strong that we shall move in a few days, perhaps tomorrow. And lest I should not be able to write you again, I feel impelled to write a few lines that may fall under your eyes when I am no more.

I have no misgivings about or lack of confidence in the cause in which I am engaged and my courage does not halt or falter. I know how American Civilization now leans on the triumph of the Government and how great a debt we owe to those who went before us through the blood and suffering of the Revolution. And I am willing, perfectly willing, to lay down all my joys in this life to help maintain this government and to pay that debt.

Sarah, my love for you is deathless. It seems to bind me with mighty cables that nothing but Omnipotence can break. And yet my love of Country comes over me like a strong wind and bears me irresistibly, with all these chains, to the battlefield.

The memories of all the blissful moments I have enjoyed with you come creeping over me, and I feel most deeply grateful to God and you that I have enjoyed them so long. And hard it is for me to give them up and burn to ashes the hopes of future years when, God willing, we might still have lived and loved together and seen our boys grown up to honorable manhood around us. I have, I know, but few and small claims upon Divine Providence, but something whispers to me — perhaps it is the wafted prayer of my little Edgar, that I shall return to my loved ones unharmed.

If I do not return, my dear Sarah, never forget how much I loved you, nor that when my last breath escapes me on the battlefield, it will whisper your name. Forgive my many faults and the many pains I have caused you. How thoughtless, how foolish I have sometimes been! How gladly would I wash out with my tears every little spot upon our happiness.

But, O Sarah! If the dead can come back to this earth and flit unseen around those they loved, I shall always be near you; in the gladdest days and in the darkest nights . . . *always* always, and if there be a soft breeze upon your cheek, it shall be my breath, as the cool air fans your throbbing temple, it shall be my spirit passing by. Sarah, do not mourn me dead; Think I am gone and wait for thee, for we shall meet again . . .

Samuel Clemens to W. D. Howells, in memory of his wife, Olivia Langdon Clemens

In 1903, still grieving over the death of her daughter Susy, Olivia Langdon Clemens fell ill. In the autumn of that year the Clemens family went to Florence, hoping that the sunny, warm climate of Italy would revive Livy's health. She died there, on June 5, 1904. To his dear friend and fellow writer, W. D. Howells, Samuel Clemens lamented, "How poor we are to-day!" and expressed his wish that he might join his beloved wife in death.

The last years of the widower's life were filled with a variety of academic honors, including honorary degrees from Yale and Oxford, impressive for a man whose formal education had been both intermittent and brief. Fame and continued work, however, did not save him from more personal tragedy. Clemens's daughter Jean died on Christmas eve, 1909, from an epileptic seizure, when she was taking a bath. Known as one of America's greatest humorists, Mark Twain's reaction to Jean's death reveals the dark side of his mind in his later years: "I never greatly envied anybody but the dead," he said, gazing at Jean. "I always envy the dead."

VILLA DI QUARTO, FLORENCE
June 6, 1904

Dear Howells,—Last night at 9:20 I entered Mrs. Clemens's room to say the usual goodnight—and she was dead—tho' no one knew it. She had been cheerfully talking, a moment before. She was sitting up in bed—she had not lain down for months—and Katie and the nurse were supporting her. They supposed she had fainted, and they were holding the oxygen pipe to her mouth, expecting to revive her. I bent over her and looked in her face, and I think I spoke—I was surprised and troubled that she did not notice me. Then we understood, and our hearts broke. How poor we are to-day!

But how thankful I am that her persecutions are ended. I would not call her back if I could.

To-day, treasured in her worn old Testament, I found a dear and gentle letter from you, dated Far Rockaway, Sept. 13, 1896, about our poor Susy's death. I am tired and old; I wish I were with Livy.

I send my love—and hers—to you all.

S.L.C.

Thomas Hardy, poem on the death of his wife, Emma

When Thomas Hardy's wife died in 1912, a flock of admiring women gathered about the famous novelist, all quite willing to console him in his grief and perhaps vie for a place as the second Mrs. Hardy. He kept them at a distance, however, by spending the next year creating a poetic homage to the first Mrs. Hardy, a surprising circumstance, since their marriage had been almost intolerable.

Even on the honeymoon it was clear that there was no real physical attraction on Emma's part. Later, she had to cope with an imperious mother-in-law (and the hold she had over her son), and she found Thomas's fiction increasingly offensive. She was so horrified by the bleakness and impropriety of *Jude the Obscure* (1895) that she forbade her husband to publish it. When he did, she shut herself off from him, occupying the same house but having nothing to do with him. But obviously the publication of *Jude the Obscure* was simply the final straw in a marriage that went bad almost at the start. When

Fanny and Robert Louis Stevenson called upon the Hardys in 1885, Fanny expressed dismay at the marriage she witnessed: "We saw [Hardy's] wife," she wrote in a letter to a friend. "What very strange marriages literary men seem to make."

Emma's death allowed Hardy imaginatively to recreate his marriage in a more romantic image. His outburst of poetic commemoration was partly a compensation for his discovery of a secret diary that his wife had kept over the last two decades of her life. In it she recorded his neglect of her as well as her own harsh opinions on his conduct, character, and literary skills. Wracked by remorse, Hardy spent the next few months producing poem after poem. He even made a sentimental pilgrimage back to St. Juliot in March of 1913 in order to recapture the feelings of his first meeting with Emma, forty-three years earlier, outside the rectory door. Ironically, her death inspired the most romantic period in his life and writing.

Without Ceremony

It was your way, my dear,
To vanish without a word
When callers, friends, or kin
Had left, and I hastened in
To rejoin you, as I inferred.

And when you'd a mind to career
Off anywhere—say to town—
You were all on a sudden gone
Before I had thought thereon,
Or noticed your trunks were down.

So, now that you disappear
For ever in that swift style,
Your meaning seems to me
Just as it used to be:
'Good-bye is not worth while!'

4

LOVE HURTS

UNREQUITED LOVE

George Eliot (Marian Evans) to Herbert Spencer

Before George Henry Lewes, there was another man in Marian Evans's life. She met him when she was editing the *Westminster Review*, a prestigious intellectual journal for which she recruited articles by feminist Harriet Martineau, philosopher (and feminist) John Stuart Mill, historian James Anthony Froude, as well as a number of Continental immigrants and refugees, including Giuseppe Mazzini, Pierre Leroux, and Karl Marx. Among this illustrious roster was Herbert Spencer, a young scientist working out his theory of social Darwinism.

The collaboration of Evans and Spencer was intense and personal. He became her nearly constant escort and companion, and his manner was both publicly and privately flirtatious. Close friends assumed a wedding announcement was imminent. So, indeed, did Marian. But when she declared her love, he beat a hasty retreat, saying that he had feared and dreaded that such a misunderstanding might happen. He said that although Marian was the "most admirable woman, mentally, I ever met," she was simply too homely to be taken as a wife. A mutual friend offered Marian a kinder explanation: "Poor Spencer, he lacks instinct, my dear, he lacks instinct—you will discover that instinct is as important as intellect."

Herbert Spencer remained a bachelor until his death at the age of eighty-six. Marian, however, had already met George Henry Lewes by the time of the debacle with Spencer. With Lewes she discovered, happily, that intellect and "instinct" can reside in the same person.

July 1852

I know this letter will make you very angry with me, but wait a little, and don't say anything to me while you are angry. I promise not to sin any more in the same way.

My ill health is caused by the hopeless wretchedness which weighs upon me. I do not say this to pain you, but because it is the simple truth which you must know in order to understand why I am obliged to seek relief.

I want to know if you can assure me that you will not forsake me, that you will always be with me as much as you can and share your thoughts and feelings with me. If you become attached to some one else, then I must die, but until then I could gather courage to work and make life valuable, if only I had you near me. I do not ask you to sacrifice anything—I would be very good and cheerful and never annoy you. But I find it impossible to contemplate life under any other conditions. If I had your assurance, I could trust that and live upon it. I have struggled—indeed I have—to renounce everything and be entirely unselfish, but I find myself utterly unequal to it. Those who have known me best have always said, that if ever I loved any one thoroughly my whole life must turn upon that feeling, and I find they said truly. You curse the destiny which has made the feeling concentrate itself on you—but if you will only have patience with me you shall not curse it long. You will find that I can be satisfied with very little, if I am delivered from the dread of losing it.

I suppose no woman ever before wrote such a letter as this—but I am not ashamed of it, for I am conscious that in the light of reason and true refinement I am worthy of your respect and tenderness, whatever gross men or vulgar-minded women might think of me.

Emily Dickinson to "Master"

Think about the Emily Dickinson you read in high school. How could that frail, pale virgin-poetess have written:

> Wild Nights—Wild Nights!
> Were I with thee
> Wild Nights should be
> Our luxury!
> . . .
> Rowing in Eden—
> Ah, the Sea!
> Might I but moor—Tonight—
> In Thee!

That's a long way from "A Bird Came Down the Walk," "I Never Saw a Moor," and other harmless poems befitting the "Belle of Amherst." Yet anyone who has read the whole of Dickinson's poetry knows that she is one of the world's greatest poets of love—and of loss.

Nor was her life as reclusive as once was thought. But to find the "real" Emily Dickinson requires undoing the censoring perpetuated after her death. When her sister, Lavinia, discovered three "Master letters" along with several hundred unpublished poems, she (like subsequent editors) embarked on a process of culling and editing. A brief portion of one of the letters was published by Mabel Loomis Todd in 1894, but the identity of the recipient was obscured and the letter was deliberately misdated to suggest it came from the pen of an old woman, a way of downplaying its romantic content.

The Master letters provide a fleeting glimpse into the unexpurgated life of Emily Dickinson. All evidence suggests that these were part of a larger correspondence that took place over the course of several years. The first letter seems to be a response to the "Master's" desire to hear from her. In this letter, both Dickinson and her anonymous correspondent are ill. The tone is formal, distant. In the final two letters, however, the tone is both intimate and heartbreaking.

Many biographers have tried to guess who this "Master" might have been: Samuel Bowles, a newspaper editor; Otis Phillips Lord, a judge; or maybe Charles Wadsworth, a minister. Dickinson had an active correspondence with many men of stature who came through Amherst. We do not know if she called one of them "Master."

Summer, 1861

Master,

If you saw a bullet hit a Bird—and he told you he was'nt shot—you might weep at his courtesy, but you would certainly doubt his word. One drop more from the gash that stains your Daisy's bosom. . . . God made me, Master. I didn't be myself. *I* don't know how it was done. He built the heart in me. Bye and bye it outgrew me—and like the little mother with the big child—I got tired holding him. I heard of a thing called "Redemption"—which rested men and women. You remember I asked you for it—you gave me something else. I forgot the Redemption . . . (I did'nt tell you for a long time—but I knew you had altered me) and was tired. . . . I am older—tonight, Master—but the love is the same—so are the moon and the crescent. If it had been God's will that I might breathe where you breathed and find the place—myself—at night—if I never forget that I am not with you—and that sorrow and frost are nearer than I—if I wish with a might I cannot re-press—that mine were the Queen's place—the love of the Plantagenet is my only apology— . . .

These things are holy, Sir, I touch them hallowed, but persons who pray—dare remark "Father!" You say I do not tell you all. Daisy "confessed—and denied not."

Vesuvius dont talk—Etna—dont— . . . One of them—said a syllable—a thousand years ago, and Pompeii heard it, and hid forever. She could'nt look the world in the face, afterward—I suppose—Bashful Pompeii! "Tell you of the want"—you know what a leech is, dont you—and you have felt the horizon hav'nt you—and did the sea—never come so close as to make you dance?

I dont know what you can do for it—thank you—Master— but if I had the Beard on my cheek—like you—and you—had Daisy's petals—and you cared so for me—what would become of you? Could you forget me in fight, or flight—or the foreign land? . . . I used to think when I died—I could see you—so I died as fast as I could—but the "corporation" are going too—so Heaven wont be sequestered at all.

Say I may wait for you—

Say I need go with no stranger to the to me—untried country. I waited a long time—Master—but I can wait more—wait till my hazel hair is dappled and you carry the cane—then I can look at my watch—and if the Day is too far declined—we can take the chances for Heaven.

What would you do with me if I came "in white"? Have you the little chest—to put the alive—in?

I want to see you more—Sir—than all I wish for in this world—and the wish—altered a little—will be my only one—for the skies.

Could you come to New England this summer? Would you come to Amherst—Would you like to come—Master?

Would it do harm—yet we both fear God? Would Daisy disappoint you—no—she would'nt—Sir—it were comfort forever—just to look in your face, while you looked in mine—then I could play in the woods—till Dark—till you take me where sundown cannot find us—and the true keep coming—till the town is full. (Will you tell me if you will?)

I did'nt think to tell you, you did'nt come to me "in white"—nor ever told me why—

> No Rose, yet felt myself a'bloom,
> No Bird—yet rode in Ether.

Anne Gilchrist to Walt Whitman

Anne Gilchrist, a genteel English widow, was the first woman to write a major defense of Whitman's work. Her "A Woman's Estimate of Walt Whitman" (1870) appeared when critics (on both sides of the Atlantic) were labeling his poetry "obscene." "Almost everybody," Whitman noted retrospectively, "was against me—the preachers, the literary gentlemen—nearly everybody . . . then this wonderful woman." Although Gilchrist had never met the poet, she wrote from the heart. Hers was criticism filled with passion, criticism as love.

But like many readers (and especially readers of Whitman's verse), Gilchrist confused the verse with the man. As poet John Keats had once warned, sometimes readers "would like to be married to a Poem and to be given away by a Novel." When Anne Gilchrist wrote to Whitman directly, she addressed him as a lover. Her steamy letter—four times the length of this excerpt—is certainly one of the most remarkable of all literary love letters. After confessing that she had never really loved her late husband, she notes that Whitman's verse has inflamed her passionate nature. She yearns to be united to him. Lest the poet miss her point, she emphasizes that "it is for [my] soul exactly as it is for [my] body." When Whitman did not respond immediately to her entreaties, she wrote again, more explicitly: "I am yet young enough to bear thee children, my darling, if God should so bless me. And would yield my life for this cause with serene joy if it were so appointed, if that were the price for thy having a 'perfect child.' "

Understandably, Whitman was abashed when he received Anne Gilchrist's confession of love. Whitman liked women but he loved men, especially "working class camerados," as biographer Charley Shively has called Whitman's lovers. Fearful that he might hurt the feelings of one to whom he felt gratitude, Whitman took six weeks to find the right note on which to respond. His answer is brief, explicit, and touching in its tactfulness. He sidesteps the issue of sexual desire by noting that his books are the real repository of his "body and spirit." He gently suggests that he would like to enter a "beautiful & delicate" epistolary relationship with her. After a few months in which she had to mend what was clearly a broken heart, Anne began to write loving, friendly, passionate, but *poetic* letters. They continued to write until July 20, 1885, a few months before Anne's death. She signed her final letter to him, simply, "my love, dear Walt."

Whitman treasured Gilchrist's devotion. When her son, Herbert Harlakenden Gilchrist, wrote to Whitman requesting that he return his mother's letters for use in a posthumous biography, Whitman demurred, preferring to keep the letters until his death in 1892. "Among the perfect women I have met," Whitman wrote to the devoted son, "I have known none more perfect in every relation, than my dear, dear friend, Anne Gilchrist."

September 3, 1871

DEAR FRIEND:

At last the beloved books have reached my hand—but now I have them, my heart is so rent with anguish, my eyes so blinded, I cannot read in them. I try again and again, but too great waves come swaying up & suffocate me. I will struggle to tell you my story. It seems to me a death struggle.

When I was eighteen I met a lad of nineteen who loved me then, and always for the remainder of his life. After we had known each other about a year he asked me to be his wife. But I said that I liked him well as my friend, but could not love him as a wife should love & felt deeply convinced I never should. . . . I knew I could lead a good and wholesome life beside him—his aims were noble—his heart a deep, beautiful, true Poet's heart; but he had not the Poet's great brain. His path was a very arduous one, and I knew I could smooth it for him—cheer him along it.

It seemed to me God's will that I should marry him. So I told him the whole truth, and he said he would rather have me on those terms than not have me at all. He said to me many times, "Ah, Annie, it is not you who are so loved that is rich; it is I who so love." And I knew this was true, felt as if my nature were poor & barren beside his.

But it was not so, it was only slumbering—undeveloped. For, dear Friend, my soul was so passionately aspiring—it so thirsted & pined for light, it had not power to reach alone and he could not help me on my way. And a woman is so made that she cannot give the tender passionate devotion of her whole nature save to the great conquering soul, stronger in its powers, though not in its aspirations, than her own, that can lead her forever & forever up and on. It is for her soul exactly as it is for her body. The strong divine soul of the man embracing hers with passionate love—so alone the precious germs within her soul can be quickened into life. And the time will come when man will understand that a woman's soul is as dear and needful to his and as different from his as her body to his body.

This was what happened to me when I had read for a few days, nay, hours, in your books. It was the divine soul embracing mine. I never before dreamed what love meant: not what life meant. Never was alive before—no words but those of "new birth" can hint the meaning of what then happened to me. . . .

O dear Walt, did you not feel in every word [of my review] the breath of a woman's love? did you not see as through a transparent veil a soul all radiant and trembling with love stretching out its arms towards you? I was so sure you would speak, would send me some sign: that I was to wait—wait.

So I fed my heart with sweet hopes: strengthened it with looking into the eyes of thy picture. O surely in the ineffable tenderness of thy look speaks the yearning of thy man-soul towards my woman-soul? But now I will wait no longer. A higher instinct dominates that other, the instinct for perfect truth. I would if I could lay every thought and action and feeling of my whole life open to thee as it lies to the eye of God. But that cannot be all at once.

O come. Come, my darling: look into these eyes and see the loving ardent aspiring soul in them. Easily, easily will you learn to love all the rest of me for the sake of that and take me to your breasts for ever and ever. Out of its great anguish my love has risen stronger, more triumphant than ever: it cannot doubt, cannot fear, is strong, divine, immortal, sure of its fruition this side the grave or the other. "O agonistic throes," tender, passionate yearnings, pinings, triumphant joys, sweet dreams—I too from you all. . . .

Good-bye, dear Walt,
ANNE GILCHRIST.

Walt Whitman to Anne Gilchrist

Washington, November 3, 1871

Dear friend,

    I have been waiting quite a long while for time & the right mood to answer your letter in a spirit as serious as its own, & in the same unmitigated trust & affection. But more daily work than ever has fallen upon me to do the current season, & though I am well & contented, my best moods seem to shun me. I wished to give to it a day, a sort of Sabbath or holy day apart to itself, under serene & propitious influences— confident that I could then write you a letter which would do you good, & me too. But I must at least show, without further delay, that I am not insensible to your love. I too send you my love. And do you feel no disappointment because I now write but briefly. My book is my best letter, my response, my truest explanation of all. In it I have put my body & spirit. You understand this better & fuller & clearer than any one else. And I too fully & clearly understand the loving & womanly letter it has evoked. Enough that there surely exists between us so beautiful & delicate a relation, accepted by both of us with joy.

Walt Whitman

Federico García Lorca to Salvador Dalí

When poet and playwright Federico García Lorca met Salvador Dalí in 1923, the tall, slender artist was wearing stylish clothes and had his hair slicked back like Rudolph Valentino. Despite such cosmopolitan airs, he was painfully shy. Lorca, on the other hand, was incredibly charismatic. "The personality of Federico García Lorca produced an immense impression on me," the painter wrote in his memoir, *Secret Life*. "The poetic phenomenon in its entirety and 'in the raw' presented itself before me suddenly in flesh and bone, confused, blood-red, viscous and sublime, quivering with a thousand fires of darkness and of subterranean biology, like all matter endowed with the originality of its own form."

For the next five years, these two prominent Spaniards enjoyed an intense friendship and a rewarding artistic collaboration. There was only one problem. Lorca pined with a sexual longing that Dalí could not fulfill. When they met, Dalí showed no interest whatsoever in women, a fact that gave Lorca reason to hope. But the more he came to know him, the more Lorca realized that Dalí was beset by deep sexual anxieties, especially fears of impotence and venereal disease. There was flirtation, perhaps even love, but the artist was reluctant to consummate the relationship.

Throughout the period of their friendship, Lorca's sensuous, surrealistic poems smoldered with repressed lust, usually conveyed in print as heterosexual longing. And Dalí painted Lorca's face and body over and over again, sometimes as the shadow-image behind his own portrait.

Unfortunately, only a few fragments of Lorca's remarkable letters to Dalí (such as the one reprinted here) have survived. Here Lorca reminisces about the time they spent together in Cadaqués, a small paradise on the Costa Brava, cut off from the rest of Spain by a mountain barrier. Dalí's house was only a few feet from the water, and here he painted while Lorca wrote.

But the sexual and emotional frustration became increasingly painful for Lorca. As this letter intimates, the two soon parted. They would not see each other again for seven years. When they finally met in Barcelona one September night in 1935, Lorca was so excited that he went off to the seaside resort of Tarragona with his friend, neglecting to appear at a special concert held in his honor.

It would be their last meeting. After Franco's fascists gained power in Spain, Lorca was singled out for harassment. For a time he hid out with friends; he was later put under house arrest. An ardent populist and Republican, Lorca had devoted himself to setting up a traveling theater company that produced both new plays and classics for peasant audiences in remote villages. He was despised by local authorities for his leftist politics as well as for his homosexuality.

In August of 1936, Federico García Lorca, the greatest writer of modern Spain, was arrested and then executed by Franco's henchmen in Granada. His body was never found.

Barcelona, July 1927

Cadaqués has the vitality and permanent neutral beauty of the place where Venus was born, *but where this has been forgotten.*

It aspires to pure beauty. The vines have disappeared and day by day are exalted the sharp edges which are like waves. One day the moon will move with the elasticity of a damp fish and the tower of the church oscillate like soft rubber over the hard or *sorrowful houses,* of lime or chewed bread. I get excited thinking about the discoveries you're going to make in Cadaqués and I remember Salvador Dalí the neophyte licking the twilight's shell without going in altogether, the pale pink shell of a crab lying on its back.

Today you're inside. From here I can hear (ay, my little boy, how sad!) the soft trickle of blood from the Sleeping Beauty of the Wood of Gadgets [in your painting of Saint Sebastian] and the crackling of two little beasties like the sounds of a pistachio nut cracked between one's fingers. The decapitated woman [in your painting *Honey Is Sweeter Than Blood*] is the finest imaginable "poem" on the theme of blood, and has more blood than all that spilt in the European war, which was *hot* blood and had no other purpose than to *irrigate* the earth and appease a symbolic thirst for eroticism and faith. Your pictorial blood and in general the whole tactile concept of your physiological aesthetic has such a concrete, well-balanced air, such a logical and true quality of pure poetry that it attains the category of *that which we need absolutely* in order to live.

One can say: "I was tired and I sat down in the shade and freshness of that blood," or: "I came down from the hill and ran all along the beach until I found the melancholy head in the spot where the delicious little crackling beasties, so useful for the digestion, gathered."

Now I realize how much I am losing by leaving you.

The impression I get in Barcelona is that everyone is playing and sweating in an effort to *forget*. Everything is confused and aggressive like the aesthetic of the flame, everything indecisive and out of joint. In Cadaqués the people feel on the ground all the sinuosities and pores of the soles of their feet. Now I realize how I felt my shoulders in Cadaqués. It's delicious for me to recall the slippery curves of my shoulders when for the first time I felt in them the circulation of my blood in four spongy tubes which trembled with the movements of a wounded swimmer.

Anne Sexton to Philip Legler

In April of 1966 Anne Sexton gave a poetry reading at Sweet Briar College in Virginia where she met Philip Legler, a young professor and poet. He was crazy about her, and after she returned home, he wrote her intense and passionate letters. Their correspondence lasted for many years. She encouraged him in his work, he complimented her on her own, and they wrote letters filled with intimacy, intensity, and friendship.

But for Anne, there was an emotional line that could not be crossed in their relationship, one Philip kept pressing. As she wrote him in 1966, "We are two of a kind, the abundance stuff that runs wild, runs as wild with love as cancer." In the letter reprinted here, she is by turns tender and witty, firm and tactful. She tries to let him down gently—for both their sakes. Even rejecting him, her letter reads like love.

14 Black Oak Road
May 19th, 1970

Dear Phil Baby,
   I will have to burn your letter as incriminating evidence . . . but that's not the point. Your letter is full of love and I wish I could keep it. I do know you love me more than most people do. Perhaps my husband more because he had to live with me. Sometimes I think he deserves an award for putting up with me. Other times I think he's pretty lucky. Lucky because I'm quite naturally a loving, affectionate person. But then, even that can get to be a bore.
   I'm sorry I put your hand in a tin box. God, I'm sorry. I didn't mean to really. You know I've never slept with anyone on a reading . . . never a one-night stand . . . never something so casual or lighthearted. I'm just not the type. I'm a pretty faithful type when you come right down to it. Sleeping with someone is almost like marrying them. It takes time and thought. If you lived in Boston or I lived where the lovely fog horns are . . . but even then I'm not sure. Just that it wasn't possible that time. I've got to be true to myself as well as to you. Further, I think I'm so busy fighting the suicide demons that I have little time for love. You saw how I go to sleep—not sleep at all. You said it: "death touched me." I hope to hell my present shrink can help me work this out before it's too late.
   I zapped into your life and I'm so glad I did. I'll never really zap out. Put me there, friend, friend, forever.
   . . . next day . . .
   I've been out killing dandelions. It's a lovely spring day. I think I'll go out into [it] again. The manager (Bob) of "Her Kind" (my rock group) is coming over for lunch, or rather bringing the lunch. I will sit in the shade (thorazine makes me

allergic to the sun) and he will sit in the sun. How I miss that!

I finished that fairy tale ("The Maiden Without Hands") last week and am thinking about doing Hansel and Gretel. My transformations of the Brothers Grimm are full of food images but what could be more directly food than cooking the kids and finally the wicked lady. Smack in the oven like a roast lamb.

Readings are accumulating for next year. I'll do few of them I hope. Enough to pull in some dough to help out but not enough to drain me too much. I find them very hard to do . . . particularly those informal classes where (as they say) I can do anything I want . . . Mostly I don't want. That's the trouble. But you, Phil, make it easy on me and helped in every way. I thank you. That's still the nicest Holiday Inn I ever stayed in. And I can remember those ghost-like fog horns. I remember too you tucking me in bed and patting my head so gently. I don't forget! Love to you, my dear,

Annie Babe

OBSTACLES

Rochester to Elizabeth Barry

John Wilmot, second earl of Rochester (1647–1680), was a poet, satirist, and member of the "court wits" who surrounded King Charles II. But he was perhaps best known for his letters, which revealed his amorous adventures and philosophy, also recounted in his *The Maimed Debauchee*. He wrote explicitly about sex, in all its varieties, and considered seduction (whether of men or women) to be a high art.

He started young. At the age of eighteen, aware that he had an aristocratic lineage but no property, he decided he needed to marry an heiress. The obvious choice was Elizabeth Malet, young, beautiful, unmarried, and with an income of two thousand pounds a year. He decided he must conquer her. Literally. One night he rode up on horseback to the house where she was exiting from a dinner party, seized her, and put her into a coach drawn by six horses. Two ladies-in-waiting were inside to receive her. Rochester returned her to her family three weeks later. It is unclear exactly what went on, but obviously Malet was a match for him. Two years later, still unmarried, she wrote ironically of her strange love life to a friend: "My Lord Herbert would have had her, my Lord Hinchingbroke was indifferent to have her, my Lord John Butler might not have her, my Lord of Rochester would have forced her, and Sir [Francis] Popham would kiss her breech to have her." Finally, she settled on Rochester, and together they had four children and, between them, countless love affairs.

His most lasting romance was with the gifted actress Elizabeth Barry. He wrote her many letters, some of which were published in *Familiar Letters* (1697), a book intended as a guide for the bourgeoisie, which was just gaining the literacy and the affluence (paper was expensive then) required for personal correspondence. Since Rochester and Elizabeth Barry were among the most famous lovers of the day, their letters were especially esteemed as models. Publishers often made up letters and claimed they were by Rochester and Barry, a surefire way to sell new letter books.

The love between Rochester and Elizabeth Barry was intense, anxiety-laden, and stormy. They were deliriously happy at first, but long separations meant multiple affairs for both of them (despite Rochester's protestations of faithfulness in the letter reprinted here).

As this letter suggests, Rochester's infidelities did not make him any less jealous of Barry's. He was not a generous man. When she tried to end their relationship, he sought revenge by taking away the child she had by him—something both legal and typical until well into the twentieth century. Her revenge was to make sexual conquests of virtually all of his friends and relatives. Only Rochester's early death put an end to a bitter lovers' rivalry that was as intense as their passion once had been.

Madam,

I know not well who has the worst on't: you, who love but a little, or I who dote to an extravagance. Sure to be half kind is as bad as to be half-witted; and madness, both in love and reason, bears a better character than a moderate state of either.

Would I could bring you to my opinion in this point. I would then confidently pretend you had too just exceptions either against me or my passion, the flesh and the devil; I mean, all the fools of my own sex, and that fat with the other lean one of yours whose prudent advice is daily concerning you, how dangerous it is to be kind to the man upon earth who loves you best. I, who still persuade myself by all the arguments I can bring that I am happy, find this none of the least, that you are too unlike these people every way to agree with them in any particular.

This is writ between sleeping and waking, and I will not answer for its being sense; but I, dreaming you were at Mrs N——'s with five or six fools and the lean lady, waked in one of your horrors, and in amaze, fright and confusion send this to beg a kind one from you, that may remove my fears and make me as happy as I am faithful.

Stendhal (Henri Beyle) to Madame Dembowski

Stendhal's *De L'Amour* (1822) is an original and provocative exploration of love. It is especially pointed on the hopelessness and folly of passion, a subject on which the novelist was an expert. He had an affair with the stunning Pietragrua, who proved to be faithless; he fell hopelessly in love with Madame Métilde Dembowski, who was uninterested in a serious relationship with him. There were other loves of less magnitude but hardly more satisfaction, and he wove all of them into *De L'Amour*, which attempts to explain not only the psychology of love but its political and social meaning.

Stendhal's two masterpieces, *The Red and the Black* (1830) and *The Charterhouse of Parma* (1839), are both political novels recounting life in early-nineteenth-century Europe. Both are written with a remarkable vitality and power. As this letter to Madame Dembowski suggests, Stendhal was not a man to live life halfway. He threw himself into his writing and into his love with full force and often suffered for that commitment. His work was condemned as sensational, scandalous, immoral, irreligious, and subversive. His ardent love was never fully reciprocated. "The heart which blazes with the flames of a volcano," he wrote in one of his letters to Madame Dembowski, "cannot please the object of its adoration; it commits follies, fails in delicacy, and burns itself away."

Varese, the 7th of June 1819

Madame,

You throw me into despair. You repeatedly accuse me of failing in delicacy—as if, on your lips, this accusation were nothing. Who would have thought, when I parted from you at Milan, that the first letter you wrote to me would begin with "monsieur", or that you would accuse me of failing in delicacy?

Ah, madame, it is easy for a man who has no passion to conduct himself always with moderation and prudence. I, too, when I can hearken to my own counsel, I believe that I am not lacking in discretion. But I am dominated by a fatal passion that leaves me no longer master of my actions. I had sworn to myself to take coach, or at least not to see you, and not to write to you until you returned: a force more powerful than all my resolutions dragged me to the places where you were. I perceive all too well that henceforth this passion is to be the great concern of my life. All interests, all considerations have paled before it. This fatal need I have of seeing you carries me away, dominates me, transports me. There are moments, in the long, solitary evenings, when, if it were necessary to commit a murder that I might see you, I would become a murderer.

In all my life I have had only three passions: ambition, from 1800–1811; love of a woman who deceived me, from 1811 to 1818; and, during the past year, this passion that dominates me and ceaselessly grows. At all seasons and amidst all distractions, anything unrelated to my passion has meant nothing to me: whether happy or unhappy, it has occupied every moment. And do you suppose that the sacrifice I have made to your conventions, of not seeing you this evening, is a little thing? Assuredly, I do not wish to make a merit of it: I present it to you only as an expiation of the wrongs of which I may have been guilty two days [a]go. This expiation means nothing to you, madame: but for me, who have spent so many frightful evenings deprived of you and without seeing you, it is a sacrifice more difficult to endure than the most horrible tortures; it is a sacrifice which, in the extreme pain of the victim, is worthy of the sublime woman to whom it is offered.

In the midst of the confusion of my whole being, into which I am thrown by the imperious necessity of seeing you, there is nevertheless one quality which I have preserved, and which I pray that destiny will continue to preserve for me, unless it seeks to plunge me, in my own esteem, into the underworld of abjection—the quality of perfect truthfulness. You tell me, madame, that I so greatly "compromised" matters on Saturday morning, that in the evening it was necessary for you to act as you did. It is the word "compromised" that wounds me to the bottom of my soul; and, if I had the good fortune to be able to pluck out the fatal affection that pierces my heart, it would be this word "compromised" that gave me the strength to do so.

But no, madame, your soul has too much nobility not to have understood mine. You were offended, and you used the first word that came to the end of your pen. I shall accept as judge, between your accusation and myself, a person whose evidence you will not reject. If Madame Dembowski, if the noble and sublime Métilde, *believes* that my conduct of Saturday morning was the least in the world *calculated* to force her, out of a just care for her reputation in this country, to take some further step, then I confess that this infamous conduct was mine, that there is a being in the world who can say that I fail in delicacy. I shall go further: I have never had any talent for seduction except in respect of women whom I did not love at all. As soon as I am in love I become timid—as you can judge from the manner in which I am always out of countenance in your presence.

If I had not started prattling on Saturday evening, everybody, even including the good padre Rettore, would have perceived that I was in love. But even if I had had a talent for seduction, I would not have employed it upon you. If success depended only upon the making of vows, I would still wish to win you for myself, and not for another being whom I had set up in my place. I would blush, I would have no more happiness, I think, even though you loved me, if I could suspect that you loved a being who was not myself. If you had faults, I could say that I did not see them: I would say, and say in truth, that I adored them: and, indeed, I can say I adore that extreme susceptibility which causes me to spend such horrible nights. It is thus that I would wish to be loved, it is thus that true love is created: it rejects in horror the idea of seduction, as a means unworthy of it, and, together with seduction, it rejects every calculation, every stratagem— including the least thought of "compromising" the beloved object in order to force her to certain further steps to its own advantage.

Had I the talent to seduce you—and I do not believe that such a talent exists—I would not use it. Sooner or later you would perceive that you had been deceived; and to lose you after having possessed you would be still more frightful, I think, than if heaven had condemned me to die without ever having been loved by you.

When a being is dominated by an extreme passion, all that he says or does in a particular situation proves nothing concerning him: what bears witness for him is the entirety of his life. Thus, madame, were I to vow all day long at your feet that I loved you, or that I hated you, this should have no influence upon the degree of credence that you decided to grant me. It is the entirety of my life that should speak. Now, although I am very little known, and still less interesting to the people who know me, yet you might enquire—for lack of another topic of conversation—whether I am known to lack either pride or constancy.

I have now been in Milan for five years. Let us assume that all that is said about my previous life is false. Five years—from the age of thirty-one to the age of thirty-six—are a fairly important interval in a man's life, especially when during these five years he has been tested by difficult circumstances. If ever you deign, madame—for lack of a better occupation—to think about my character, then deign to compare these five years of my life with five years taken from the life of any other individual. You will find lives much more brilliantly talented, lives much more fortunate: but that you will find a life more full of honour and constancy than mine, this I do not believe. How many mistresses had I in Milan, in five years? How many times have I weakened on a point of honour? Well, I would have disgracefully failed in honour if, in my relations with a being who cannot make me draw my sword, I had in the least sought to "compromise" her.

Love me if you will, divine Métilde, but in God's name do not despise me. Such torment is beyond my strength to endure. In your manner of thinking, which is very just, if you despised me it would be impossible for you ever to love me.

With a soul as lofty as yours, what surer way could there be of earning your displeasure than that which you accuse me of having taken? I so much fear to displease you that the moment when I first saw you, on the evening of the 3rd—the moment which should have been the sweetest of my life—was, on the contrary, one of my most wretched, by reason of the fear I had of displeasing you.

Elizabeth Barrett to Robert Browning

In 1845, when Robert Browning began to write to Elizabeth Barrett, he was thirty-two and she thirty-eight. She was a famous poet who had praised his work in print; he wrote to express his gratitude. Soon they had a full-blown correspondence, which he pressed into a friendship and then, persistently, into love. In the process, he also transformed himself, for when he met Elizabeth he, too, was still living under his parents' roof, relying on them for financial support and daily care.

Aesthetically, Robert most often deferred to Elizabeth's judgment, quoting admiringly from her poems far more often than she from his. But as this letter makes clear, Elizabeth's self-confidence as a poet was in contrast to her fearfulness as her father's daughter. Here she lists the ways in which her siblings have tried (and failed) to rebel against their father. Here she succumbs to a sense of hopelessness. Nor is she comfortable dreaming a fairy-tale ending, as if she's some kind of stereotypical damsel waiting for the knight in shining armor who can save her from the tower and the evil wizard who holds her captive there. She sardonically dismisses Robert's "gold-headed nails of chivalry, which won't hold to the wall through this summer." She wryly jokes about Sleeping Beauty and Cinderella. "I have no spell," she notes in another letter, "for charming the dragons."

Yet the dragons *were* charmed. Elizabeth and Robert escaped together to the sunshine of Florence. They lived out their life together there as happy lovers, proud parents, and productive poets. It is impossible not to read high romance in the epistolary story of the Brownings, a story first published in 1899 by their son (aptly nicknamed "Pen"): "Ever since my mother's death these letters were kept by my father in a certain inlaid box, into which they exactly fitted, and where they have always rested, letter beside letter, each in its consecutive order and numbered on the envelope by his own hand."

January 15, 1846
Thursday night

Ever dearest—how you can write touching things to me—&
how my whole being vibrates, as a string, to these!—How have
I deserved from God and you all that I thank you for? Too
unworthy I am of all! Only, it was not, dearest beloved, what
you feared, that was "horrible," . . . it was you *supposed*,
rather!—It was a mistake of yours. And now we will not talk of
it any more.

Friday morning

. . . For the rest, I will think as you desire: but I have thought a
great deal, & there are certainties which I know; & I hope we
both are aware that nothing can be more hopeless than our
position in some relations & aspects, though you do not guess
perhaps that the very approach to the subject is shut up by
dangers, & that from the moment of a suspicion entering *one
mind*, we should be able to meet never again in this room, nor
to have intercourse by letter through the ordinary channel. I
mean, that letters of yours, addressed to me here, would
infallibly be stopped & destroyed—if not opened. Therefore it
is advisable to hurry on nothing—on these grounds it is
advisable.

What should I do if I did not see you nor hear from you,
without being able to feel that it was for your happiness? What
should I do for a month even? And then, I might be thrown
out of the window or its equivalent—I look back shuddering to
the dreadful scenes in which poor Henrietta was involved who
never offended as I have offended . . years ago which seem as
present as today. She had forbidden the subject to be referred
to until that consent was obtained—& at a word she gave up
all—at a word. In fact she had no true attachment, as I
observed to Arabel at the time: a child never submitted more
meekly to a revoked holiday. Yet how she was made to suffer—
Oh, the dreadful scene!— only because she had seemed to feel
a little. I told you, I think, that there was an obliquity . . an

eccentricity—or something beyond . . on one class of subjects.
I hear how her knees were made to ring upon the floor,
now!—she was carried out of the room in strong hysterics, &
I, who rose up to follow her, though I was quite well at that
time & suffered only by sympathy, fell flat down upon my face
in a fainting-fit. Arabel thought I was dead.

I have tried to forget it all—but now I must remember—&
throughout our intercourse *I have remembered*. It is necessary
to remember so much as to avoid such evils as are evitable, &
for this reason I would conceal nothing from you. Do *you*
remember, besides, that there can be no faltering on my 'part,'
& that, if I should remain well, which is not proved yet, I will
do for you what you please & as you please to have it done.
But there is time for considering!

Only . . as you speak of 'counsel,' I will take courage to tell
you that my SISTERS KNOW—. Arabel is in most of my
confidences, & being often in the room with me, taxed me
with the truth long ago—she saw that I was affected from
some cause—& I told her. We are as safe with both of them as
possible—& they thoroughly understand that if *there should be
any change it would not be* YOUR fault . . I made them
understand that thoroughly. From themselves I have received
nothing but the most smiling words of kindness &
satisfaction—(I thought I might tell you so much,—) they
have too much tenderness for me to fail in it now. My
brothers, it is quite necessary not to draw into a dangerous
responsibility: I have felt that from the beginning, & shall
continue to feel it—though I hear, & can observe that they are
full of suspicions & conjectures, which are never unkindly
expressed. I told you once that we held hands the faster in this
house for the weight over our heads. But the absolute
knowledge would be dangerous for my brothers: with my
sisters it is different, & I could not continue to conceal from
them what they had under their eyes—and then, Henrietta is
in a like position—It was not wrong of me to let them know
it?—no?—

Yet of what consequence is all this to the other side of the
question? What, if *you* should give pain & disappointment

where you owe such pure gratitude—But we need not talk of these things now. Only you have more to consider than *I*, I imagine, while the future comes on. . . .

My life was ended when I knew you, & if I survive myself it is for your sake:— *that* resumes all my feelings & intentions in respect to you. No 'counsel' could make the difference of a grain of dust in the balance. It *is so*, & not otherwise. If you changed towards me, it would be better for you I believe—& I should be only where I was before. If you do *not* change, I look to you for my first affections & my first duty—& nothing but your bidding me, could make me look away.

Virginia Stephen to Leonard Woolf

Virginia Stephen was thirty years old when she wrote this remarkable letter to Leonard Woolf, essentially warning him about what he might expect from marriage to her. She tells him "brutally," as she says, that she "feel[s] no physical attraction in you." Not content with that, she spells it out: "There are moments—when you kissed me the other day was one—when I feel no more than a rock." So much for pandering to the male ego!

Idealistic in her view of marriage, Virginia Stephen did not want either of them entering into one under false pretenses. And she knew that she could not promise any man sexual attraction or satisfaction. As a child, she was repeatedly molested by her older half-brothers. As a result, she had a lifelong revulsion toward many aspects of the physical, including eating and sexuality.

For whatever personal reasons, Leonard was not dissuaded by a letter that would have sent most men packing. The marriage was pretty much as Virginia had forewarned. There was intellectual excitement and companionship, compassion, accomplishment, and even times of great joy. They worked well together at the Hogarth Press and enjoyed a lively intellectual circle. There were also her severe depressions, with which Leonard attempted to cope. There was no real sexual relationship, and Leonard accepted Virginia's long and passionate romance with Vita Sackville-West.

In 1944, three years after his wife's suicide, Leonard fell in love again, this time with Trekkie Parsons. It was a very different kind of relationship than any he had had before. "You have turned a passive, neutral existence into a life of passionate happiness," he wrote to Parsons. "To know you and love you has been the best thing in my life."

Asheham, Rodmell, Sussex
May 1st, 1912

Dearest Leonard,

To deal with the facts first (my fingers are so cold I can hardly write) I shall be back about 7 tomorrow, so there will be time to discuss—but what does it mean? You can't take the leave [from the Foreign Service], I suppose if you are going to resign certainly at the end of it. Anyhow, it shows what a career you're ruining!

Well then, as to all the rest. It seems to me that I am giving you a great deal of pain—some in the most casual way—and therefore I ought to be as plain with you as I can, because half the time I suspect, you're in a fog which I don't see at all. Of course I can't explain what I feel—these are some of the things that strike me. The obvious advantages of marriage stand in my way. I say to myself, Anyhow, you'll be quite happy with him; and he will give you companionship, children, and a busy life—then I say By God, I will not look upon marriage as a profession. The only people who know of it, all think it suitable; and that makes me scrutinise my own motives all the more. Then, of course, I feel angry sometimes at the strength of your desire. Possibly, your being a Jew comes in also at this point. You seem so foreign. And then I am fearfully unstable. I pass from hot to cold in an instant, without any reason; except that I believe sheer physical effort and exhaustion influence me. All I can say is that in spite of these feelings which go chasing each other all day long when I am with you, there is some feeling which is permanent, and growing. You want to know of course whether it will ever make me marry you. How can I say? I think it will, because there seems no reason why it shouldn't—But I don't know what the future will bring. I'm half afraid of myself. I sometimes feel that no one ever has or ever can share something—It's the thing that makes you call me like a hill, or a rock. Again, I want everything—love, children, adventure, intimacy, work. (Can you make any sense out of this ramble? I am putting down one thing after another.) So I go from being half in love with you, and wanting you to be with me always, and know everything about me, to the extreme of wildness and aloofness. I sometimes think that if I married you, I could have everything—and then—is it the sexual side of it that comes between us? As I told you brutally the other day, I feel no physical attraction in you. There are moments—when you kissed me the other day was one—when I feel no more than a rock. And yet your caring for me as you do almost overwhelms me. It is so real, and so strange. Why should you? What am I really except a pleasant attractive creature? But it's just because you care so much that I feel I've got to care before I marry you. I feel I must give you everything; and that if I can't, well, marriage would only be second-best for you as well as for me. If you can still go on, as before, letting me find my own way, as that is what would please me best; and then we must both take the risks. But you have made me very happy too. We both of us want a marriage that is a tremendous living thing, always alive, always hot, not dead and easy in parts as most marriages are. We ask a great deal of life, don't we? Perhaps we shall get it; then, how splendid!

One doesn't get much said in a letter, does one? I haven't touched upon the enormous variety of things that have been happening here—but they can wait.

D'you like this photograph?—rather too noble, I think. Here's another.

Yrs.
VS

Conrad Aiken to
Clarissa Lorenz

P oet, novelist, and essayist, Conrad Aiken (1889–1973) was a prolific and brilliant letter writer. Especially in love, he wrote extraordinary letters that served as an inspiration and a source for his work.
He never intended to publish his letters nor even made carbons of
them (as many writers do). Both he considered to be betrayals of
privacy and friendship. Only late in his life did he suggest to a friend
that his letters might be collected and published after all. Perhaps he,
too, realized that his letters rank as small classics of the love letter
genre: "You with your vegetable cart and your old coat (for rain) —
but I can't finish the sentence. All I want to do is BEGIN sentences
like that. And end them with a kiss, complete surrender, complete
abdication."

The object of this sumptuous epistolary prose was Clarissa
("Joan") Lorenz, a musician and a free-lance journalist who met
Conrad Aiken in 1926 when she interviewed him for a story. Omi-
nously, he dubbed her "Lorelei Two." There had been another wife
("Lorelei One"), Jessie McDonald Aiken. Inevitably, there would be a
"Lorelei Three," Mary Hoover Aiken, whom he married in 1937. In
between there were other women, but apparently he did not number
them.

The letter reprinted here is just one in the amazing rush of words
that he used to woo his Clarissa. Who could resist such vital prose
and poetry? But Clarissa was nervous, and the courtship exchange
ranged from ecstasy to anxiety (sometimes both emotions emerging
at once).

In *Ushant* (1952), an autobiographical essay published first with
pseudonyms and then, in 1971, shortly before Aiken's death, reissued
with the real names, Aiken rehearsed his life and realized that most
of his love life had been a mess. He had wandered through love as
through a "maze-like pattern" of being "over and over again unfaithful to pretty much everything" and everyone. More than most, Aiken's letters read like warm-ups for his writing; they read like brilliant performances rather than real communications, something the
writer himself realized only too late.

Jeake's House, Rye
November 24–25, 1926

Darling,

I don't complain, protest, murmur, object, cavil, whine,
moan, plead, nor do I tear my teeth, gnash my hair, bite the
chair-rungs, shake my fist at the heavens-deaf-to-my-
imprecations, nor do I grovel like a whipped cur, nor cry in
my secret heart of hearts, nor shut my lips with stoic
fortitude: none of these things; but if I had you here, WENCH,
HUSSY, STRUMPET, by godfry I'd wring your neck. Swelp me
bob I would. Do you really think it's humane? No, by god, I
don't. You really think she ought to have written you sooner?
You know bloody well she should have. There, there, little boy,
don't cry. Besides, think of the nice little accumulation of
letters there'll be *tomorrow* morning: maybe *three* all at once.
Tomorrow and tomorrow and tomorrow. Dryad, come out of
your oaktree—rise from your pool, blue nymph. And now I go
out in search of a nice dark wet sewer.

Here lies one whose heart was fract-
ured (otatatòi) by a world of fact.
Jackinthepulpit prays above him:
only the weeds and sewerworms love him.

Rats will nibble his ears and fingers;
His eyes are shut; but near him lingers
Whimpering little his tethered ghost
and mourns for the one he loved the most.

Where is she, who should be sitting
Here on the sewerlid with her knitting?
Gone with the rosebud, gone forever,
While *he* waits here in Pluto's river.

Will she come back, and will she find him?
Kiss him, or with her fair arms bind him?
No, she forgets him, she is fickle
(Alas, alas) as the new moon's sickle.

The sparrow brings him a withered leaf,
The mole with blind eyes weeps for grief;
Jackinthepulpit tolls his bell;
The ghost is released and flies to hell.

Who shall we pray for, him or her?
Pray for the one who remembers, sir.
And let that other be cursed forever
With the sight and sound of Pluto's river.

And let her constant comrade be
The cry from the cross, Sabacthani.
This be her curse, until she come,
To find her lover and bring him home.

So, now.   C

And now, by gosh, I do feel betrayed. Here's Thursday
morning—THANKSGIVING, if you please—and after
dreaming all night about letters that didn't come, and waiting
till nine to go out, so as to give the mail time to arrive, THEN I
go down and find—   C.

THE GOOD FIGHT

Fyodor Dostoyevsky to Anya G. Dostoyevskaya

Remember *Crime and Punishment?* The grim philosophical tome about Raskolnikov, the man who thinks he's a Superman and kills an old woman to prove it, and Sonya, the Prostitute with the Heart of Gold, who decides (six hundred pages later) to follow him to Siberia? Now imagine getting a love letter from its author.

The letter reprinted here is an almost too-perfect embodiment of the writer. Another man would have been quicker than Dostoyevsky in his explanation of how he managed to gamble away the whole thirty thalers that his wife had sent him and how she's going to need to visit the pawnbroker's again in order to send him more money for his "literary" tour of the Continent and England and how—yes, yes, dear Anya, angel Anya, all-forgiving Anya—he has given up gambling forever. (Even more remarkable, soon after this letter he really *did* give up his gambling!)

Dostoyevsky had more than his share of writerly neuroses. In his youth, he was arrested for his socialism, sentenced to death, and made to wait, hands tied, for his turn before the firing squad. He was reprieved at the last moment, only to discover it had all been a macabre charade (no execution had ever been intended). His sentence was commuted to four years of hard labor in Siberia, where he contemplated his brink-of-death experience, underwent a religious crisis, and converted from socialism to Russian Orthodoxy. In 1857 he married Mariya Dmitriyevna Isayeva, whom he called a "knight in female clothing," but with whom he had a notably unhappy relationship until her death from tuberculosis in 1864.

Two years later Dostoyevsky hired an attractive twenty-year-old stenographer, Anya Grigorevna. As he dictated one of his semiautobiographical novels to her, he realized she was falling in love with him. He proposed immediately. She was intelligent and efficient, good at handling pesky creditors and anxious publishers. And besides, anyone who could fall in love with the author of *The Gambler* would probably be willing to pawn the family silver.

By his accounts and those of his biographers, it was a happy marriage, even if it fell into the stereotypical pattern of the erratic artist-husband and his capable, patient, all-suffering wife. After his death, Anya wrote a memoir of their life together, edited and indexed his works, and organized the "Dostoyevsky Room" at the Pushkin Library in Moscow. Marriage to one of the great Russian novelists was, apparently, consolation enough for his colossal moods, his gambling, drunkenness, and occasional infatuations with other women.

No one ever said it was going to be easy. "Remember, too, Anya," Dostoyevsky writes in this letter, "that there are misfortunes that carry their own punishment."

Wiesbaden, Friday, April 28, 1871

Anya, for the sake of Christ, for the sake of Lyuba [their daughter], for the sake of our whole future, don't start worrying and getting all upset—read this letter carefully to the end. You will see at the end that disaster isn't really a reason for despair, but on the contrary, something may even have been gained by it which will be much more valuable than the price paid for it! And so calm yourself, my angel, hear me out—read this to the end. For Christ's sake, don't fall to pieces.

You, my precious one, my lifelong friend, my heavenly angel, you have, of course, gathered that I have lost everything—the whole of the 30 thalers you sent me. Remember that you are my only salvation and that there is no one else in the world who loves me. Remember, too, Anya, that there are misfortunes that carry their own punishment. As I write this, I am wondering: What will this do to you? How will you take it? I hope nothing terrible will happen to you! And if you feel sorry for me at this moment, don't, that would make it even worse for me.

I didn't dare wire you nor do I dare now, after your latest letter in which you write that you will be worrying about me. I can just imagine how it would have been had you received a telegram tomorrow saying *Schreiben sie mier* . . . what would have become of you then!

Ah, Anya, why did I have to go?

Here is how it happened today. First of all, I got your letter at 1 P.M., but not the money. Then I went home and wrote you an answer (a nasty, cruel letter; why, I almost reproach you in it). I suppose you will get it tomorrow, Saturday, if you stop by the post office not earlier than 4 o'clock. I took my letter to the post office and there the man told me again that there was no money for me; it was then two-thirty. But when I came by again, for the third time, at four-thirty, he gave me the money, and when I asked at what time it had arrived, he replied very calmly, "Around 2 o'clock." So why didn't he give it to me when I was there before, well after two? Then, when I saw that

I had to wait until half past six for the next train out of here, I headed for the casino.

Now Anya, you may believe me or not, but I swear to you that I had no intention of gambling! To convince you of that, I will confess everything to you: when I wired you asking you to send me 30 thalers instead of 25, I thought I might yet risk another 5 thalers, but I was not sure I would do even that. I figured that if any money were left over, I would bring it back with me. But when I got the 30 thalers today, *I did not want to gamble* for two reasons: (1) I was so struck by your letter and imagined the effect it would have on you (and I am imagining it now!) and (2) I dreamed last night of *my father* and he appeared to me in a terrifying guise, such as he has only appeared to me twice before in my life, both times prophesying a dreadful disaster, and on both occasions the dream came true. (And now, when I think of the dream I had three nights ago, when I saw your hair turn white, my heart stops beating—ah, my God, what will become of you when you get this letter!)

But when I arrived at the casino, I went to a table and stood there placing imaginary bets just to see whether I could guess right. And you know what, Anya? I was right about ten times in a row, and I even guessed right about Zero. I was so amazed by this that I started gambling and in 5 minutes won 18 thalers. And then, Anya, I got all excited and thought to myself that I would leave with the last train, spend the night in Frankfurt, and then at least I would bring some money home with me! I felt so ashamed about the 30 thalers I had *robbed* you of! Believe me, my angel, all year I have been dreaming of buying you a pair of earrings, which I have not yet given back to you. You had pawned all your possessions for me during these past 4 years and followed me in my wanderings with homesickness in your heart! Anya, Anya, bear in mind, too, that I am not a scoundrel but only a man with a passion for gambling.

(But here is *something else* that I want you to remember, Anya: I am through with that fancy forever. I know I have written you before that it was over and done with, but I never felt the way I feel now as I write this. Now I am rid of this delusion and I would bless God that things have turned out as disastrously as they have if I weren't so terribly worried about you at this moment. Anya, if you are angry with me, just think of how much I've had to suffer and *still* have to suffer in the coming three or four days! If, sometime later on in life you find me being ungrateful and unfair toward you—just show me this letter!)

By half past nine I had lost everything and I fled like a madman. I felt so miserable that I rushed to see the priest (don't get upset, I did *not* see him, no. I did *not*, nor do I intend to!). As I was running toward his house in the darkness through unfamiliar streets, I was thinking: "Why, he is the Lord's shepherd and I will speak to him not as to a private person but as one does at confession." But I lost my way in this town and when I reached a church, which I took for a Russian church, they told me in a store that it was not Russian but sheeny. It was as if someone had poured cold water over me. I ran back home. And now it is midnight and I am sitting and writing to you. (And I won't go to see the priest, I won't go, I swear I won't!)

I had one and a half thalers left in small change. That would have been enough for a telegram (15 groschen) but I am afraid to send it. I don't know how you will take it! And so I decided to write you a letter and send it off the next day at 8 A.M., and to make sure that you get it on Sunday without delay, I am sending it directly to our home address rather than *poste restante*. (For, what if, expecting me to come, you didn't bother to go to the post office?) But I still may send you another letter *poste restante* tomorrow, though I will be rather late in getting it off. But I will write you for sure the day after tomorrow—on Sunday.

Anya, save me once more and for the last time—send me another 30 (thirty) thalers. I will arrange things in such a way that it will be enough. I will be very economical. If you can manage to send it on Sunday, even late, I will be able to come back on Tuesday, or, at the latest, on Wednesday.

Anya, I prostrate myself before you and kiss your feet. I

realize that you have every right to despise me and to think: "He will gamble again." By what, then, can I swear to you that *I shall not*, when I have already deceived you before? But, my angel, I know that you would die (!) if I lost again! I am not completely insane, after all! Why, I know that, if that happened, it would be the end of me as well. I won't, I won't, I won't, and *I shall come straight home!* Believe me. Trust me for this *last time* and you won't regret it. Mark my words, from now on, for the rest of my life, I will work for you and Lyubochka without sparing my health, and *I shall reach my goal!* I shall see to it that you two are well provided for.

If you cannot manage to send the money on Sunday, send it on Monday as early as possible. In that case, I will be with you around noon on Wednesday. Don't worry if you cannot send it on Sunday, and don't think too much about me, that would be *too much*, I don't deserve it!

But what can happen to me? I am tough to the point of coarseness. More than that: it seems as if I have been completely morally regenerated (I say this to you and before God), and if it had not been for my worrying about you the past three days, if it had not been for my wondering every minute about what this would do to you—I would even have been happy! You mustn't think I am crazy, Anya, my guardian angel! A great thing has happened to me: I have rid myself of the abominable delusion that has *tormented* me for almost 10 years. For ten years (or, to be more precise, ever since my brother's death, when I suddenly found myself weighted down by debts) I dreamed about winning money. I dreamt of it seriously, passionately. But now it is all over! This was the *very* last time! Do you believe now, Anya, that my hands are untied?—I was tied up by gambling but now I will put my mind to worthwhile things instead of spending whole nights dreaming about gambling, as I used to do. And so my *work* will be better and more profitable, with God's blessing! Let me keep your heart, Anya, do not come to hate me, do not stop loving me. Now that I have become a new man, let us pursue our path together and I shall see to it that you are happy!

And Lyuba, Lyuba, oh, how despicably I have behaved! But I

am thinking only of you. I can just imagine how you will feel when you read this! And even before you get this letter, how much you will worry when you find I have not come back, and the things you will imagine! Will they bring you this letter in time? And what if it gets lost! But how could it get lost since my telegram sent to the same address reached you? But to make sure, I will also send a few lines addressed to *poste restante* tomorrow and will mail it during the day.

I keep wondering: will I get a letter from you tomorrow or won't I? Probably not! You are expecting me back tomorrow so why should you write?

If you *cannot* send me the money on Sunday, write me a letter. I would be so happy to receive even a few lines in your hand, even if you cursed me in them. If you cannot manage to write on Sunday, send me a letter the first thing on Monday together with the money (that is, if you haven't already sent the money on Sunday). In any case, your letter will reach me before the money and it would make me so happy to hear from you!

Anya, when I think about how you will feel when you get this letter, it makes me go all cold inside. That is the only thing that causes me suffering. As for the rest—the boredom, the loneliness, and the uncertainty—I am sure I can put up with all of that. I deserve worse! I will try to keep myself busy; in the three days ahead, I'll get off two letters that I have to write—to Katkov and to Maikov! But believe me, Anya, our resurrection has come about and believe, too, that now I shall reach my goal and make you happy!

I kiss you both and hug you, forgive me, Anya!

From now on, all yours,
Fyodor Dostoyevsky

P.S. I *shall not go* and see the priest, in no event, whatever happens. He is a witness of things that took place long ago and that time has vanished. It would be painful to me even to meet him!

P.S.S. Anya, my eternal joy, my only happiness—don't worry, don't torment yourself, preserve yourself for me!

Don't worry about that accursed, insignificant 180 thalers. It is true that this leaves us without money once again, but not for long, though, not for long (possibly Stellovsky will save us). To be sure, we are faced with the appalling necessity of pawning things again, which you find so odious! But this is the last time, the very last time! Back home I'll make money, I know I will! If only we could get back to Russia quickly! I will write Katkov and implore him to *advance* the date of payment, and I am certain that he will be responsive.

In the name of God, don't worry about me (ah, you are an angel, and, even if you cursed me, you would be sorry for me), yet I know that you will worry. But you may be at peace: I shall be regenerated in these three days and start a new life. Oh, how anxious I am to be back together with you! The only thing that frightens me is the thought of how you will take this letter. But of one thing you can be sure—of my infinite love for you. And from now on I will never do anything that will make you miserable.

P.S.S.S. I will remember this as long as I live and each time I think of it I will bless you, my angel! Let there be no mistake, now I am yours, all yours, undividedly yours. Whereas, up till now, *one-half* of me *belonged* to that accursed delusion.

Marcel Proust to Geneviève Straus

Marcel Proust loved best in his writing, both in the monumental *Remembrance of Things Past* (1913–1927) and in his letters. In his life, there was sexual confusion and conflict that he never fully resolved. He had a series of close friendships with heterosexual men after whom he pined in vain. He had a brief affair with Louisa de Mornand, who then left him to return to her lover. And in his lifelong relationship with Geneviève Straus, he acted out the various guises of a lover—ardent seducer, faithful servant, spurned suitor—without ever fully living the part.

Widow of composer Georges Bizet, Geneviève Straus was twenty years older than Proust. She was a brilliant woman who presided over the most important salon in Paris, where musicians, artists, writers, journalists, and politicians all came together to discuss the issues and events of the day.

As the letter reprinted here makes clear, the two fought bitterly, but he found it impossible not to love her. Even after he retired into seclusion to write his masterpiece, he continued his correspondence with Geneviève. It was to her that he announced the completion of the first draft: "You will read me—more of me than you will want—for I've just begun—and finished—a whole long book."

Thursday, upon leaving you.

Madame,

I love mysterious women, since you are one, and I have often said so in *Le Banquet*, in which I would often have liked you to recognize yourself. But I can no longer love you wholly, and I will tell you why, though it's useless, but you know how one spends one's time doing things that are useless or even quite harmful, especially when one loves, even if less. You believe that in making oneself too accessible one lets one's charms evaporate, and I think that's true. But let me tell you what happens in your case. One usually sees you with twenty people, or rather through twenty people, for the young man is farthest away from you. But let us suppose that after a good many days one succeeds in seeing you alone. You only have five minutes, and even during those five minutes you are thinking of something else.

But that's nothing so far. If one speaks to you of books, you find it pedantic, if one speaks to you of people, you find it indiscreet (if one informs) and curious (if one enquires), and if one speaks to you of yourself, you find it ridiculous. And so one is a hundred times on the point of finding you a lot less delicious, when suddenly you grant some little favour that seems to indicate a slight preference, and one is caught again. But you are not sufficiently imbued with this truth (I don't believe you are imbued with any truth): *that many concessions should be granted* to platonic love. A person who is not in the least sentimental becomes amazingly so if he is reduced to platonic love. As I wish to obey your pretty precepts condemning bad taste, I won't go into detail. But give it a thought, I beseech you. Have some indulgence towards the ardent platonic love borne you, if you still deign to believe and to countenance it, by

> your respectfully devoted
> Marcel Proust

John Middleton Murry to Katherine Mansfield

They made a dashing literary couple. She was a brilliant short story writer. He was a poet, novelist, and editor. He lectured on her work and founded journals in which he published her fiction. But like most fairy-tale romances, this one had a more realistic underside, one that turned on the perennial question of who will do the housework. "So often this week, I've heard you and [your friends] talking while I washed dishes," Mansfield wrote angrily to Murry. "And you calling (whatever I am doing), '*Tig*, isn't there going to be tea? It's five o'clock,' as though I were a dilatory housemaid." Mansfield was particularly incensed when Murry began to espouse his friend D. H. Lawrence's views on the *naturally* unequal roles of men and women. The two had some public rows on this subject. Never one to pass up good material, Lawrence used the feuding couple as the prototype for the failed lovers Gerald and Gudrun in *Women in Love.*

Whether or not Lawrence's portrayal was accurate, it is clear that Mansfield and Murry had a rocky relationship, from beginning to end. When Mansfield was stricken with tuberculosis in her early thirties, she spent several winters in sunny parts of Europe and then entered the Gurdjieff Institute in Fontainebleau, France, hoping for a cure. Murry did not accompany her. He pleaded financial exigency and emotional insecurity and stayed back home in England.

There's no way to know from their correspondence exactly what was going on. Was there someone else? Was he afraid to see her in her debilitated condition? Was he simply too neurotic to travel? Did he miss the signs that her illness was serious? All are plausible explanations. In letter after letter, Mansfield pleaded with him to visit and berated him for abandoning her. Finally, in 1923, Murry did come, but it was almost too late. She died on the night of their reunion.

> Chalet des Sapins,
> Montana-sur-Sierre, Valais
> Thursday evening February 9 1922.

My darling Worm,

I must write to you though the letter will never be posted. Your express letter has just arrived in answer to my telegram. I must somehow kill the time by thinking that I am near you.

I deserve the letter. It's the most awful one you've ever sent me.

I deserve the letter. I mean my action deserves the letter. But my soul doesn't. Darling, I'm a difficult person. I don't understand myself. I don't know myself. You know me better than I do, probably. But I'll try to explain.

I hadn't prepared myself at all for the possibility of your staying there. Subconsciously, I shirked it. When I knew you were going to stay there, I instinctively shirked it again—the change, the uprooting. And I was able to, simply because your presence was in the house with me. We weren't apart. (There's an enormous difference, darling, in feeling between the one who stays and the one who goes. The one who stays is in a familiar place—everything here told me of your presence.) The day after I sent that letter, I knew it was all wrong. It was meant to be true: it wasn't put up. But that was just because I wasn't yet free to feel your absence. The next day I knew it was impossible for us to be apart. I began to be anxious every hour of the day: I had lost my mate.

Don't say I was 'claiming my freedom as an artist'—such an idea never entered into my head. If you think that, you've got it all wrong. I wasn't claiming any freedom; I don't want, never have for a year now even dreamed of wanting 'freedom'. I was just shirking, shrinking from being uprooted. That was bad enough, I know; but it's better at any rate than claiming 'freedom as an artist'. If I pleaded my novel, I pleaded it (unconsciously) only as an excuse for my shrinking. As a matter of fact, it took me exactly four days to realise that I *couldn't work at all* without your presence. I worked just so long as your presence remained, not a moment longer.

I hate defending myself to you, my darling. I feel I'm not worth it; you're a so much finer being than I am. But yet I want you to know the truth about me. I'm not bad. I do believe in the last year most of the badness has gone out of me, and that I am in most ways your worthy Boge. But one thing, instead of growing better, grows worse & worse. I am more and more frightened of the world: more terrified of moving: of venturing a finger into the cogs. The last four years have taken away what little courage I had—and I never had any. That is a ghastly confession to make for a man who is well, to his wife who is ill. I am utterly ashamed. But what can I do? I fight against it. But when the moment comes I'm just petrified with fear. I *can't* move.

And I forsake you. It's terrible; it's even more terrible that I somehow deceive myself. If you had said to me, as you very nearly did, 'Bogey, why don't you come *with me* to Paris?' the only answer I could have made, if I'd been honest, was: 'I'm *afraid, afraid*'. Well, I've confessed—there's nothing else to confess. It's my very soul. It's fear makes me a miser even. I'm terrified of what may happen.

There's only one thing greater than my fear—that is my love. My love will always conquer my fear—but it can't do it immediately. It needs the full force of my love to do it and it takes days for that to emerge out of its dark hiding places. And in these days you have despaired of me again.

Wig precious, I shall never write anything truer of myself than this. Don't lose faith in me; I couldn't live unless you believed in me. But remember my fear—help me to fight it.

Your
Boge.

Vita Sackville-West to Virginia Woolf

This testy (and delightful) note was written seventeen years into the relationship between Vita Sackville-West and Virginia Woolf. It is a classic "good fight" letter in that it not only forces the Beloved to pay attention (who could ignore the porpoise on the marble slab?); it also tries to remind the Beloved of happier times, a shared and delicious moment before acrimony, recrimination, or simple indifference set in. The letter worked. Virginia answered two days later: ". . . Yes, I well remember buying rolls for breakfast at Vézelay."

But life was desperate for Virginia by 1939. *The Years* (1937) had taken too long and been too difficult to write; it had shaken her artistic confidence and taken its psychic toll. Her nephew, Julian Bell, had been killed in the Spanish Civil War. Nazism and fascism were rampant. Exhausted and spent, she somehow produced *Three Guineas* (1938), a powerful feminist argument against the masculine values that lead to war. But the book caused an argument with Vita, who accused her of deliberately mispresenting facts in order to make her point. Virginia would not let the matter drop. She insisted that they had to fight it out, "whether with swords or fisticuffs," because, whatever the book's faults, it was most "certainly an honest book." Their argument went on.

So did the war. By October of 1940, both of Virginia's residences in London had been wrecked by German bombs. Strangely, Virginia experienced an odd euphoria. Then, she plunged into depression. Vita was unaware of her friend's dangerous mental state when she received Virginia's letter of March 22, 1941. In this final missive, Virginia inquired after Vita's dying birds, pet budgerigars. "Do they all die in an instant? When shall we come? Lord knows—" Six days later, Virginia killed herself.

Sissinghurst Castle,
Kent.
23rd April 1939

This is Sissinghurst 250—is that Museum 2621?—Is that
Virginia? This is Vita speaking,—yes: Vita,—a person you once
reckoned as a friend—Oh, had you forgotten? Well, dig about
in your memory and perhaps you will remember a porpoise
on a marble slab.—Yes, it is pronounced Veeta, not Vaita—Now
you remember, do you? You remember a thunderstorm at
Vézalay [September 1928] and the ceilings of Long Barn gently
swaying around?

The purpose of this message is manifold. Its principal
object is to say that I don't like being cut off from you and
thus am making an attempt to get into touch. Will you and
Leonard ever come here, on your way down to Rodmell? I
would so like Leonard to see my garden. You, I know, are no
gardener, so I confine this interest to Leonard. I do wish you
would both come.

Signed
Sibyl Colefax

5

THE END
OF LOVE

George Gordon, Lord Byron, to Lady Caroline Lamb

When Caroline Lamb met Byron she noted in her diary that he was "mad, bad and dangerous to know." She also prophesied, "That beautiful pale face will be my fate." It was, for about three months, at which point he grew tired of her.

But she was hardly a poor, pathetic woman victimized by England's most notorious rogue. On the contrary, she was a well-known coquette with conquests of her own. Among her circle of friends, she had a host of pet names: The Sprite, Ariel, the Squirrel, the Bat, the Little Savage, the Fairy Queen. For a time, Byron was captivated. She was, he noted, "the most absurd, perplexing, dangerous, fascinating little being alive."

Although brief, their affair was notably eventful. Not known for her discretion, Lady Caroline was soon linked with Lord Byron in the local gossip, which aroused the ire of her husband. Caroline was forbidden to see her lover. Her mother-in-law, Lady Melbourne, was particularly vehement on this account, and Caroline suspected that the grande dame (she was sixty) was herself attracted to the twenty-four-year-old poet. It was not a pleasant dalliance but a messy, cumbersome affair. There were histrionics, tirades, threats; Caroline attempted suicide (or pretended to). More to the point, Byron had someone else waiting in the wings. In 1811, he had encountered his half-sister Augusta again. By 1812 (when the letter reprinted here was written) he and Augusta had become constant companions. In 1814 Augusta gave birth to a daughter, presumably Byron's. All England was scandalized. Byron fled abroad.

Six years later, Caroline still pined. Writing to a mutual friend, she asked "how Byron looks, what he says, if he is grown fat, if he is no uglier than he used to be, if he is good-humored or cross-grained, pulling his brows down—if his hair curls or is straight as somebody said, if he is going to stay [abroad] long . . ."

August 1812[?]

My dearest Caroline—

If tears, which you saw & know I am not apt to shed, if the agitation in which I parted from you, agitation which you must have perceived through the *whole* of this most nervous *nervous* affair, did not commence till the moment of leaving you approached, if all that I have said & done, & am still but too ready to say & do, have not sufficiently proved what my real feelings are & must be ever towards you, my love, I have no other proof to offer.

God knows I wish you happy, & when I quit you, or rather when you from a sense of duty to your husband & mother quit me, you shall acknowledge the truth of what I again promise & vow, that no other in word or deed shall ever hold the place in my affection which is & shall be most sacred to you, till I am nothing.

I never knew till *that moment*, the *madness* of—my dearest & most beloved friend—I cannot express myself—this is no time for words—but I shall have a pride, a melancholy pleasure, in suffering what you yourself can hardly conceive—for you do not know me.—I am now about to go out with a heavy heart, because—my appearing this Evening will stop any absurd story which the events of today might give rise to—do you think *now* that I am *cold & stern, & artful*—will even *others* think so, will your *mother* even—that mother to whom we must indeed sacrifice much, *more* much more on my part, than she shall ever know or can imagine.

"Promises not to love you" ah Caroline it is past promising—but I shall attribute all concessions to the proper motive—& never cease to feel all that you have already witnessed—& more than can ever be known but to my own heart—perhaps to yours—May God protect forgive & bless you—ever & even more than ever

yr. most attached
BYRON

P.S.—These taunts which have driven you to this—my dearest Caroline—were it not for your mother & the kindness of all your connections, is there anything on earth or heaven would have made me so happy as to have made you mine long ago? & not less *now* than then, but *more* than ever at this time— you know I would with pleasure give up all here & all beyond the grave for you—& in refraining from this—must my motives be misunderstood—? I care not who knows this— what use is made of it—it is to *you* & to *you* only that they owe yourself, I was and am *yours*, freely & most entirely, to obey, to honour, love—& fly with you when, where, & how you yourself *might* & *may* determine.

Percy Bysshe Shelley to Harriet Shelley

Shelley's Dear Jane to his pregnant wife is one of the more remarkable documents in the history of literary love letters. First, note the tone. You'd think that *he* were the one who had been betrayed and abandoned. "My dear, Harriet," he adds in a postscript, "you must not do me injustice. You have done so. I expect you to repair it." He then audaciously includes a request, "I am in want of stockings, hanks & Mrs. W[ollstonecraft]'s posthumous works." Amazing! He dismisses her fears about childbirth ("I do not apprehend the slightest danger from your approaching labour"), then complains he's out of hankies.

220

She was decimated. "The man I once loved is dead. This is a vampire," she wrote her anguish to a friend. Harriet never recovered from her husband's defection. In 1816 she penned a suicide note to her sister, with whom she entrusted her two small children: "Too wretched to exert myself, lowered in the opinion of everyone, why should I drag on a miserable existence?"

London, October 3, 1814

Harriet you mistake—you obstinately mistake me. I never stated that I had conferred pecuniary benefits on you or that I derived from such sources a claim to your confidence & regard. I had hoped that the more substantial benefits of intellectual improvement, & the constant watchfullness of a friendship, ill understood it seems, would not have been degraded by so mean & common a mistake.

I perceive that your irritated feelings have led you into this injustice towards me. If my friendship is thus rejected I cherish little hope of any advantage arising to either of us from our intercourse. I was deeply solicitous that what has taken place should have been avoided that although united to one perfectly adapted to my nature by a lasting and intense affection, you should have perceived that I continued to be mindful of your happiness, that I would have superintended the progress of your mind, & have assisted you in cultivating an elevated philosophy, to which without the interest I have taken in your improvement, it is probable that you never would have aspired.—If you inflexibly resist these advances of kindness, if in return for my intentions you overwhelm me with contumely & reproach—what hope remains of a favorable issue to my ill requited attempts?

I am united to another; you are no longer my wife. Perhaps I have done you injury, but surely most innocently & unintentionally in having commenced any connexion with you.—That injury whatever be its amount was not to be avoided. If ever in any degree there was sympathy in our feelings & opinions wherefore deprive ourselves in future of the satisfaction which may result, by this contemptible cavil—

these unworthy bickerings. Unless a sincere confidence be accorded by you to my undesigning truth, our intercourse for the present must be discontinued. You derive more pain than advantage from the irritations produced by my visits. The interest which I take in you is disturbed by no feelings which prevent me from calmly calculating on your happiness.

Collect yourself I entreat you: remember what I am: recall your recollections of my character. The hint respecting my duty to settle the property on you which your letter contains proves how little you can appreciate it. —You have little need to fear that I shall fail in real duty.

> Affectionately yours
> P.B. Shelley

I hope that you will attend to the preservation of your health: I do not apprehend the slightest danger from your approaching labour: I think you may safely repose confidence in Sim's skill [Harriet's physician]. Your last labour was painful, but auspicious. I understand that cases of difficulty after that are very rare.

My dear Harriet, I am anxious for your answer, you must not do me injustice you have done so I expect you to repair it. I see Hookham tonight. I am in want of stockings, hanks & Mrs. W[ollstonecraft]'s posthumous works.

I cannot keep the engagement made at 3 tomorrow. I hear that my personal safety would be endangered by appearing there—Will you inform me where I can call upon the persons.

Stendhal (Henri Beyle) to Comtesse Clementine Curial

Love letters are virtually the only "public" space in which it is permissible for us to explore our deepest self, excavate our feelings, and express our most private emotions. Writing such letters, we often come to appreciate our own complexities and understand that the real purpose of writing letters is to fall a little bit in love with our self. In this process, the actual Beloved is mostly an innocent bystander.

Nowhere is this more apparent (comically so) than in the "Dear John" letter that Stendhal wrote to himself on June 24, 1824. Dissatisfied with his lover's reticence, he penned a "My dear Henri" letter that does everything that the perfect Dear John should do: it takes the blame for the end of love, it praises the Beloved, it promises tender interest until the end of one's life, it hints that the Beloved was the best thing that ever happened to one, it offers (of course!) friendship. Ah, yes, friendship. If love is self-love, the function of a Dear John is to help the Beloved preserve self-love even after the magic potion of passion has been withdrawn.

Had Stendhal really believed his passionate affair with Comtesse Clementine Curial was over, he never could have written such a letter. This letter borders on parody with its formulaic presentation of all of the requisite features of a Dear John. (No one who has ever been decimated by a Dear John/Dear Jane has paused to consider the letter's generic requirements.) Stendhal's affair with Comtesse Curial lasted another two years. When it did end, there was no room for humor.

Clementine Curial was married to a cruel and abusive man fourteen years her senior when she met Stendhal in 1824. They fell almost immediately and passionately into love, so much so that they forgot all caution. Once, she even hid him in her cellar for several days in order that they could be together whenever her jealous husband left the house. She was consumed by love for Stendhal, yet unable to leave her husband. She was a mother at a time when law allowed a father full control over his children, especially in the case of separation or divorce. Torn between desire and the reality of her situation, Curial attempted suicide in 1826. When that failed, she made a final break from Stendhal, unable to continue a love that brought so much pain.

The real end of the relationship (unlike this feigned Dear John) left Stendhal in a depression that felt like living death. He recovered, true to form, by writing. In *Promenades dans Rome* he was able to reminisce about happier times spent in Italy and soothe himself with the tame pleasures of research. Carefully, even tenderly, he wrote himself into life and self-love once more.

Paris, the 24th of June 1824, at noon

You can have no notion of the black thoughts into which your silence has plunged me. I was thinking that yesterday night, when you were packing, you might have found the time to write me three lines, which you could have put into the box at Laon. When no letter came yesterday, I hoped for one this morning. "Whilst changing horses at S_____," I said to myself, "she will have asked for a sheet of paper." But no: occupied solely with her daughter, she forgets the being who can no longer think of anything but her!

As I pondered at my desk, with the shutters closed, my black grief found entertainment in composing the following letter which you will perhaps write to me before long—for, after all, what would it cost you to write me a few words? Here, then, is the letter which I shall have the sorrow to read:

"My dear Henri, you exacted from me a promise to be sincere. This opening to my letter already enables you to foretell what remains to be said. Do not take it too greatly to heart, my dear friend. Bear in mind that, in default of keener sentiments, I shall always be bound to you by the sincerest friendship, and shall always take the tenderest interest in whatever may befall you. You realise, my dear friend, from the tone of this letter that a very sincere trust in you has taken that place in my heart which was formerly occupied by feelings of another sort. I like to believe that this trust will be justified, and that I shall never have to repent what I have been to you.

"Farewell, my dear friend, let us both be reasonable.

Accept the friendship, the tender friendship, that I offer you, and do not fail to come and see me when I return to Paris.

"Farewell, my friend . . ."

Agnes von Kurowsky to Ernest Hemingway

The face and physique of Ernest Hemingway, whether as virile young soldier or virile old writer, have become icons of American Modernist *machismo*. His fiction, with its laconic heroes, and his life, with its succession of wives, have come to symbolize tough-guy love. Yet before he was twenty, Hemingway had learned the lesson of the brokenhearted.

As a young soldier in 1918, his leg full of shrapnel, Hemingway fell in love with the vivacious, attractive Agnes von Kurowsky, an American nurse serving with the Red Cross in Milan. He had just turned nineteen; she was twenty-six. For him, it was a first serious relationship. Von Kurowsky was engaged to a doctor back home and was surrounded by admiring soldiers in Italy.

Despite the disparity in age and experience, Hemingway started saving money for the marriage. Once he went home to America, "Ag" began to demur, writing him letters about her busy social life back in Italy and, most significant, commenting in both serious and jocular fashion about the difference in their ages. She wrote him the "Ernie, dear boy" letter reprinted here after she fell for an aristocratic Italian officer.

Hemingway believed that you could get rid of pain by writing about it. In "A Very Short Story" he lambastes a nurse he calls "Luz" who ignobly dumps the good young man to whom she had protested undying love. But Scott Donaldson, one of Hemingway's biographers, has suggested that writing the story did not rid Hemingway of his pain. For whatever deep-seated reasons, Hemingway could not overcome his fear of making himself vulnerable. He spent the rest of his life dumping friends and wives before they could hurt him. In his trademark style, Hemingway later commented on Agnes von Kurowsky: "I loved her once and then she gypped me."

March 7, 1919

Ernie, dear boy,

I am writing this late at night after a long think by myself, & I am afraid it is going to hurt you, but, I'm sure it won't harm you permanently.

For quite awhile before you left, I was trying to convince myself it was a real love-affair, because, we always seemed to disagree, & then arguments always wore me out so that I finally gave in to keep you from doing something desperate.

Now, after a couple of months away from you, I know that I am still very fond of you, but, it is more as a mother than as a sweetheart. It's alright to say I'm a Kid, but, I'm not, & I'm getting less & less so every day.

So, Kid (still Kid to me, & always will be) can you forgive me some day for unwittingly deceiving you? You know I'm not really bad, & don't mean to do wrong, & now I realize it was my fault in the beginning that you cared for me, & regret it from the bottom of my heart. But, I am now & always will be too old, & that's the truth, & I can't get away from the fact that you're just a boy—a kid.

I somehow feel that some day I'll have reason to be proud of you, but, dear boy, I can't wait for that day, & it is wrong to hurry a career.

I tried hard to make you understand a bit of what I was thinking on that trip from Padua to Milan, but, you acted like a spoiled child, & I couldn't keep on hurting you. Now, I only have the courage because I'm far away.

Then—& believe me when I say this is sudden for me, too— I expect to be married soon. And I hope & pray that after you have thought things out, you'll be able to forgive me & start a wonderful career & show what a man you really are.

> Ever admiringly & fondly
> Your friend,
> Aggie

Katherine Anne Porter to Matthew Josephson

These two "Dear John" letters written by Katherine Anne Porter to Matthew Josephson early in 1931 illustrate the nature of their tempestuous on-again, off-again affair, as well as Porter's remarkable flair for the perfect image. Alluding to his promiscuity ("you have found someone or something new to play with"), she accuses him: "You are like a good golfer who chooses just the right club to hit the ball in a certain way."

With Matthew Josephson, Katherine Anne Porter could easily have fallen into the pattern that crippled her writing career until the end of her life. She favored extremely complicated relationships that were so consuming they impeded her work. Instead of writing fiction, she lived in the swirl of love's histrionic excess and had to support herself in any way she could—with journalism, ghostwriting, and copyediting. Certainly the affair with Josephson was emotionally gripping. He was so handsome that Hemingway once said of him, "If I looked like Matty, I wouldn't need to be a writer." He used the safety of marriage—he was a father of small children—as a screen for his compulsive philandering. He had no scruples about telling whatever lies were required for seduction. In short, he was exactly the kind of man to whom Porter was attracted.

But there was one crucial difference. Whereas her other unsatisfactory lovers kept her from writing, Josephson recognized her talent and encouraged it. He would listen spellbound to her stories about her relatives, ancestors, and neighbors in Indian Creek, Texas, and he would sit her down and tell her, "Write! Write!"

Porter would later say that he had been the first and one of the few men ever to show interest in her work. He became her mentor and her muse. During the two brief years of their affair, Porter wrote some of her best fiction, including such memorable stories as "The Jilting of Granny Weatherall" and "Flowering Judas." No wonder she had such a difficult time saying good-bye.

January 7, 1931

When I first knew you, you were just emerging from the Zola
period . . . Later, remember, you were the man of action
warring single-handed against great cities. Later when you
feared I might stubbornly keep on being in love with you when
the occasion that called for me had passed, you wrote that
"our emotional feats" were of no consequence compared to
the realistic businesses of life such as running a household,
begetting young and writing books. We were to be machines, I
remember distinctly, functioning with hair's breadth
precision. I wasn't deceived then, dear Matthew, and still I'm
not when you decide that we must all be romantic rather than
decorous. One might be both if one's nature was such? I think
it means merely that you have found someone or something
new to play with, and this point of view may be for the
moment useful to you? You are like a good golfer who chooses
just the right club to hit the ball in a certain way?

• • • •

You do wrong to be so angry with a friend who loves you as I
do, and you mustn't burst into abuse, elegies and eternal
farewells regularly as you do whenever I forget myself and take
the liberty of writing to you as frankly and freely as I do to
other persons. Why cannot you grant to your friends the
freedom you give yourself of criticism and comment. And as
for MY rhetoric? I am being continually humbled and
confounded by the complicated brilliance of your style. It
wasn't acid and brimstone—not at all these. I was in an
excellent but I see now foolhardy humor. And it wasn't pretty
of you—I can't say graceful, for that word is gradually being
destroyed for me—to answer by a general flight under cover of
such words as psychosis, vengeance, vomiting, spewing—oh,
come now, Matthew. You'll have to do better than this. I did
not mean to insult you; I was perfectly aware I was writing a
provocative letter, but it was not a bitter one. But this has
happened before. You have written frightfully wounding things
to me, or have said them. And then I answered with edged

words, and you were grieved and astonished and wounded, and wounded that I was wounded—and yes, really, to flee is one answer for such persistent wronging of the human heart.

Let me answer your thousandth farewell with the thousand and first. But I do not mean it and you need not. Am I among all your friends to be the only one not permitted to quarrel even a little with you, and make it up again. . . .

Out of this well-renovated bosom of tenderness I send you my affection. In the hope that Mr. Rousseau will make a fine book. Better than *The Portrait,* and *The Portrait* was better than Zola . . . and remember what we thought of Zola.

Above all, no more good-byes.

Nelson Algren to Simone de Beauvoir

Simone de Beauvoir, author of *The Second Sex* (1949), one of the most influential feminist books of the twentieth century, said that she did not personally come to understand the subjugation of women until a 1947 trip to America. Her women friends in France were intellectuals, typically single or without children, whereas on her American lecture tour she was hosted by men whose wives sat silently by, serving food, tending children, catering to the needs of guests, rarely voicing an idea themselves.

On the same trip, Beauvoir met and fell in love with hard-boiled Chicago novelist Nelson Algren. She called him "Crocodile"; he called her "Crazy Frog." She said he was the "only truly passionate love in my life." They both acknowledged that their love inspired their best work. Algren's *The Man with the Golden Arm* (1949) won a National Book Award. Beauvoir followed *The Second Sex* (1949; 1953, in English) with a *roman à clef, The Mandarins* (1954), for which she received the Prix Goncourt.

But there were problems. Algren was moody and difficult, a heavy drinker and a gambler, who lived in squalid rooms in a Chicago tenement. Although Beauvoir referred to Algren as her "husband" (a term she reserved only for him), her feelings for him did not prevent her from returning to her life in Paris, a life of salon intellectuals, art, and politics, all centering around Jean-Paul Sartre, her longtime companion. She and Sartre had not had a sexual relationship in years; he was constantly in the company of other women. Yet, in the words of Beauvoir's biographer, Deirdre Bair, Beauvoir and Sartre were to remain a "professional couple" until the end of their lives. Beauvoir explained to Algren that her relationship to Sartre did not diminish her love for Algren and proposed a long-distance relationship (writing twice a week, visits twice a year). Algren wanted to be her husband in a more conventional sense. Still in love, he called off their transcontinental romance. The end of the love affair between Anne (a French intellectual) and Lewis (an American writer) in *The Mandarins* records one of the final conversations between the Crazy Frog and the Crocodile.

Although the relationship ended, neither writer could forget the other. An interviewer once made the fatal mistake of asking the seventy-two-year-old Algren about the way Beauvoir had quoted from some of his letters in her memoirs. The elderly writer fell into an uncontrollable rage: "Love letters should be private . . . But this woman flung the door open and called in the public and the press." Algren then noted that he had saved all of the 1442 pages of love letters that Beauvoir had written to him. "You can't commercialize half and keep the other half sacrosanct. Let's make it all public!" he exclaimed. Afraid that Algren's temper tantrum might not be safe for a man of his age and physical condition, the reporter quickly withdrew. The next day friends found Algren's body. He had died of a heart attack.

November 1, 1952

One can still have the same feelings for someone and still not allow them to rule and disturb one's life. To love a woman who does not belong to you, who puts other things and other people before you, without there ever being any question of your taking first place, is something that just isn't acceptable. I don't regret a single one of the moments we had together. But now I want a different kind of life. . . . The disappointment I felt three years ago, when I began to realize that your life belonged to Paris and to Sartre . . . [has] become blunted by time. What I've tried to do since is to take my life back from you. My life means a lot to me, I don't like its belonging to someone so far off, someone I see only a few weeks every year.

BETRAYED AND ABANDONED

Mary Wollstonecraft to Gilbert Imlay

Mary Wollstonecraft went further than any other eighteenth-century thinker in advancing the cause of improved women's education and social equality. In *A Vindication of the Rights of Woman* (1792), she analyzed the way in which the eighteenth-century legal definition of the *feme covert* ("hidden woman") meant that all of a married woman's property, assets, and even her physical person belonged to her husband. In contrast, she believed marriage should be based on mutual respect and affection, not wifely subordination and obedience.

She did not come by these principles easily. As a child, she tried to protect her mother from marital violence. In 1784, in her early twenties, she helped her sister to escape an equally unhappy and abusive marriage. She and her dear friend, Fanny Blood, set up an alternative school based on feminist principles, and then, in 1785, she watched Fanny die in childbirth.

Several years later, when she moved to France, Wollstonecraft fell in love with an American novelist who had fought in the Revolutionary War, a charming adventurer named Gilbert Imlay, with whom she thought she had found the perfect marriage of minds. The two lived together in an idyllic cottage at Neuilly on the Seine while she wrote *A Historical and Moral View of the Origin and Progress of the French Revolution* (1794). Then she became pregnant and bore their daughter Fanny out of wedlock. Imlay took off. "Amongst the feathered race, whilst the hen keeps the young warm, her mate stays by to cheer her," she wrote, "but it is sufficient for man to condescend to get a child, in order to claim it.—A man is a tyrant!"

Alone with an infant amid the French Terror and ill with consumption, Wollstonecraft entrusted her daughter to a friend and tried to kill herself. Learning of the suicide attempt, Imlay refused either to terminate the relationship or to resume it. She wrote him several Dear John letters, seeking a closure that she hoped might restore her equilibrium. She even made a trip to rural Scandinavia where she hoped to snatch "some moments of exquisite delight, wandering through the woods, and resting on the rocks." There she wrote *Letters Written During a Short Residence in Sweden, Norway, and Denmark* (1795), a delightful travel memoir that revealed none of the year's anguish nor presaged her second suicide attempt upon returning to England. She threw herself into the Thames, only to be fished out, unconscious, by strangers. Recovering at the home of friends, disgusted by Imlay's continuing cowardice, Wollstonecraft wrote him a last good-bye: "I part with you in peace." Finally, she was able to go on with her own life.

London

As the parting from you for ever is the most serious event of my life, I will once expostulate with you, and call not the language of truth and feeling ingenuity!

I know the soundness of your understanding—and know that it is impossible for you always to confound the caprices of every wayward inclination with manly dictates of principle.

You tell me "that I torment you."—Why do I?—Because you cannot estrange your heart entirely from me—and you feel that justice is on my side. You urge, "that your conduct was unequivocal."—It was not.—When your coolness has hurt me, with what tenderness have you endeavoured to remove the impression!—and even before I returned to England, you took great pains to convince me, that all my uneasiness was occasioned by the effect of a worn-out constitution—and you concluded your letter with these words, "Business alone has kept me from you.—Come to any port, and I will fly down to my two dear girls with a heart all their own."

With these assurances, is it extraordinary that I should

believe what I wished? I might—and did think that you had a struggle with old propensities; but I still thought that I and virtue should at last prevail. I still thought that you had a magnanimity of character, which would enable you to conquer yourself.

_____ , believe me, it is not romance, you have acknowledged to me feelings of this kind.—You could restore me to life and hope, and the satisfaction you would feel, would amply repay you.

In tearing myself from you, it is my own heart I pierce—and the time will come, when you will lament that you have thrown away a heart, that, even in the moment of passion, you cannot despise.—I would owe every thing to your generosity—but, for God's sake, keep me no longer in suspense!—Let me see you once more!

Charlotte Brontë to Constantine Héger

Charlotte Brontë went abroad to study languages but ended up learning a heartbreaking lesson in love. After she and her sister Emily were called home from Brussels because of their aunt's death, Charlotte returned alone to Belgium, where she studied French, worked as an assistant governess, and fell hopelessly in love with Professor Constantine Héger. Again she had to leave the Continent earlier than planned, this time because of increasing friction between herself and Madame Héger. Although it is impossible to know just what transpired between the twenty-six-year-old woman and the older, married professor, it is certain that, upon her return to the family home in Haworth, Yorkshire (England), she suffered enormously when Héger refused to correspond with her. In her own words, all that was left for her was "lasting estrangement and unbroken silence."

After writing him many times and being disappointed to receive no answer, she forced herself to wait six months before she wrote again. The letter reprinted here marks the end of her self-imposed six months of "epistolary celibacy." In this letter, she promises to wait another six months before she writes again.

She filled the interstices between her letters with fiction writing. First, she finished a novel, appropriately called *The Professor*, for which she never found a publisher during her lifetime. Then in 1847 she published *Jane Eyre* and was immediately recognized as one of the most powerful and original voices of her generation. Sadly, success was tempered by the deaths in rapid succession of her brother, Branwell, and her sisters Emily and Anne. Again she got through tragedy by writing—first a novel called *Shirley* (1849), then *Villette* (1853), based on her time in Brussels. Writer Harriet Martineau read *Villette* and pronounced it a novel about "the need of being loved."

Once relegated to high-school English classes, Charlotte Brontë's novels are now almost as widely appreciated as they were when they were written. Poet and critic Matthew Arnold wrote well when he noted in a letter to a friend that Brontë's mind was filled with "hunger, rebellion and rage."

November 18th, 1845

Monsieur,

The six months of silence have run their course. It is now the 18th of Novr.; my last letter was dated (I think) the 18th of May. I may therefore write to you without failing in my promise.

The summer and autumn seemed very long to me; truth to tell, it has needed painful efforts on my part to bear hitherto the self-denial which I have imposed on myself. You, Monsieur, you cannot conceive what it means; but suppose for a moment that one of your children was separated from you, 160 leagues away, and that you had to remain six months without writing to him, without receiving news of him, without hearing him spoken of, without knowing aught of his health, then you would understand easily all the harshness of such an obligation.

I tell you frankly that I have tried meanwhile to forget you, for the remembrance of a person whom one thinks never to see again, and whom, nevertheless, one greatly esteems, frets too much the mind; and when one has suffered that kind of anxiety for a year or two, one is ready to do anything to find peace once more. I have done everything; I have sought occupations; I have denied myself absolutely the pleasure of speaking about you—even to Emily; but I have been able to conquer neither my regrets or my impatience. That, indeed, is humiliating—to be unable to control one's own thoughts, to be the slave of a regret, of a memory, the slave of a fixed and dominant idea which lords it over the mind. Why cannot I have just as much friendship for you, as you for me—neither more nor less? Then should I be so tranquil, so free—I could keep silence then for ten years without an effort.

My father is well but his sight is almost gone. He can neither read nor write. Yet the doctors advise waiting a few months more before attempting an operation. The winter will be a long night for him. He rarely complains; I admire his patience. If Providence wills the same calamity for me, may He at last vouchsafe me as much patience with which to bear it! It seems to me, Monsieur, that there is nothing more galling in great physical misfortunes than to be compelled to make all those about us share in our sufferings. The ills of the soul one can hide, but those which attack the body and destroy the faculties cannot be concealed. My father allows me now to read to him and write for him; he shows me, too, more confidence than he has ever shown before, and that is a great consolation.

Monsieur, I have a favour to ask of you: when you reply to this letter, speak to me a little of yourself, not of me; for I know that if you speak of me it will be to scold me, and this time I would see your kindly side. Speak to me therefore of your children. Never was your brow severe when Louise and Claire and Prosper were by your side. Tell me also something of the School, of the pupils, of the Governesses. Are Mesdemoiselles Blanche, Sophie, and Justine still at Brussels? Tell me where you travelled during the holidays—did you go to the Rhine? Did you not visit Cologne or Coblentz? Tell me, in short, my master, what you will, but tell me something. To write to an ex-assistant governess (No! I refuse to remember my employment as assistant governess—I repudiate it)—anyhow, to write to an old pupil cannot be a very interesting occupation for you, I know; but for me it is life.

Your last letter was stay and prop to me—nourishment for half a year. Now I need another and you will give it me; not because you bear me friendship—you cannot have much—but because you are compassionate of soul and you would condemn no one to prolonged suffering to save yourself a few moments' trouble. To forbid me to write to you, to refuse to answer me, would be to tear from me my only joy on earth, to deprive me of my last privilege—a privilege I never shall consent willingly to surrender. Believe me, my master, in writing to me it is a good deed that you will do. So long as I believe you are pleased with me, so long as I have hope of receiving news from you, I can be at rest and not too sad. But when a prolonged and gloomy silence seems to threaten me with the estrangement of my master—when day by day I await a letter, and when day by day disappointment comes to fling me back into overwhelming sorrow, and the sweet delight of seeing your handwriting and reading your counsel escapes me as a vision that is vain, then fever claims me—I lose appetite and sleep—I pine away.

May I write to you again next May: I would rather wait a year, but it is impossible—it is too long.

I must say one word to you in English. I wish I could write to you more cheerful letters, for when I read this over I find it to be somewhat gloomy—but forgive me, my dear master—do not be irritated at my sadness—according to the words of the Bible: 'Out of the fulness of the heart, the mouth speaketh,' and truly I find it difficult to be cheerful so long as I think I shall never see you more. You will perceive by the defects in this letter than [sic] I am forgetting the French language—yet I read all the French books I can get, and learn daily a portion by heart—but I have never heard French spoken but once since I left Brussels—and then it sounded like music in my ears—every word was most precious to me because it reminded me of you—I love French for your sake with all my heart and soul.

Farewell, my dear Master—may God protect you with special care and crown you with peculiar blessings.

C.B.

Oscar Wilde to Lord Alfred Douglas

The gay, gilt and gracious lad has gone away—and I hate everyone else; they are tedious," Oscar Wilde wrote to and of Lord Alfred Douglas in 1894. What is remarkable about this letter is that it was written a year after Douglas had carelessly allowed some of Wilde's love letters to fall into the hands of a blackmailer. Yet Wilde forgave him. Indeed, he worried that Douglas might be angry with *him:* "No money, no credit, and a heart of lead."

The same pattern of love and forgiveness is evident in the heart-breaking letter of June 4, 1897, reprinted here. It was written a month after Wilde's release from two years' imprisonment for sodomy. When he wrote this letter, he was crushed in body and spirit. In *De Profundis* (1905), a long letter to Douglas that he wrote while in jail and later published as a kind of apologia for his behavior, Wilde is clear-sighted about the key role that Lord Alfred Douglas played in his ruin. Yet barely released from prison and responding to a letter written by Douglas, Wilde finds it impossible not to love.

Wilde deserved better than he got from Douglas, yet he could not bring himself to repudiate the passion of his life. "I don't regret for a single moment having lived for pleasure. I did it to the full, as one should do anything that one does. . . . I lived on honeycomb."

Hôtel de la Plage, Berneval-sur-Mer
Friday, 4 June 1897   2:30

My dear Boy,

I have just got your letter, but Ernest Dowson, Dal Young, and Conder are here, so I cannot read it, except the last three lines. I love the last words of anything: the end in art is the beginning. Don't think I don't love you. Of course I love you more than anyone else. But our lives are irreparably severed, as far as meeting goes. What is left to us is the knowledge that we love each other, and every day I think of you, and I know you are a poet, and that makes you doubly dear and wonderful. My friends here have been most sweet to me, and I like them all very much. Young is the best of fellows, and Ernest has a most interesting nature. He is to send me some of his work.

We all stayed up till three o'clock; very bad for me, but it was a delightful experience. Today is a day of sea-fog, and rain—my first. Tomorrow I go with fishers to fish, but I will write to you tonight.

Ever, dear boy, with fondest love

Oscar

Liane de Pougy to Natalie Barney

Liane de Pougy was raised at the Convent of the Sacred Heart at Rennes, but left while still in her teens to marry a naval officer. Once, in a fit of jealousy, her husband fired his revolver at her, grazing her wrist. After she left him, she supported herself as a courtesan, but often displayed the scar as a symbol of her distrust of men.

Nor was she entirely trusting of women. After Natalie Barney sent her an anonymous love note, Liane staged a meeting in which another courtesan greeted Natalie, posing as Liane. Watching from behind a curtain, Liane saw Natalie enter, dressed as a page, and drop adoringly to her knee. When Natalie looked up and discovered the other courtesan, she was furious. She calmed down only when Liane appeared and invited her to return the next morning, promising to be alone and addressing Natalie in the always seductive *tu,* the French familiar pronoun with its hint of intimacies to come.

The relationship lasted for two full, exciting years. Although each woman would accuse the other of unfaithfulness at one time or another, they remained friends long after their affair was over and continued to think of one another with affection. After Liane published *The Sapphic Idyll* (1901), she wrote to Natalie: "*The Idyll* has seen the light and the public is scrambling, that's the word, for these scraps of us and our former desires."

Natalie continued to live an independent and controversial life as a writer, free thinker, and feminist. Liane married, became respectable, and, after the death of her husband, took vows as a third-order nun under the name Sister Marie-Madeleine de la Pénitence. Before her death in 1950, she had repented her earlier life and confessed that "Natalie has been my greatest sin." Natalie's reminiscences were less puritanical but perhaps no different from Liane's. "Liane," she said, "was my greatest sensual pleasure."

1899

I am learning so much about you. Ugh. You present yourself as Flossie. You don't even have the courage to use your name and to show yourself without a mask. If you are ashamed of what you are doing, why do you do it?

And I who thought you so beautiful and who believed in you. And you are thinking about coming to me.

I am worth more than you, Flossie-Natty. I'm prettier, you are ugly with your yellow skin and reddish eyes. Your head of hair, yes, it's ashamed of the rest of you. Your heart . . .

doesn't exist. You're stuffed with phrases, and you're believed, and paid attention to.

I don't want to think about you anymore for a very long time. Your reputation is sullied everywhere and from all sides. There is nothing real in you. What I used to love doesn't exist and I'm mad at you for having made me discover it . . .

Take care that I never run into you, for I would take off your mask in front of everybody.

Good-bye.

I no longer believe.

I no longer hope.

I no longer love.

Aline Bernstein to Thomas Wolfe

Aline Bernstein met Thomas Wolfe aboard the *Olympic* on a return trip from Europe in August of 1925. He was twenty-five, she forty-four; he was a Christian from North Carolina, she an urban Northeastern Jew; he was a novice writer, she a successful stage and costume designer. He thought her "the most beautiful woman who ever lived," and for eleven years, the two were tempestuously in love. In over 1,900 pages of love letters they recorded all the moods of their complicated and conflicted relationship.

Wolfe was a talented young man, haunted by despair and depression. His letters explore these moods, as well as recount in precise and voluminous detail all that he saw and heard and felt and experienced on his various travels away from Bernstein. Continually he works at fine-tuning their relationship, sometimes requesting that they become "just friends," at other times trying to revive a passion that he has seemingly worked to destroy. Bernstein's letters, too, chart the pendulum swings of their relationship against the backdrop of the changing art scene of New York and Europe in the twenties and thirties. She is surer of the relationship, promises undying love, and eventually succumbs to a wrenching and humiliating epistolary pattern—he withdrawing, she beseeching, he apologizing, she forgiving, and on and on. She tried to hang on for years after it was clear that there was no longer any relationship and that they had very different ideas of love. For her, love meant total commitment to and absorption in someone else; for him, love was mostly an excuse for self-exploration. More than once, he wrote her letters as long as sixty pages, and forgot to mail them: "Thus I think of you all the time, begin a letter, sleep, write, add to the letter, and finally, wondering in horror how it shall ever get to you, I remember suddenly that there are postage stamps, and strange things called ships, in which I don't believe."

Berlin
Hotel Esplanade
August 11, 1928

My Dear:

We arrived yesterday, could not get rooms at Adlon Hotel, a nasty place anyway, and came here which is lovely.—Your letter came here, I was so afraid you would come to the Adlon and miss me that I bribed every official and flunkey in the place, so when I came in at lunch time I found a boy waiting with your letter.

I had been hoping so desperately that you would come although I knew it would be very difficult for both of us, and very disquieting. I am in a constant agony of longing for you, and it seems so strange to me, if you love me so, that you would not take this journey to see me, even if you do not care to see Berlin (a very peculiar reason, isn't it?) I do not seem to be able to put into words the love and longing I have for you. I feel now that I will never be satisfied with this loving friendship you talk so much about. The phrase stings me to helpless anger.

I am your true love until I die, how dare you write me to make "other arrangements for my happiness." That is what you wrote. Have you no sense! Ever since you parted from me, you write that you love me, and never once have you said you would come back to me. Except in "loving friendship." Well, once for all, that means nothing and you know it.

As you see, I feel bitter, angry and horribly discouraged. This whole summer has been a prolonged agony, except for the times I have been able to lose myself in pictures, and what will be the consequence of it all. God knows I only hope that you will benefit by it. I am also discouraged that you drift so endlessly. How about your work? Wasn't that the idea behind our separation this summer? Tom dear forgive me, but I am so hurt that you didn't come to meet me here, when you could.

For heaven's sake do something, you are now in the most precious time of your life, and it seems to me you are doing the same thing you did four years ago, aimlessly wandering. Possibly I am wrong and that sort of thing is necessary to you. I think I know, but must be mistaken.

—We came from Prague here by aeroplane yesterday. It was a strange and terrible experience, and I hoped several times the God damn plane would smash and go down. This is not fancy talk as you call it, but the truth. The wind was blowing a gale, and we had what is called a very rough passage. It was terrible, nothing that a ship does in the most violent storm could compare to the plunges and leaps of the plane. The earth was wonderful to look at from above, so perfectly designed. I felt deathly sick but could not vomit, and for the last hour of the ride had a steady sharp pain in my heart and was a beautiful indigo blue color when we landed. . . . The strangest thing was that I had no sensation of fear at all. And if it weren't for the awful sickness it must be a marvellous way to travel. I had some tea when we got settled in the hotel, and stayed nearly an hour in a very hot bath, finally got warm, and went to bed. But the bed swayed, and my head nearly cracked all night. No more flying for me for some time.—I wish to God I could sink into some state of insensibility.

I don't know what to do if I go on being wracked this way by my feeling. I wish I could be so noble that I would be happy just because you have your freedom, or whatever you choose to call it, and are doing what you please. I'm not that noble, in spite of the Carlsbad cure. As I feel I don't think it is in me to do any more beautiful shows, in spite of your advice. I also do not think it is in me to make another home for my family, and root up my old one. Isn't it funny to have reached my age and be all at sea! And here I go giving advice to you about settling to work. More people than I, have lived through it. Without you I am finished with it.

You must dread getting a letter from me now, they are all so painful, but I guess not so painful as to see me. Do you think you ever will again?—When I think that you are being untrue to me with women, I have murder in my heart.—I am true to you and me and love forever. I went to the museum here for an hour this morning, it is very fine. Some magnificent paintings. My head hurt so from the flight I couldn't stay very long. Fortunately I can get off by myself, occasionally. Phil comes along, when I look at pictures. I am sending you a lovely Egyptian head. Berlin is much lovelier than I had thought, I took a little one horse hack and drove around. I will get up very early tomorrow, as the galleries all close at one o'clock Saturday and 3 other days. The pictures seem to be grand. Will know better tomorrow.

I hope you will let me know where to write you, will go on sending mail to Munich till further notice. You will find a great collection from me there. If I feel no happier soon what shall I do? Just go on. Well, my darling an ache only aches the person who has it, I found that out by now. Time is a dream—

I love you   Aline

AFTER GREAT PAIN

Edith Wharton to W. Morton Fullerton

W• Morton Fullerton possessed many virtues as a lover and a friend, but constancy was not among them. He seemed to think of his social life as an elaborate game and took a certain pride in the complexity of the interrelationships that he was able to spin. His love life, one might say, was a giant spiderweb in which he lived elegantly, if predatorily, at the center.

Biographer Leon Edel has suggested that Fullerton enjoyed the part he played in a complex romantic triangle with Edith Wharton and Henry James. James knew, admired, and possibly fell in love with the handsome young man several years before he introduced him to Wharton. As this letter makes clear, after the full-blown passion of a romance, Fullerton tired of Wharton but kept her dangling, unwilling either to end the relationship cleanly or to continue it at its early level of commitment and companionship. Wharton began to feel like she had become merely a convenience. He stored books and papers at her house, dropped in when he felt like it, but also broke engagements at will, and refused to make any plans for the future. Since he cultivated a similarly fickle relationship with James, Fullerton's mailbox was filled with importuning letters from two of America's most famous writers.

For Wharton the lack of closure in the relationship was the most painful part. Decimated by Fullerton's cowardice and inconstancy, she ended up writing the letters that finally—years after the relationship had begun to falter—ended the affair, presumably on a note of friendship. Perhaps inevitably, she turned for consolation to Henry James, the one friend she knew would understand.

53 Rue de Varenne
Tuesday, Winter 1910

When I received your note of last night I was really alarmed,
& sent a line to your hotel at 9 o'c this morning, to beg you to
rest for a day or two, & to ask if there was anything I could do
to help you *in any way,*—but you were not there!

What am I to think?—

When I don't write you for two or three days (purposely)
you write & telephone to know what is the matter. When I *do*
write, & ask if I can help you, or see you for a moment, you
tell me that you are too ill—and when I sent to your hotel at 9
A.M., *you are not there!*

You know what I must think—what I have thought during
these last mysterious three months, when again & again,
seeing how things were, I gave you every chance for an easy
transition to *amitié!*—

I don't know why you refused; but since you did, I must ask
you now—*implore you*—not to build up any more of these
elaborate *échafaudages* [structures] of pretexts, like last
Saturday's St. Germain!—*Mon pauvre ami, comprends donc
que je comprends, que je t'aime, que je suis toujours la tendre
amie que tu retrouvera quand tu en aura besoin* [My poor
friend, believe that I understand, that I love you, that I am
always the affectionate friend that you will find when you are
in need]—but spare me these little hurts. They are so
unneeded—and every time an incident like this happens, I am
sick again with all the accumulated sickness of these last
unintelligible months—

I hear you say: "What! I haven't the right to be absent from
my hotel at 9 in the morning, or any other hour?"—You have
every right, Dear, over every moment of your time, & every
feeling.—Only don't tell me the night before: "I am too ill to
see you."

Don't you understand that what hurts me is not *the fact* of
the change, which I find myself able to accept with a kind of
cheerful stoicism that reassures me?—It's not that, Dear, but
the pain, the unutterable pain, of thinking you incapable of

understanding my frankness & my honest desire to let you lead your own life.—You say: "I will be all you have the right to expect."—If I have any rights, I renounce them.—Don't write me in that way again . . . The one thing I can't bear is the thought that I represent to you *the woman who has to be lied to* . . . And if I think this, it is your own conduct that has brought it about.—*Vous l'avez voulu*—

Don't answer. It's useless.—I am your *camarade*—

Colette to Léon Hamel about Henri de Jouvenel ("Sidi")

Colette, the great French novelist of passion, nicknamed her second husband "Sidi" after the first and most enduring love of her life, her mother, Sido. Colette has written rapturously of her mother's walled garden—private, luxuriant, rich with lush blossoms and wafting maternal love. She has written far more cynically of love between the sexes, and even when she fell for Henri de Jouvenel, she suspected their love was only a temporary state of affairs.

When she met de Jouvenel in 1911 she was already notorious for the publication of her *Claudine* series. Her first husband, Henri Gauthier-Villars ("Willy"), had urged her to write the books and then published the series under his own name. Later, editors and the public realized that Colette was the actual author, and she became simultaneously famous and notorious, since the *Claudine* series is a semi-autobiographical account of an innocent schoolgirl exposed to the world's lust and longing. Colette continued to attract scandal in her stage career by acting (sometimes seminude) as a mime or giving dramatic recitations. She also attracted attention by living openly and flamboyantly with an older lover, "Missy" (marquise de Belbeuf), the niece of Napoléon III. When de Jouvenel, the coeditor of *Le Matin*, wanted her named literary editor of the Paris newspaper, at least one member of the staff threatened to resign because he did not want his name associated in any way with this well-known "courtesan."

During World War I, Colette turned her attention to writing journalistic reports of the effects of the war on the lives of ordinary citizens. The sensitivity of her stories won her loyal and adoring readers. After the war, she devoted herself increasingly to her writing, while de Jouvenel became involved in politics and, in 1922, served as a delegate to the League of Nations. He was away more and more often. Both took other lovers. When he died of a heart attack in 1935, the couple had not seen each other for over a decade, and Colette admitted that she would not have recognized him on the street. This letter to friend Léon Hamel indicates that already in 1912 Colette and de Jouvenel were making their good-byes.

Tours, June 26, 1912

. . . If you see Paul Barlet, he will tell you what strange days I've been living through, and what the effect can be on a man without willpower when he gets what he wants and what he wants is a definitive separation. Four days of conversation boil down to something like this:

> *Jouvenel:* We have to separate.
> *Colette:* Yes!
> *J.:* Life together . . .
> *C.:* . . . is impossible.
> *J.:* That wouldn't prevent our remaining good friends!
> *C.:* On the contrary!
> *J.:* So we are going to separate . . .
> *C.:* At once!
> *J.:* Oh! there's no need to hurry.
> *C.:* Yes, yes, it's absolutely urgent.
> *J.:* Absolute is hardly the word . . .
> *C.:* Absolute! The first of July we'll make a clean break.

Each will go his own way. If, for my part, there is an emotional change, that is to say, if I meet someone beddable and friendly, then simple loyalty would make it my duty . . .

J.: Certainly. But meanwhile . . .

C.: Meanwhile, I move to Paul Barlet's in the rue La Fontaine.

J.: That's unnecessary, and even stupid. You're better off here.

C.: No. Good night, Sidi.

J.: But . . . Where are you going?

C.: Where I belong. You yourself have told me . . .

J.: Oh, well! What I've said is not of great importance . . . Wouldn't you like to play a game of cards?

C.: Cards? With pleasure.

J.: . . . Four thousand five hundred!

C.: *Bravo!* Upon which . . . *adieu,* Sidi.

J.: But . . . what are you doing this evening? If it wouldn't revolt you to have dinner chez Laurent in the open air, the weather is good, and I'd so much like to stay with you . . .

Etc., etc.

I am showing you, dear Hamel, the comic side. Unhappily, there are others. But I've passed the dead point. Meantime, Sauerwein, very appropriately, has sent me here to cover the Guillotin trial. I arrived yesterday evening. The legal press flutters around me, Henri de Robert has adopted me, and all goes well. Sidi took me to the railway station looking like a lost dog. I don't despair of treating him as frivolously as I did Hériot.

I'll be coming back Saturday, probably . . . I count on you unendingly. And I comfort myself with the thought that I shall need you. No one, at this moment, is closer to me than you.

Joy Harjo
to _____

In her collection *In Mad Love and War* (1990), Muscogee Creek poet Joy Harjo writes fiercely and powerfully of the loves that hurt or destroy. "I don't believe in promises, but there you are, / balancing on a tightrope of sound," she writes in "Bleed Through." Or, again, in "The Bloodletting":

> How am I to stop you with
> stark words, promises
> glued together with blood,
> or with the smell of love
> a distant memory?

"Transformations," reprinted here, is a letter-poem in which, like many of Harjo's poems, love and hatred are inextricably fused together.

Born in Oklahoma in 1951, Harjo is a poet and scriptwriter as well as a professional musician (she plays tenor sax, an instrument whose sound often wails through her poetry). She began to write while a student at the University of New Mexico, where she also gave birth to the first of her two children.

Long drives in the pickup, the desert in the moonlight, scorching sunsets, rock music blasting the dawn, the erotic landscape of women's bodies: this is the terrain of Harjo's mad love and poetry.

Transformations

This poem is a letter to tell you that I have smelled the hatred you have tried to find me with; you would like to destroy me. Bone splintered in the eye of one you choose to name your enemy won't make it better for you to see. It could take a thousand years if you name it that way, but then, to see after all that time, never could anything be so clear. Memory has many forms. When I think of early winter I think of a blackbird laughing in the frozen air; guards a piece of light. (I saw the whole world caught in that sound, the sun stopped for a moment because of tough belief.) I don't know what that has to do with what I am trying to tell you except that I know you can turn a poem into something else. This poem could be a bear treading the far northern tundra, smelling the air for sweet alive meat. Or a piece of seaweed stumbling in the sea. Or a blackbird, laughing. What I mean is that hatred can be turned into something else, if you have the right words, the right meanings, buried in that tender place in your heart where the most precious animals live. Down the street an ambulance has come to rescue an old man who is slowly losing his life. Not many can see that he is already becoming the backyard tree he has tended for years, before he moves on. He is not sad, but compassionate for the fears moving around him.

That's what I mean to tell you. On the other side of the place you live stands a dark woman. She has been trying to talk to you for years.
You have called the same name in the middle of a nightmare, from the center of miracles. She is beautiful. This is your hatred back. She loves you.

REMEMBRANCE OF LOVE PAST

Émilie du Châtelet to Duc de Richelieu

Émilie du Châtelet showed early promise of great intellect and was fortunate enough to have a wise and doting father who educated her in a manner commensurate with her intelligence. She was married at the age of eighteen to the marquis du Châtelet, a regimental colonel from a famous old family that was no longer particularly affluent. He was happy with the large dowry and the independent income that Émilie brought to the marriage, and like many members of his class, he regarded jealousy as bad manners. He expected that she, like he, would lead her own intellectual and amorous life, although he had a lifelong habit of chiding his wife when she took lovers whom he deemed unworthy of her.

The husband very much approved his wife's selection of Louis François Armand du Plessis, Duc de Richelieu. Richelieu was the grandnephew of Cardinal Richelieu, commander-in-chief of the French armies in the field, one of France's most important statesmen, and unquestionably the most accomplished *roué* of his day. Émilie had known the younger Richelieu virtually her whole life. Their families were distantly related by marriage, and they had been good friends before they were lovers and remained friends after. She wrote to him at least weekly until her death, letters filled with tenderness, concern, and love. Even in 1739, when she was madly in love with Voltaire, Émilie could write to her old friend, Richelieu: "I am sure that no one has felt more than I have the value of your friendship."

[1739]

It is the privilege of friendship to see one's friend in every condition of his soul. I love you sad, gay, lively, oppressed; I wish that my friendship might increase your pleasures, diminish your troubles and share them. There is no need on that account to have real misfortunes or great pleasures. No events are necessary, and I am as much interested in your moods and flirtations as other people are in the good fortune or bad fortune of the people they call their friends . . .

I do not know whether it is flattering to you to say that you are as agreeable far off as near by; but I know very well that it is thought to be a great merit by a lonely person, who, in renouncing the world, does not wish to renounce friendship, and who would be very sorry if a necessary absence made a breach between her and you.

I discover in your mind all the charms and in your society all the delights which the whole world has agreed to find there; but I am sure that no one has felt more than I have the value of your friendship. Your heart has prepossessed mine. I believed there was none other but myself who knew friendship in a measure so keen, and I was provoked by the proofs I wished to give you of it, sometimes on account of my scruples, at other times from fear, always in defiance of myself.

I could not believe that anyone so amiable, so much sought after, would care to disentangle the sentiments of my heart from all my faults. I believed that I had known you too late to obtain a place in your heart; I believed, also, I confess it, that you were incapable of continuing to love anyone who was not necessary to your pleasures and could not be useful to you— you, unique and incomparable man, understand how to combine everything; delicious friendship, intoxication of love, all is felt by you and spreads the sweetest charm over your fine destiny.

I confess to you that if, after having made me give myself up to your friendship, you should cease—I do NOT say to love me—but to tell me of it; if you should allow such a breach to appear in your friendship, if the remarks or witticisms of people who find me pleasing today and who will perhaps be displeased with me tomorrow, make the least impression on you, I should be inconsolable. I should be most unfortunate if you do not keep your friendship for me, and if you do not continue to give me proofs of it. You would make me repent of the candor with which I speak, and my heart does not wish to know repentance.

Until I write again, dear friend, goodbye. There is no perfect happiness for me in the world until I can unite the pleasure of enjoying our friendship with that of loving him to whom I have devoted my life.

Charles Dickens to Mrs. Maria Sarah Beadnell Winter

A famous writer receives a lot of fan mail. Alone one night, sitting before the fire, Charles Dickens had begun the tedious task of answering his correspondence when he noticed an envelope that made his heart skip a beat. It was addressed to him in a handwriting he had not seen in over twenty years. "I opened [the letter] with the touch of my young friend David Copperfield when he was in love," Dickens wrote in reply to the unexpected missive from his first love, Maria Sarah Beadnell, now married to Henry Winter and a mother of two daughters.

Writing in 1855, "Mrs. Winter" recalled their young love and her devotion in the most romantic terms, carefully editing out her youthful flirtations with other men. Nor did she mention how the relationship had ended, when her affluent parents opposed her match to a penniless parliamentary reporter with literary aspirations.

Now England's most popular novelist, Dickens had never fully recovered from his broken heart. The letter reprinted here is his initial response to this surprising letter from a woman he thought he would never see again. In it he recounts the events of the decades since he last saw her. Although much of what he says is matter-of-fact, even documentary, the whole is tinged by a tone of nostalgia and regret.

Perpetually dissatisfied in his marriage to the patient Catherine Hogarth, mother of his ten children, Charles was only too eager to participate in a fantasy of young love come again. He and Maria began a flirtation by letter, both luxuriating in long-ago love. He recreated Maria as she had been in their youth—tender, beautiful, wearing "a sort of raspberry coloured dress with a little black trimming at the top." She warned him that she was now a "toothless, fat, old and ugly" matron.

With much anxiety and anticipation, they met. He quickly discovered that Maria's description of herself was more accurate than his fantasy had been. She was older now—and so was he.

Deprived of his vision of love as the fountain of youth, Dickens beat a hasty retreat, suggesting that Maria and his wife might make nice friends.

TAVISTOCK HOUSE
Saturday, Tenth February 1855

MY DEAR MRS. WINTER,

I constantly receive hundreds of letters in great varieties of writing, all perfectly strange to me, and (as you may suppose) have no particular interest in the faces of such general epistles. As I was reading by my fire last night, a handful of notes was laid down on my table. I looked them over, and, recognising the writing of no private friend, let them lie there and went back to my book. But I found my mind curiously disturbed, and wandering away through so many years to such early times of my life, that I was quite perplexed to account for it. There was nothing in what I had been reading, or immediately thinking about, to awaken such a train of thought, and at last it came into my head that it must have been suggested by something in the look of one of those letters. So I turned them over again—and suddenly the remembrance of your hand came upon me with an influence that I cannot express to you. Three or four and twenty years vanished like a dream, and I opened it with the touch of my young friend David Copperfield when he was in love.

There was something so busy and so pleasant in your letter—so true and cheerful and frank and affectionate—that I read on with perfect delight until I came to your mention of your two little girls. In the unsettled state of my thoughts, the existence of these dear children appeared such a prodigious phenomenon, that I was inclined to suspect myself of being out of my mind, until it occurred to me, that perhaps I had nine children of my own! Then the three or four and twenty years began to rearrange themselves in a long procession between me and the changeless Past, and I could not help considering what strange stuff all our little stories are made of.

Believe me, you cannot more tenderly remember our old days and our old friends than I do. I hardly ever go into the City but I walk up an odd little court at the back of the Mansion House and come out by the corner of Lombard Street. Hundreds of times as I have passed the church there— on my way to and from the Sea, the Continent, and where not—I invariably associate it with somebody (God knows who) having told me that poor Anne [Maria's sister] was buried there. If you would like to examine me in the name of a good-looking Cornish servant you used to have (I suppose she has twenty-nine great grandchildren now, and walks with a stick), you will find my knowledge on the point, correct, though it was a monstrous name too. I forget nothing of those times. They are just as still and plain and clear as if I had never been in a crowd since, and had never seen or heard my own name out of my own house. What should I be worth, or what would labour and success be worth, if it were otherwise!

Your letter is more touching to me from its good and gentle associations with the state of Spring in which I was either much more wise or much more foolish than I am now—I never know which to think it—than I could tell you if I tried for a week. I will not try at all. I heartily respond to it, and shall be charmed to have a long talk with you, and most cordially glad to see you after all this length of time.

I am going to Paris to-morrow morning, but I propose being back within a fortnight. When I return, Mrs. Dickens will come to you, to arrange a day for our seeing you and Mr. Winter (to whom I beg to be remembered) quietly to dinner. We will have no intruder or foreign creature on any pretence whatever, in order that we may set in without any restraint for a tremendous gossip.

Mary Anne Leigh we saw at Broadstairs about fifty years ago. Mrs. Dickens and her sister, who read all the marriages in the papers, shrieked to me when the announcement of hers appeared, what did I think of *that?* I calmly replied that I thought it was time. I should have been more excited if I had known of the old gentleman with seven thousand a year, uncountable grown-up children, and no English grammar.

My mother has a strong objection to being considered in the least old, and usually appears here on Christmas Day in a juvenile cap which takes an immense time in the putting on. The Fates seem to have made up their minds that I shall never see your Father when he comes this way. David Lloyd is altogether an imposter—not having in the least changed (that I could make out when I saw him at the London Tavern) since what I suppose to have been the year 1770, when I found you three on Cornhill, with your poor mother, going to St. Mary Axe to order mysterious dresses—which afterwards turned out to be wedding garments. That was in the remote period when you all wore green cloaks, cut (in my remembrance) very round, and which I am resolved to believe were made of Merino. I escorted you with native gallantry to the Dress Maker's door, and your mother, seized with an apprehension—groundless upon my honour—that I might come in, said emphatically: "And now, Mr. Dickin"—which she always used to call me—"We'll wish *you* good morning."

When I was writing the word Paris just now, I remembered that my existence was once entirely uprooted and my whole Being blighted by the Angel of my soul being sent there to finish her education! If I can discharge any little commission for you, or bring home anything for the darlings [Mrs. Winter's children], whom I cannot yet believe to be anything but a delusion of yours, pray employ me. I shall be at the Hotel Meurice—locked up when within, as my only defence against my country and the United States—but a most punctual and reliable functionary, if you will give me any employment.

My Dear Mrs. Winter, I have been much moved by your letter; and the pleasure it has given me has some little sorrowful ingredient in it. In the strife and struggle of this great world where most of us lose each other so strangely, it is impossible to be spoken to out of the old times without a softened emotion. You so belong to the days when the qualities that have done me most good since, were growing in my boyish heart that I cannot end my answer to you lightly. The associations my memory has with you made your letter more — I want a word — invest it with a more immediate address to me than such a letter could have from anybody else. Mr. Winter will not mind that. We are all sailing away to the sea, and have a pleasure in thinking of the river we are upon, when it was very narrow and little. — Faithfully your friend.

Fred Vaughan to Walt Whitman

F or the one I love lay sleeping by my side, under the same cover in the cool night," Walt Whitman wrote. "And in the stillness his face was inclined toward me, while the moon's clear beams shone, / And his arm lay lightly over my breast — and that night I was happy." These lines from the "Calamus" poems in *Leaves of Grass* were most certainly written for Fred Vaughan, an illiterate working-class street lad with whom Whitman used to swim and frolic in Brooklyn's East River. The two were lovers during the late 1850s, years when Whitman's "barbaric yawp" sounded "over the roofs of the world" and Fred Vaughan learned to read, write, and appreciate the lectures of Emerson.

Whitman was the teacher, but he also listened to Vaughan and learned. His famous, colloquial poetic style was partly based on the spare, direct, forceful language of working-class men like Vaughan. More directly, Vaughan's love inspired what biographer Charley Shively has called "the most intense and successful celebration of gay love in our language."

After 1859, Vaughan and Whitman separated, but neither could forget the love they had shared. Vaughan moved in with another man for a time, and then, in 1862, got a woman pregnant and felt duty-bound to marry her. "I shall have no show! I have invited no company. *I want you to be there,*" Vaughan wrote, imploring Whitman's attendance at the wedding ceremony.

Whitman went on to become the most celebrated and controversial poet of his day. Vaughan worked at a series of jobs (elevator operator, salesman) and struggled to support his growing family. Despite separation, the two men kept in touch over the years. After Whitman suffered a stroke, Vaughan wrote him the letter reprinted here, among the most moving love letters ever penned. Written over twenty years after he left the poet's house, this letter shows Vaughan reminiscing about his earlier love for Whitman. The poet's absence fills Vaughan with tender pain like a persistent toothache that nags and spreads and never quite goes away. "Please do not criticize my grammar, nor phraseology," he pleads, "it was written too heartfelt to alter."

Brooklyn
November 16, 1874

Dear Walt—

I promised to write to you a week ago Sunday evening and did not do it.—I have no apology to offer.—Years ago Dear Walt—(and looking back over the tombstones it seems centuries)—Father used to tell me I was lazy. Mother denied it—and in latter years—(But O' my friend still looking over tombstones).—I used to tell your Mother you was lazy and she denied it.—You have assented yourself. I have confirmed my Father.

O, Walt, what recollections will crowd upon us both individually and in company from the above. To me the home so long long past—the brother—sisters—the sea—the return—New York, the Stage box—Broadway.—Walt—the Press—the Railroad. Marriage. Express—Babies—trouble. *Rum*, more trouble—more *Rum*—estrangement from you. More *Rum*.—Good intentions, sobriety. Misunderstanding and more *Rum.*

Up and down, down and up. The innate manly nature of myself at times getting the best of it and at other times entirely submerged. Now praying now cursing.—Yet ever hoping—and even now my friend after loosing my hold of the highest rung of the ladder of fortune I ever reached and dropping slowly but surely from rung to rung until I have almost reached the bottom, I still hope—

From causes too numerous and complex to explain *except verbally*, I found myself in June last in Brooklyn possessed of a wife and four boys—ages 12—9—4 years—and one of 8 months—no money, no credit—no friends of a/c and no furniture—Well, I am writing with my own pen, ink and paper on my own table, in a hired room, warmed by my own fire and lighted by my own oil—my wife sleeping on a bed near me and the Boys in an adjoining room.—

I have just got through supper after a hard days work and have to start again in the morning at 7 o'clock and am glad of it.—I am living on Atlantic ave one door above Classon ave and have been down past our old home several times this summer taking Freddie with me.—

There is never a day passes but what I think of you. So much have you left to be remembered by a Broadway stage—a Fulton ferry boat, a bale of cotton on the dock. The "Brooklyn Daily Times"—a ship loading or unloading at the wharf.—a poor man fallen from the roof of a new building, a woman & child suffocated by smoke in a burning tenement house. All—all to me speak of thee Dear Walt.—Seeing them my friend the part thou occupiest in my spiritual nature—I feel assured you will forgive my remissness of me in writing—My love my Walt—is with you always.—

I earnestly pray God that he may see fit to assuage your sufferings and in due time restore your wonted health and strength owing to *"impecuniosity"* (The first time I ever seen that word was in a letter from R. W. Emerson to you while we were living in Classon Ave, excusing himself as I now do). I cannot promise to come and see you soon. But, Walt should you become seriously ill, promise to telegraph to me immediately.

My Father is dead. Brother Burke is dead. I have not heard from Mother in 10 months.—My wife is faithful-loving-honest.

true. and one you could dearly love. Ever yours, — Fred. —

Walt — please do not criticize my grammar, nor
phraseology — it was written too heartfelt to alter. Fred.

Paul Laurence Dunbar to Alice Ruth Moore Dunbar

The young poet Paul Laurence Dunbar (1872–1906) first wrote to Alice Ruth Moore in 1895. His own reputation as a poet was growing and he was eager to communicate with other African-American writers. He expressed admiration for "some lines and a sketch" of hers that had appeared in the *Monthly Review*. He introduced himself by letter, asked her views on a range of racial and literary questions, and expressed his hope that they might strike up a literary correspondence. Three years later, they were married.

Both were exceptional people. Alice was a poet, short-story writer, journalist, and educator, as well as a founding member of the National Association of Colored Women. Her literary reputation extended far beyond her native New Orleans to Boston and New York, where her work appeared in prestigious newspapers. She would go on (under the name Alice Dunbar-Nelson) to become a major American writer, teacher, and lecturer on African-American culture.

Paul was a poet, a newspaper editor, essayist, and novelist. He worked with both Booker T. Washington and W. E. B. Du Bois in support of Tuskegee Institute and other projects, and was invited by President William McKinley to participate in his inauguration. After their marriage, both continued to write and to participate in black political and social causes and organizations.

But the relationship was fraught with problems. Despite failing health from consumption, Paul was unwilling to slow down the pace of his writing or lecturing, driving himself beyond human endurance and often venting his stress and sense of frustration on his wife. He was prone to bitterness and even despair, especially since white audiences enjoined him to read his "dialect poetry" or "Negro poetry," when he sought recognition for his more serious work. He also suffered from severe bouts of depression, now known to be a symptom of tuberculosis. A mistaken nineteenth-century idea that alcohol was good for the lungs helped him rationalize excessive drinking, which threatened to ruin his public career and contributed to the dissolution of his marriage.

This poignant letter was written in 1903, one year after Alice left Paul, but before their divorce was final. The letter is filled with longing, remembrance, and, still, some shred of hope. But the turmoil of their marriage had proven too much for her. She had her own life to lead, her own career as a writer, and could not sacrifice herself yet again to a man who broke promises as often as he made them.

This was Paul's final appeal to Alice for reconciliation. She did not answer the letter.

Boston, Mass. May 7th, 1903

Little Girl:

I hardly know how to begin writing to you. It has been so long since I could call you 'little girl,' but whether you like it or not, whether your freedom is too sweet to give up or not I must say that I was reading at Salem yesterday for one of the oldest woman's clubs in Mass. and the joy of the success was so great that I felt I must share it with you. You are always with me and the past is like a black dream.

Perhaps I should not have dared write this letter had not our situation been brought home to me by meeting a Mrs. Hay, a friend of Leila's, in Salem. She knew Leila's whole story for she has stopped at the hotel (with the impossible name) which James ran. She spoke of Leila's coming up unexpectedly to see him and of his resentment and she sent love and sympathy to the deserted wife! My God, how I felt, Alice, there must be some plane upon which we can come together. I have been a coward and a dastard but I love you, may I call you wifelums again?

Won't you meet me some where and talk it over? Don't be influenced by your friends. The very ones who would have been the quickest to advise you to remain away from me are the quickest to take me up, here, and it has been so everywhere.

After the first two weeks of our separation, a separation that

I have not yet realized, there has not been a day when with heartache I have not longed for you my wife. Nothing can take you away from me. Nothing can unmarry us. Don't you remember when we used to say that we had married for eternity?

I am a broken hearted man, but, thank God, you are mine. Will you meet at Sallie Brown's or some place in New York within the next four days? Meet me please and I shall stay here for a day or two to await your answer. What ever that may be, answer.

I am here at 221 West Newton St. with Posey Marshall. Answer me for God's sake.

Goodnight, little wife.

Hubbins

6

FALLING IN LOVE AGAIN

Benjamin Franklin to Madame Helvétius

It may be difficult to imagine the venerable Founding Father with the funny glasses and the key on his kite string as a *roué*, but Benjamin Franklin was pretty inventive in the romantic department as well. As one biographer notes, "women were attracted to him as surely as iron filings to a magnet, a circumstance which men with less appeal tended to report with disapproval." With his common-law wife, Deborah Read, he had a contented if not happy marriage. He called her a "good & faithful Helpmate." She preferred not to follow him on his travels across the Atlantic; he preferred to live abroad as if he were a bachelor, especially when spending time amid the salons of France. He and his wife had two children together; he acknowledged two additional, illegitimate children.

He and Madame Helvétius became close friends in 1777, when he was living in Passy, France, after the death of his wife. Born Anne-Catherine de Ligniville d'Autricourt, she was the widow of Claude-Adrien Helvétius, one of the Encyclopedists, an important group of French writers and intellectuals. A dazzling conversationalist, Madame Helvétius enjoyed Franklin's company. Apparently he fell in love with her; or, at least, proposed to her. She declined the proposal, despite this delightful letter in which he tried to assuage her feelings of loyalty toward her late husband.

He did not long rue her rejection. Word of Franklin's amorous conquests spread so quickly that he felt called upon to defend himself to his stepniece back home in Boston: "You mention the Kindness of the French Ladies to me. I must explain that matter," he began. "Somebody, it seems, gave it out that I lov'd Ladies; and then everybody presented me their Ladies (or the Ladies presented themselves) to be *embrac'd,* that is to have their Necks kiss'd. For as to kissing of Lips or Cheeks it is not the Mode here, the first is recon'd rude, & the other may rub off the Paint. The French Ladies have however 1000 other ways of rendering themselves agreeable; by their various Attentions and Civilities, & their sensible Conversation. 'Tis a delightful People to live with.''

Mortified at the barbarous resolution pronounced by you so positively yesterday evening, that you would remain single the rest of your life, as a compliment due to the memory of your husband, I retired to my chamber. Throwing myself upon my bed, I dreamt that I was dead, and was transported to the Elysian Fields.

I was asked whether I wished to see any persons in particular; to which I replied, that I wished to see the philosophers. "There are two who live here at hand in this garden; they are good neighbors and very friendly towards one another." "Who are they?" "Socrates and Helvétius." "I esteem them both highly, but let me see Helvétius first, because I understand a little of French, but not a word of Greek." I was conducted to him; he received me with much courtesy, having known me, he said, by character, some time past. He asked me a thousand questions relative to the war, the present state of religion, of liberty, of the government in France.

"You do not inquire, then," said I, "after your dear friend, Madame Helvétius; yet she loves you exceedingly; I was in her company not more than an hour ago." "Ah," said he, "you make me recur to my past happiness, which ought to be forgotten in order to be happy here. For many years I could think of nothing but her, though at length I am consoled. I have taken another wife, the most like her that I could find; she is not indeed altogether so handsome, but she has a great fund of wit and good sense; and her whole study is to please me. She is at this moment gone to fetch the best nectar and ambrosia to regale me; stay here awhile and you will see her." "I perceive," said I, "that your former friend is more faithful to you than you are to her; she has had several good offers, but refused them all. I will confess to you that I loved her extremely; but she was cruel to me, and rejected me peremptorily for your sake." "I pity you sincerely," said he, "for she is an excellent woman, handsome and amiable. But do not the Abbé de la Roche and the Abbé Morelett visit her?" "Certainly they do; not one of your friends has dropped her acquaintance." "If you had gained the Abbé Morelett with a bribe of good coffee and cream, perhaps you would have succeeded; for he is as deep a reasoner as Duns Scotus or St. Thomas; he arranges and methodizes his arguments in such a manner that they are almost irresistible. Or, if by a fine edition of some old classic, you had gained the Abbé de la Roche to speak *against* you, that would have been still better; as I always observed, that when he recommended anything to her, she had a great inclination to do directly the contrary."

As he finished these words the new Madame Helvétius entered with the nectar, and I recognized her immediately as my former American friend, Mrs. Franklin! I reclaimed her, but she answered me coldly: "I was a good wife to you for forty-nine years and four months, nearly half a century; let that content you. I have formed a new connection here, which will last to eternity.

Indignant at this refusal of my Eurydice, I immediately resolved to quit those ungrateful shades, and return to this good world again, to behold the sun and you! Here I am: let us *avenge ourselves!*

Mary Wollstonecraft to William Godwin

Mary Wollstonecraft had been burned badly by love before she met fellow philosopher William Godwin. She had borne a daughter out of wedlock only to be abandoned by the child's father, Gilbert Imlay; she had spent two years of her life in a suicidal depression after he rejected her. She questioned whether she was suited for love.

In the remarkable letter reprinted here, we see one of England's greatest philosophers using an elaborate conceit to express her most intimate fears about falling in love again. In her "fable," a sycamore tree, shivering in winter and envious of the thick boughs of the evergreens that surround her, decides to send forth her buds prematurely on a balmy springlike day. The weather turns, frost comes, and the sycamore's leaves shrivel and die. Wollstonecraft yearns to love again, but she remembers too keenly what it feels like to be frozen out. She no longer trusts herself to distinguish "February from April."

Her fears were natural but unfounded. Godwin turned out to be the perfect man for her. Like Wollstonecraft, he was an avowed feminist. Like her, he had also denounced the institution of marriage. And like her, he was lonely and looking for love. After she gave him a copy of her most recent book, a travel book about her time in Scandinavia, he began to woo her ardently. "If ever there was a book calculated to make a man in love with its author," Godwin observed later in his *Memoir of the Author of "A Vindication of the Rights of Woman,"* "this appears to me to be the book."

When Mary became pregnant in 1797, the two decided to marry, despite their philosophical reservations, and Mary even modified her ideas on matrimony. "A husband is a convenient part of the furniture of a house," she admitted, happy in her relationship with Godwin, "unless he be a clumsy fixture." She meant it as a compliment to the man with whom she felt intellectually, emotionally, and physically content for the first time in her life.

Tragically, the marriage ended only a few months after it began, when Mary died of septicemia following the birth of their daughter. Godwin was utterly bereft. He shut out the world and began to write his memoir of his late wife, vowing to keep her memory alive. He moved all of his books and papers into Mary's study and, until his own death forty years later, continued to work in her room, among her belongings, amid her papers, beneath the magnificent portrait of her by John Opie.

London
August 19, 1796

As I was walking with Fanny [Wollstonecraft's daughter] this morning, before breakfast, I found a pretty little fable, directly

in my path; and, now I have finished my review, I will tran-
scribe it for thee.

A poor Sycamore growing up amidst a cluster of Evergreens,
every time the wind beat through her slender branches,
envied her neighbours the foliage which sheltered them from
each cutting blast. And the only comfort this poor trembling
scrub could find in her mind (as mind is *proved* to be only
thought, let it be taken for granted that she had a mind, if not
a soul) was to say, Well; spring will come soon, and I too shall
have leaves. But so impatient was this silly plant that the sun
could not glisten on the snow, without her asking, of her more
experienced neighbours, if this was not spring? At length the
snow began to melt away, the snow-drops appeared, and the
crocus did not lag long behind, the hepaticas next ventured
forth, and the mezereon began to bloom.

The sun was warm—balsamic as May's own beams. Now
said the Sycamore, her sap mounting, as she spoke, I am sure
this is spring. Wait only for such another day, said a fading
Laurel; and a weather-beaten Pine nodded, to enforce the
remonstrance.

The Sycamore was not headstrong, and promised, at least,
to wait for the morrow, before she burst her rind.

What a tomorrow came! The sun darted forth with
redoubled ardour; the winds were hushed. A gentle breeze
fluttered the trees; it was the sweet southern gale, which Willy
Shakespear felt, and came to rouse the violets; whilst every
genial zephyr gave birth to a primrose.

The Sycamore no longer regarded admonition. She felt that
it was spring; and her buds, fostered by the kindest beams
immediately came forth to revel in existence.

Alas! Poor Sycamore! The morrow a hoar frost covered the
trees, and shrivelled up thy unfolding leaves, changing, in a
moment the colour of the living green—a brown, melancholy
hue succeeded—and the Sycamore drooped, abashed; whilst a
taunting neighbour whispered to her, bidding her, in future,
learn to distinguish February from April—

Whether the buds recovered, and expanded, when the
spring actually arrived—the Fable sayeth not—

George Sand to Gustave Flaubert about Charles Marchal

George Sand (Amandine-Aurore Lucille Dupin, Baronne Dudevant) was sixty-seven years old when she wrote to her friend Gustave
Flaubert about her young lover, Charles Marchal. "And what, you
want me to stop loving?" she asks rhetorically. For George Sand, living was loving, loving was living—and she did both abundantly.

Probably her most notorious affair was with Alfred de Musset, a
French poet and playwright whom she met shortly after she left her
husband. He was twenty-two, she almost thirty. It began as a literary
friendship, with his sending her a fan letter about her novel, *Indiana*
(1832), one of a series of romantic novels in which she dramatized
the problems of an independent woman in a world of social con-
straint and social convention. Soon he was writing her passionate
entreaties: "Pity me, but do not despise me. If my name is written in
a corner of your heart, do not efface the impression, however faint
and feeble it may be. . . . There are days when I could kill myself."
She had endured a brutal marriage; she had taken other lovers; she
had suffered heartbreak. But with Alfred, she wrote a friend, "I am
happy, very happy. . . . His intimacy is as delightful to me as his love
for me is precious. After all, you see, there is nothing really good in
the world but that."

The two lived and loved together publicly and went off to Venice on
a kind of honeymoon, although there had been no marriage. She
wrote; he spent his nights gambling and visiting bawdy houses. When
he fell ill, George Sand had an affair with the handsome Dr. Pagello
who came to tend him. De Musset left; George Sand and Pagello each
wrote to him; he wrote to each of them. There were reconciliations,
departures, reconciliations, departures. After Alfred's death in 1857,
she wrote her version of their love story, *Elle et Lui* (1859); Paul de
Musset responded with a more sympathetic account of his brother
in *Lui et Elle* (1860). It was all quite public, passionate, and complicated—and set up the pattern of intricate love that continued for the
rest of George Sand's life.

When she wrote to Flaubert in 1871, she was explaining not only her past life of love but her present affair. The object of her affections, this time, was the "Mastodon," Charles Marchal, a huge, robust, jolly painter two years younger than her son. She was pushing seventy, and she liked him because he took her "as I am." She called him her "great big springtime." And as one biographer has suggested, he loved her "lightly, healthily and well." May we all be so fortunate!

14 September, 1871, Nohant

And what, you want me to stop loving? You want me to say that I have been mistaken all my life, that humanity is contemptible, hateful, that it has always been and always will be so? And you chide my anguish as a weakness, and puerile regret for a lost illusion? You assert that the people has always been ferocious, the priest always hypocritical, the bourgeois always cowardly, the soldier always brigand, the peasant always stupid? You say that you have known all that ever since your youth and you rejoice that you never have doubted it, because maturity has not brought you any disappointment; have you not been young then? Ah! We are entirely different, for I have never ceased to be young, if being young is always loving.

What, then, do you want me to do, so as to isolate myself from my kind, from my compatriots, from my race, from the great family in whose bosom my own family is only one ear of corn in the terrestrial field? And if only this ear could ripen in a sure place, if only one could, as you say, live for certain privileged persons and withdraw from all the others!

But it is impossible, and your steady reason puts up with the most unrealizable of Utopias. In what Eden, in what fantastic Eldorado will you hide your family, your little group of friends, your intimate happiness, so that the lacerations of the social state and the disasters of the country shall not reach them? If you want to be happy through certain people—those certain people, the favorites of your heart, must be happy in themselves. Can they be? Can you assure them the least security?

Will you find me a refuge in my old age which is drawing near to death? And what difference now does death or life make to me for myself? Let us suppose that we die absolutely, or that love does not follow into the other life, are we not up to our last breath tormented by the desire, by the imperious need of assuring those whom we leave behind all the happiness possible? Can we go peacefully to sleep when we feel the shaken earth ready to swallow up all those for whom we have lived? A continuous happy life with one's family in spite of all, is without doubt relatively a great good, the only consolation that one could and that one would enjoy. But even supposing external evil does not penetrate into our house, which is impossible, you know very well, I could not approve of acquiescing in indifference to what causes public unhappiness.

All that was foreseen. . . . Yes, certainly, I had foreseen it as well as anyone! I saw the storm rising. I was aware, like all those who do not live without thinking, of the evident approach of the cataclysm. When one sees the patient writhing in agony is there any consolation in understanding his illness thoroughly? When lightning strikes, are we calm because we have heard the thunder rumble a long time before?

No, no, people do not isolate themselves, the ties of blood are not broken, people do not curse or scorn their kind. Humanity is not a vain word. Our life is composed of love, and not to love is to cease to live.

Colette to
Marguerite Moreno
about
Maurice Goudeket

Colette wrote flamboyantly, passionately, erotically about love and lived a life as rich and various as any. In 1925, already in her fifties, she fell headlong, heedlessly, foolishly into love as if (as she says) she were a teenager again. The object of her desire was Maurice Goudeket—a "skunk," she called him, "who looks like a classical Satan." He was twenty years younger than she, a pet of numerous women in the theater and fashion worlds of Paris. As a youth, he had read but a few pages of one of Colette's novels when he proclaimed to his parents, "I am going to marry that woman. She is the only one in the world who can understand me." Even madly in love, Colette was wise enough to think this was a recipe for disaster.

She was wrong. The two met at the home of Colette's dear friend, Marguerite Moreno, and got off to a rocky start. Initially Goudeket was put off by the way Colette reclined full length before him and displayed all of her well-known affectations of speech and manner. "At first," he said many years later, "I thought you were playing the part of Colette. But after thirty years with you, I now believe that you *are* Colette." *Thirty years.* Maurice was with Colette when she died in 1954.

June 11, 1925

What am I doing? Heavens, I'm spinning. And I use this verb as a planet would. Yes, I'm spinning. I've seen roses, honeysuckle, forty degrees Centigrade of dazzling heat, moonlight, ancient wisteria enlacing the door of my old home in Saint-Sauveur. I've seen the night over Fontainebleau. And as I said, I'm spinning. Beside me there is a dark boy at the wheel. I'm on my way back to Paris, but shall I stay there? The dark boy beside me is still at the wheel, and how strange everything is! And how good I am, and how amazed I am, and what wise improvidence in my behavior! Oh yes, I'm spinning!

As you can see, you must not worry about me. From time to time I am uneasy about myself, and I give a start, prick up my ears, and cry out, "But what are you doing?" and then I refuse to think any more about it . . .

Just now, on the telephone, an enlightened Chiwawa, enlightened by the dark, dark, dark boy, sang my praises. The era of frankness is back and the cards are on the table. But, my Marguerite, how strange it all is! . . . I have the fleeting confidence of people who fall out of a clock tower and for a moment sail through the air in a comfortable fairy-world, feeling no pain anywhere . . .

Paris, June 21, 1925

Ah! la la, and la la again! And never la la enough! Your friend is very proper, believe it. She is in a fine, agreeable mess, and up to her chin, her eyes, and farther than that! Oh! the satanism of tranquil creatures—and I'm speaking of the kid Maurice. Do you want to know what he is? He's a skunk, and a this and a that, and at the same time a chic chap with a satiny hide. That's the mess I'm in . . .

Jack London to Charmian Kittredge

Reeling from the Dear John sent to him by Anna Strunsky, Jack London insisted he would continue to write about love but would never again succumb to its influence: "Henceforth I shall dream ro-

mances for other people and transmute them into bread & butter."
Almost exactly one year later, writing to Charmian Kittredge, London
noted: "I always held, always I say, that there were rare loves, such as
the Browning love, once in a generation of folks. But I little dreamed
that such a love would be my love affair. And it is, it is!"

The object of such "reverent wonder" was a handsome, adventurous woman who early took as her personal motto, "Love dangerously." Rebellious and high-spirited, Charmian Kittredge met London
on her own terms. Aware that he liked to challenge friends in contact
sports, she once engaged him in a duel, complete with foil, face mask,
protective breastplate, and a very short skirt. In front of the "Crowd,"
Jack's circle of freewheeling friends, Charmian beat him handily. He
grabbed and kissed her—and later wooed her aggressively, passionately, and epistolarily, in letter after letter, each one more extravagant
than the last. He was sure their love was fated, "inevitable." "The
hour is already too big to become anything less than the biggest," he
wrote.

Although Anna Strunsky was named correspondent in his divorce
from Bessie, it was Charmian whom he loved and whom he married
the day after the divorce became final. The couple continued to live
and love daringly, if not exactly dangerously. They traveled, wrote,
and explored the world together. They insisted that friendship and
equality were the basis for their marriage together. Of course, marriage did not always live up to this romantic ideal. Yet the man who
had publicly renounced love in his twenties went on, after marriage
to Charmian, to equally publicly celebrate it: "Sometimes," he wrote
in *The Star Rover* (1915), "I think that the story of man is the story of
the love of woman."

Oakland
Thursday, Sept. 24, 1903

Nay, nay, dear Love, not in my eyes is this love of ours a
small and impotent thing. It is the greatest and most powerful
thing in the world. The relativity of things makes it so. That I
should be glad to live for you or to die for you is proof in itself
that it means more to me than life or death, is greater, far
greater, than life or death.

That you should be the one woman to me of all women; that
my hunger for you should be greater than any hunger for food
I have ever felt; that my desire for you should bite harder than

any other desire I have ever felt for fame and fortune and such things;—all, all goes to show how big is this our love.

As I tell you repeatedly, you cannot possibly know what you mean to me. The days I do not see you are merely so many obstacles to be got over somehow before I see you. Each night as I go to bed I sigh with relief because I am one day nearer you. So it has been this week, and it is only Monday that I was with you. To-day I am jubilant, my work goes well. And I am saying to myself all the time, "To-night I shall see her! To-night I shall see her!"

My thoughts are upon you always, lingering over you always, caressing you always in a myriad ways. I wonder if you feel those caresses sometimes!

Our love small! Dear, it might be small did the love of God enter into my heart, and the belief in an eternity of living and an eternity of the unguessed joys of Paradise. But remember my philosophy of life & death, and see clearly how much my love for you & your love for me must mean to me.

Ah Love, it looms large. It fills my whole horizon. Wherever I look I feel you, see you, touch you, and know my need for you. And there is no love of God to lessen my love for you. I love you, you only & wholly. And there are no joys of a future life to make of less value the joy I know and shall know through you. I clutch for you like a miser for his gold, because you are everything and the only thing. Remember, I must die, and go into the ground, and cease to feel and joy & know; and remember, each moment I am robbed of you, each night & all nights I am turned away from you, turned out by you, give me pangs the exquisiteness of which must be measured by the knowledge that they are moments and nights lost, lost, lost forever. For my little space of life is only so long. To-morrow or next day I cease forever; and the moment I am robbed of you and the night I must be away from you will never, never come again. There is no compensation. It is all dead and utter loss.

So I live from day to day like an unwilling prodigal. I am wasting my substance and I cannot help it—nor am I wasting it even in riotous living. My fortune of life is only so large. How large I know not, but no matter how large, the sum of the

hours & moments which compose it is determined. Each lost
moment, is a moment squandered. My fortune is diminished
that much without return. And so, day by day, helplessly, I
watch the bright-minted moments flowing out and see the day
of my bankruptcy approaching which is the day when I shall
have no more moments perforce must die.

But it is even harder. For I know I am twenty-seven, at the
high-tide of my life and vigor; and I know that these wasted
moments now are the brightest-minted of all my moments.

I have not wandered through all this in order to plead for
something I have not & might have, but to show how large to
me, in the scheme of life, bulks this love of ours.

Sherwood Anderson to Eleanor Copenhaver

Sherwood Anderson, who wrote so poignantly of loneliness and
lovelessness in *Winesburg, Ohio* (1919), was himself a three-time loser
at love and marriage when he met Eleanor Copenhaver, a business
executive working on the national board of the YMCA. He was fifty-
three, she thirty-three. His third marriage was collapsing, he was
fearful about the reception of a new book, *Hello Towns!*, and he was
even more fearful about entering into another marriage: "Where love
may be life-giving," he wrote to Eleanor early in their relationship,
"marriage may be destructive. It is to me." For four years, until their
marriage in 1933, they lived apart, she traveling for business, he living anonymously in small midwestern towns, gathering material for
stories and novels. They met sporadically and often impulsively. The
one constant was his letters. He wrote once or twice a day, over 1,400
letters over the course of their relationship, and then in 1932 he
wrote her secretly each day, never mailing the letters but hiding them
so that she would find them after his death.

In the letter that follows we see the way in which Anderson's fiction
fused with his life. He is writing a story, "No God," about an older
man who has already been burned badly by a previous marriage

when he meets and falls in love with a younger woman. Here Anderson tries to understand his own confused feelings of love and fear, and writing the fiction makes him fall even more deeply in love with Eleanor, the woman who inspires it.

Sherwood and Eleanor's marriage was not fairy-tale perfect. She was deeply saddened when she realized she could not conceive a child; he suffered depression and self-hatred at those times when his work didn't sell and he had to rely on her for emotional and financial support. Painful times, depressions, readjustments, but, through it all, a kind of love that felt to him like a miracle. "To love and then not to love is a tragedy always happening to people," he wrote to Eleanor in 1929, soon after they met. "The not loving, the separation, is like a major physical operation. I feel now like a convalescent."

October 21, 1929
Washington

Dearest Eleanor—

I hope you will not be bothered by a stream of letters. I keep wanting to write you, feeling you, in some odd way, a part of what I am trying to do.

Temporarily the tone of the book has slipped. It is because now I must get ahold of something else.

The two people directly concerned are Jim LaForge and Mildred Edgerton. He is forty and she is 22.

I have now to bring her more fully into the picture, make her live in it.

Of course the only thing I can do is to go right on. I will have to see if she is willing to come to life in the pages.

I think Jim has rather.

You have said, with that turn of yours for saying things that sometimes miss but sometimes do strip pretensions bare, that I was a woman expert. Of course you must know, being a woman, that I am a muddler in that field. If a man has got, as that mill woman said, a few women between the sheets, that doesn't mean much.

In that other thing I wrote before I left home and that I repudiated later, I over-emphasized the importance of what goes on between sheets. I knew that afterwards, or at least was pretty sure of it.

Just the same it can be very lovely, bringing out the loveliness of people.

Maybe that's all we want of each other, the niceness inside, when it is inside, given.

I wish you had told me, in your letter, why I inhibit you. It would be so fine of you if you would just write it all out.

Besides being whatever I am, I am also, must be, a bit of a scientist too. Dear one, I presume I have muddled so much and so long in the world of feeling that just now I want to see.

I mean I want people to tell me things.

I have been trying here, when I have seen people, to stand a little aside. I have tried to say to myself—"Now be nice. Don't condemn people or judge them. Stop, look and listen."

Perhaps I am trying not to be hit by any more trains.

If I knew more about what you felt about me, I surely would know more of what Mildred felt about Jim.

He takes women but is afraid of them. He has had a marriage that turned out badly. "There is no use," he thinks, "saying, 'It was her fault or my fault.' "

His wife is dead. He has been living alone for a long time. He sees this woman Mildred.

He is drawn to her but is suspicious of his own feeling. If, being with her outdoors, the landscape becomes suddenly lovelier because she is there, he remembers that it was once so with him because of the presence of another woman.

Look out.

Am I getting into another mess of lies?

I wish you were here so I could talk to you. I know you could tell me a lot. I shall just have to work on and perhaps, when I see you again, seeing you will make me know whether I am going right or wrong.

There is a kind of intelligence down in you and is deeper seated than in anyone else I know.

Is that an illusion?

Franz Kafka to Milena Jesenská

Kafka had a knack for falling in love with one woman when he was engaged to marry another—a good way to ensure that he would never marry. Technically, he was still engaged to Julie Wohryzek, a woman he met in a tuberculosis sanitarium, when he was approached by the twenty-four-year-old Milena Jesenská, a writer who hoped to translate his stories into Czech. At the time of their meeting, Milena was unhappily married to a doctor but insisted she was not ready for divorce. Perhaps because she was safely married, Kafka felt free to express his love for her in a way he could not to his other lovers. "I am just walking around here between the lines [of my letter], under the light of your eyes, in the breath of your mouth as in a beautiful happy day." For a time, Franz Kafka was in love again.

In this early letter to Milena, he relates his past failures at love, perhaps hoping to scare her off. Milena was convinced she could weather his moods and his bouts of misogyny; she even believed she could cure him of his depressions and uncertainties and make him a happy man. Kafka was tempted by her strength and sureness, but then fell back into his more accustomed despair. Although in love with her, he broke off the relationship decisively, shortly before his death. "Love," Kafka once said, "has as few problems as a motorcar. The only problems are the driver, the passengers, and the road."

Monday

Now the explanation promised yesterday:

I don't want to (Milena, do help me! Do understand more than I say!) I don't want to (this isn't stammering) come to Vienna, because I couldn't stand the mental strain. I'm mentally ill, the disease of the lung is nothing but an overflowing of my mental disease. I've been ill like this since the 4, 5 years of my first two engagements (at first I couldn't explain to myself the cheerfulness of your last letter, only later did the explanation occur to me, I keep forgetting it: You're so young, after all, perhaps not yet 25, possibly only 23. I'm 37, almost 38, almost a short generation older, almost white-haired from the past nights and headaches).

I won't spread out before you the long story with its veritable forests of details of which I'm still afraid, like a child, only without the child's power of forgetting. What the three engagements had in common was that everything was all my fault, quite undoubtedly my fault. Both girls I made unhappy and—I'm talking here only about the first, about the second I cannot speak, she's sensitive, and any word, even the kindest, would be the most appalling offence to her, something I understand—and actually only because through her (who, had I insisted, would perhaps have sacrificed herself) I couldn't become lastingly happy, calm, determined, capable of marriage, although I had repeatedly and quite voluntarily assured her of it, although I sometimes loved her desperately, although I know nothing more desirable than marriage in itself. Almost five years I battered at her (or, if you prefer, at myself)—well, fortunately, she was unbreakable, Prussian-Jewish mixture, a strong invincible mixture. I wasn't all that robust, after all she only had to suffer, whereas I battered *and* suffered.

~

Enough, I can't write any more, explain any more, although I'm only at the beginning, although I should describe the mental disease, should mention other reasons for not coming. A telegram has arrived: "Meeting place Karlsbad, eighth, please communicate by letter." I confess, when I opened it, it made a terrible face, although behind it stands the most unselfish, most quiet, modest being and although it all goes back to my wanting it. I can't make this clear just now, for I can't refer to a description of the disease. This much is certain at the moment: I will leave here on Monday. From time to time I glance at the telegram and can hardly read it, it's as though a secret were written underneath, blurring the writing on top, and reading: Travel via Vienna! A clear command but without any of the terror of commands.

I won't do it, even from the practical point of view it's senseless to take the long route via Linz and then even farther via Vienna instead of the short one via Munich. I'm making a test: On the balcony is a sparrow which expects me to throw some bread from the table on to the balcony, instead of which I drop the bread beside me on the floor in the middle of the room. It stands outside and from there in the semi-darkness sees the food of its life, terribly tempting, it's shaking itself, it's more here than there, but here is the dark and beside the bread am I, the secret power. Nevertheless it hops over the threshold, a few more hops, but farther it doesn't dare go and in sudden fright it flies away. But with what energy does this wretched bird abound, after a while it's back again, inspects the situation, I scatter a little more to make it easier for it and—if I hadn't intentionally-unintentionally (this is how the secret powers work) chased it away with a sudden movement, it would have got the bread.

The fact is that my vacation expires toward the end of June and that as a transition—it's also getting very hot here, which in itself wouldn't disturb me much—I'd like to be somewhere else in the country. She too wants to leave, now we're supposed to meet there, I'll stay a few days and then perhaps a few more days in Konstantinsbad with my parents, then I'll go to Prague. When I survey these journeys and compare them with the condition of my head, I feel much as Napoleon would have felt if, on preparing his plans for the Russian campaign, he had known the precise outcome at the time. When, some time ago, your first letter arrived, I think it was shortly before the planned wedding (the plans for which incidentally were exclusively *my* doing) I was pleased and showed it to her. Later—no, nothing more and I won't tear up this letter again, we seem to have certain qualities in common except that I haven't a stove at hand and from a sign or two am almost afraid that I once sent a letter to the girl in question on the back of one of these unfinished letters.

But all this is immaterial, even without the telegram I wouldn't have been able to come to Vienna, on the contrary the telegram works rather as an argument in favour of the journey. I shall certainly not come, but on the other hand should I—it won't happen—to my own terrible surprise arrive in Vienna, then I'll need neither breakfast nor supper, but rather a stretcher on which I can lie down for a while.

Farewell, it won't be an easy week here.

Yours
F

If you'd like to write me a word, Karlsbad, *Poste Restante.* No, not till Prague.

What sort of enormous schools are these in which you teach, 200 students, 50 students. I'd love to have a window-seat in the last row for an hour, then I'd renounce any meeting with you (which indeed won't take place anyhow) renounce all journeys and—enough, this white paper, that won't come to an end, burns one's eyes out, and this is why one writes.

Ernest Hemingway to Mary Welsh

The loves of Ernest Hemingway are almost as much a feature of the twentieth-century American literary landscape as his novels. We know that he had four wives; that he liked to have a new one waiting in the wings before he left the previous one; that, later, he said he regretted ever having left his first wife; that he had one son by his first marriage, two by his second.

Less superficial features of his life come through letters such as this one to Mary Welsh, who would become the fourth and final "Mrs. Hemingway." There is a stark emotionalism here, a flagrant declaration of love, an almost childlike beseeching that love will be returned in kind.

The letter was written from Hemmeres, Germany, where Hemingway was traveling as a war correspondent with the troops responsible for the liberation of Paris. At the time, he was married to Martha Gellhorn, a fine war correspondent and novelist herself; but by 1944 it was abundantly clear to both that their marriage was over. He disliked the way she was more dedicated to her writing than to him. When Martha shipped out to Europe as the only passenger on a cargo ship filled with dynamite, Ernest waited in New York for flight orders to the front and contemplated making some changes in his life.

Mary Welsh was the name of that change. She was an attractive, thirty-six-year-old American working as a reporter at the London Bureau of *Time, Life,* and *Fortune,* unhappily married, and having an affair with Irwin Shaw, an acquaintance of Hemingway's. Hemingway entered a London restaurant frequented by the foreign press, saw Shaw with an attractive blonde, and came over to his table. When Shaw introduced Hemingway to Mary Welsh, Hemingway asked her to lunch. To her companion's annoyance, Welsh accepted. After a car accident left Hemingway with a severe concussion and injured knees, he was forced to postpone his tour of duty as an observer in Europe and used the time to begin a romance. He immediately recognized that she was the kind of tough, competent woman that he liked and desperately needed to keep his increasingly erratic moods, severe depressions, and chronic alcoholism in check.

After Hemingway left for Europe, their letters cemented what began in London. He was in love again, and so was she. They anticipated the liberation of Paris and appreciated the personal symbolism of the historic event: what better place for a reunion of two war correspondents who had been scarred in love's battles? She joined him in Paris. They stayed in Room 31 at the Ritz, where, as Mary Welsh wrote later, they lived "on little besides Lanson Brut champagne and the wonder of being together again."

The spelling errors are all, inimitably, Hemingway's.

September 13th [1944] after dinner

My Beloved:

This is only a note to tell you how much I love you. We have had dinner and there was nothing spiritous to drink—the celebration haveing out-cleaned us yest. and no new alcoholic centers taken. There are lots of troops around tonight and can sleep without challenging (or throwing one's true love out of bed). Stevie is writing his girl a masterful letter about how American Women Do Not Appreciate What A Soldier—A Man

Trained to Kill—goes through and Expects in Return—and reading me excerpts and I am just happy and purring like an old jungle beast because I love you and you love me. I hope you were quite serous Pickle because I am as committed as an armoured column in a narrow defile where no vehicle can turn and without parallel roads. I am committed horse, foot, and guns—so take good care of you for me, and for us and we will fight the best one we, or anyone, could ever fight—for what we spoke about—and against loneliness, chickenshit, death, injustice, un-understanding sloth (our old enemy), substitutions, all fear, and many other worthless things—and in favour of you sitting up straight in bed lovelier than any figure head on the finest, tallest ship that ever drew on canvas or heeled over to a wind; and in favour of kindness, permanence, loveing each other and fine loveing nights, and days, in bed. Pickle I love you very much and am your partner, friend, and true love.

It is not so cold tonight but the poor dog is so sad. I try to explain about things to him but the dog knows he should handle the cattle and the pigs and loves his master. He knows I'm good but all his world is gone to pieces and he lies out in the barn and is heart-broken. I've had the cows milked so they do not hurt and fed the cat. But it is very sad about the dog. Have had the place all cleaned up (though that will not last)— but I wish the people would come back and take care of their dog. They are worthless and selfish to go away like that and don't deserve such a fine dog. They only had two books—one on Wild Beasts of Germany—a nice book—and one on the Olympic games in Berlin in 1936. Not a nice book but with some lovely pictures. Have read them both and cursed the Brazilian tonight to his face for a fool and an imposition. He is like a little child who wants to ride in a racing motor car and then wants the car to stop in the race so he can make pee-pee.

Dearest Mary. . . . Please love me very much and always take care of me Small Friend the way Small Friends take care of Big Friends high in the sky and shining and beautiful. Oh Mary darling I love you very much.

NOTES

INTRODUCTION

PAGE 1— *"The moment my eyes"*—Wharton is here quoting Emerson. See *The Letters of Edith Wharton*, ed. R. W. B. Lewis and Nancy Lewis (New York: Charles Scribner's Sons, 1988), p. 12. See also R. W. B. Lewis, *Edith Wharton: A Biography* (New York: Harper & Row, 1975).

PAGE 1— *"Do you want"; "I vowed I wouldn't"*—Edith Wharton to W. Morton Fullerton, June 8, 1908, *Letters of Edith Wharton*, pp. 150, 151.

PAGE 1— *"I am like one"*—Wharton to Fullerton, July 1, 1908, *Letters of Edith Wharton*, p. 158.

PAGE 2— *"I don't know"*—Wharton to Fullerton, Mid-April 1910, *Letters of Edith Wharton*, p. 207.

PAGE 2— *"My life was better"*—Wharton to Fullerton, Mid-April 1910, *Letters of Edith Wharton*, p. 208.

PAGE 2— *"I enclose"*—Wharton to Fullerton, 11 May 1914, *Letters of Edith Wharton*, p. 325.

PAGE 2— *"Mrs. Wharton begs"*—Anna Bahlmann to W. Morton Fullerton, 5 September 1915, *Letters of Edith Wharton*, p. 360.

PAGE 3— *If literature is*—The most sophisticated analysis of "the letter as literature, literature as a letter" is Linda S. Kauffman's *Discourses of Desire: Gender, Genre, and Epistolary Fictions* (Ithaca: Cornell University Press, 1986).

PAGE 4— *Once in 1924*—*Letters of Edith Wharton*, p. 3.

PAGE 4— *"I dreamed"*—Quoted in James Nagel and Henry Serrano Villard, *Hemingway in Love and War: The Lost Diary of Agnes von Kurowsky, Her Letters, and Correspondence of Ernest Hemingway* (Boston: Northeastern University Press, 1989), p. 120.

PAGE 4— *"Writing has always"*—*Hemingway in Love and War*, p. 119.

PAGE 5— *"a love so big"*—*The Master Letters of Emily Dickinson*, ed. R. W. Franklin (Amherst, MA: Amherst College Press, 1986), Letter 2 (early 1861), p. 22.

PAGE 5— *"If you saw"*—*The Master Letters of Emily Dickinson*, Letter 3 (summer 1861), p. 32.

PAGE 6— *"For I do love"*—*The Love Letters of Mark Twain*, ed. Dixon Wecter (New York: Harper & Brothers, 1949), p. 79. *Cf.* Leland Krauth, "Self-Portraiture in Samuel Clemens' Courtship," unpublished paper.

PAGE 7—*As Ross Chambers*—Ross Chambers, *Story and Situation: Narrative Seduction and the Power of Fiction* (Minneapolis, MN: University of Minnesota Press, 1984).

PAGE 7— *"Writing," as Jean Cocteau*—Quoted in Joseph Barry, *French Lovers: From Héloïse and Abelard to Beauvoir and Sartre* (New York: Arbor House, 1987), p. 278.

PAGE 7—*As Carolyn Heilbrun*—Carolyn Heilbrun, *Writing a Woman's Life* (New York: W. W. Norton Company, 1988).

PAGE 8—*Their love affair*—*Letters of Edith Wharton*, p. 17.

PAGE 8—*"should write better"*—Wharton to Fullerton, August 26, 1908, *Letters of Edith Wharton*, p. 162.

PAGE 8—*"Your sonnet is"*—Oscar Wilde to Lord Alfred Douglas, January 1893[?], in *Selected Letters of Oscar Wilde*, ed. Rupert Hart-Davis (Oxford: Oxford University Press, 1979), p. 107.

PAGE 9—*"I beg you"*—Quoted in Jack Lindsay, *Daily Life in Roman Egypt* (New York: Barnes & Noble Books, 1963), p. 30.

PAGE 9—*"God knows when"*—The lover remains anonymous. See *The Letters of John Cheever*, ed. Benjamin Cheever (New York: Simon & Schuster, 1988), p. 337.

PAGE 9—*As Roland Barthes*—Roland Barthes, *A Lover's Discourse: Fragments*, trans. Richard Howard (New York: Farrar, Straus & Giroux, 1978), pp. 13–17.

PAGE 9—*"These thousands of lonely soldiers"*—John Steinbeck to Gwyndolyn Steinbeck, Fall 1943 and July 1949, *Steinbeck: A Life in Letters*, ed. Elaine Steinbeck and Robert Wallsten (New York: Viking Press, 1975), pp. 256–257, 263–264.

PAGE 9—*"Parting is not"*—John Steinbeck to Elaine Scott, July 23, 1949, *Steinbeck*, p. 368.

PAGE 9—*"I look down the tracks"*—Zelda to F. Scott Fitzgerald, Spring 1919 or 1920, quoted in Nancy Milford, *Zelda: A Biography* (New York: Harper & Row, 1970), p. 76.

PAGE 10—*"I wish I had"*—Nathaniel Hawthorne to Sophia Peabody, December 5, c. 1839, *The Hawthorne Centenary Edition, Volume XV: The Letters: 1813–1843*, ed. Thomas Woodson, L. Neal Smith, and Norman Holmes Pease (Columbus: Ohio State University Press, 1984), p. 69.

PAGE 10—*"I love you laughingly"*—Quoted in Anaïs Nin, *Henry and June* (San Diego, CA: Harcourt Brace Jovanovich, 1986), pp. 84–85.

PAGE 10—*"The hour is already"*—Jack London to Charmian Kittredge, June 1903, in *The Letters of Jack London, Volume I: 1896–1905*, ed. Earle Labor, Robert C. Leitz III, and I. Milo Shepard (Stanford: Stanford University Press, 1988), p. 368.

PAGE 11—*"I may be thinking"*—quoted in Robert E. Hemenway, *Zora Neale Hurston: A Literary Biography* (Chicago: University of Illinois Press, 1977), p. 308.

PAGE 11—*"Here was beauty"*—quoted in Cynthia Earl Kerman and Richard Eldridge, *The Lives of Jean Toomer: A Hunger for Wholeness* (Baton Rouge, LA: Louisiana State University Press, 1987), p. 124.

PAGE 11—*John Steinbeck tells*—John Steinbeck to Elaine Scott, August 16, 1949, *Steinbeck*, pp. 376–377.

PAGE 11—*Elizabeth Barrett writes*—Elizabeth Barrett to Robert Browning, January 1846, in *The Letters of Robert Browning and Elizabeth Barrett Browning, 1845–1846: Volume One* (Cambridge, MA: Harvard University Press, 1969), p. 194.

PAGE 11—*"You have no idea"*—Conrad Aiken to Clarissa Lorenz, November 9–14, 1926, *Selected Letters to Conrad Aiken*, ed. Joseph Killorin (New Haven, CT: Yale University Press, 1978), p. 123.

PAGE 12—*"But I see you"*—Robert Schumann to Clara Schumann, 1838, quoted in *Love Letters*, ed. Antonia Fraser (1976; rpt. London: Barrie and Jenkins, 1976), p. 64.

PAGE 12—*"I began observing"*—Conrad Aiken to Clarissa ["Joan"] Lorenz, November 7, 1926, *Selected Letters of Conrad Aiken,* p. 122.

PAGE 12—*"If I am moving"*—Napoléon Bonaparte to Josephine, 10 Germinal, Year IV (1796), quoted in *Love Letters,* pp. 73–74.

PAGE 12—*"Love that does not"*—Katherine Anne Porter to William Goyen, June 19, 1951, quoted in Joan Givner, *Katherine Anne Porter: A Life* (New York: Simon & Schuster, 1982), p. 379.

PAGE 13—*"While I sit here"*—Quoted in Mary Kathleen Benet, *Writers in Love: Katherine Mansfield, George Eliot, Colette, and the Men They Lived With* (Boston: G. K. Hall, 1984), p. 50.

PAGE 13—*"I want a brighter"*—John Keats to Fanny Brawne, July 3, 1819, *The Complete Poetical Works of John Keats,* ed. Horace Scudder (Cambridge: The Riverside Press, 1899), p. 131.

PAGE 13—*In the best love letters*—Janet Gurkin Altman, in *Epistolarity: Approaches to a Form* (Columbus, OH: Ohio University Press, 1982), pp. 186–87, notes the paradoxical nature of letters, including the ways in which letters are, simultaneously, both a bridge and a barrier between correspondents.

PAGE 13—*"You are the voice"*—Wallace Stevens to Elsie Moll, February 15, 1901, *The Letters of Wallace Stevens,* ed. Holly Stevens (New York: Alfred A. Knopf, 1966), p. 131.

PAGE 13—*Gertrude Stein explored*—Professor Linda Wagner-Martin, who is currently writing a biography of Gertrude Stein (forthcoming, William Morrow Publishers), generously showed me the poem that she discovered in one of Gertrude Stein's notebooks, entitled "Why I Do Not Live in America, 1928." The poem is dated July–August 1928 (Belley). Quoted by permission of the Beinecke Library and the Estate of Gertrude Stein.

PAGE 13—*"There is never a day"*—Fred Vaughan to Walt Whitman, November 16, 1874, in *Calamus Lovers: Walt Whitman's Working Class Camerados,* ed. Charles Shively (San Francisco: Gay Sunshine Press, 1987), p. 50.

PAGE 14—*"I don't know whether"*—Quoted in Joan Givner, *Katherine Anne Porter: A Life,* p. 203.

PAGE 14—*The young poet Anne Gray Harvey*—Anne Sexton to W. D. Snodgrass, April 1959; to Philip Legler, May 4, 1966, quoted in *Anne Sexton: A Self-Portrait in Letters,* ed. Linda Gray Sexton and Lois Ames (Boston: Houghton Mifflin, 1977), pp. 71 and 293–294.

PAGE 14—*"You carry away"*—Quoted in *Henry and June: From the Unexpurgated Diary of Anaïs Nin* (New York: Harcourt Brace Jovanovich, 1986), p. 15.

PAGE 14—*"to excess, to distraction"*—Letter of November 13, 1774, quoted in *Love Letters,* pp. 79, 186.

PAGE 14—*"I have met with women"*—John Keats to Fanny Brawne, July 8, 1819, *The Complete Poetical Works,* p. 382.

PAGE 14—*"Writers make love"*—*Henry and June: From the Unexpurgated Diary of Anaïs Nin,* p. 54.

PAGE 15—*"The man I once"; "Too wretched to exert myself—"* Harriet Shelley's letters of November 20, 1814 and November ?9, 1816, in *The Letters of Percy Bysshe Shelley,* ed. Frederick L. Jones (Oxford: Oxford at the Clarendon Press, 1964), I, 421, 520.

PAGE 15—*"The woman in me"*—Jack London to Anna Strunsky, February 11, 1902, *Letters of Jack London,* p. 278.

PAGE 15—*"Maybe I am having"*—Henry Miller to Brenda Venus, October 1976, *Dear, Dear Brenda: The Love Letters of Henry Miller to Brenda Venus;* text by Brenda Venus, ed. Gerald Seth Sindell (New York: William Morrow, 1986), p. 77.

PAGE 16— *"horrors at night"*—Ernest Hemingway to Pauline Pfeiffer, December 3, 1926, *Ernest Hemingway: Selected Letters, 1917–1961,* ed. Carlos Baker (New York: Charles Scribner's Sons, 1981), p. 234.

PAGE 17— *"Can you arrange"*—Edith Wharton to Morton Fullerton, November 27, 1909, *Letters of Edith Wharton,* p. 193.

PAGE 18— *"like tearing off"*—Quoted in Candace Serena Falk, *Love, Anarchy, and Emma Goldman* (New Brunswick, NJ: Rutgers University Press, 1984), p. 227.

PAGE 19— *"should always write"*—Quoted in *Ernest Hemingway,* p. x.

PAGE 19— *"Your heart beat"*—Herman Melville to Nathaniel Hawthorne, November 17?, 1851, *The Letters of Herman Melville,* ed. Merrell R. Davis and William H. Gilman (New Haven, CT: Yale University Press, 1960), p. 142.

PAGE 19—*Molly Hallock Foote*—Quoted in Carroll Smith-Rosenberg, "The Female World of Love and Ritual: Relations Between Women in Nineteenth-Century America," in *Disorderly Conduct: Visions of Gender in Victorian America* (New York: Oxford University Press, 1985), pp. 55, 58, and 62–63.

PAGE 20— *"In our advancing years"*—Quoted in Nigel Nicolson, *Portrait of a Marriage* (New York: Bantam Books, 1973), p. 250.

PAGE 20— *"What am I doing?"*—Colette to Marguerite Moreno, June 11, 1925, *Letters from Colette,* trans. Robert Phelps (New York: Farrar Straus & Giroux, 1980), p. 89.

PART 1. FALLING IN LOVE

PAGES 23–24— *"For about two thousand"; "Never before these"; "Sappho . . . broke"*—Sappho to Anactoria. The quotations come from *Sappho: One Hundred Lyrics by Bliss Carman* (London: Chatto and Windus, 1907), pp. viii, ix, and xiii.

PAGE 25— *"die at her feet"*—*The Love Letters of Mr. H. and Miss R., 1775–1779,* ed. Gilbert Burgess (Chicago: Stone and Kimball, 1895).

PAGE 28— *"poor Rice"*—John Keats to Fanny Brawne. James Rice (1792–1832), lawyer, was a close friend of Keats; Rice also suffered frequent ill health.

PAGES 29–31—*Nathaniel Hawthorne and Sophia Peabody*—See, Arlin Turner, *Nathaniel Hawthorne, A Biography* (New York: Oxford University Press, 1980).

PAGE 32— *"What seems to me"*—Quoted in *The Letters of Gustave Flaubert, 1830–1857,* ed. Francis Steegmuller (Cambridge, MA: Belknap Press of Harvard University Press, 1980), p. xi.

PAGE 34— *"the kind Ariosto speaks of"*—Flaubert probably means Aretino, who wrote erotic sonnets.

PAGES 34–35— *The Love Letters of Juliette Drouet to Victor Hugo,* ed. Louis Gimbaud, trans. Lady Theodora Davidson (New York: McBride, Nast & Co., 1914).

PAGE 36— *"Wilde wanted"*—and subsequent quotes from Richard Ellmann, *Oscar Wilde* (New York: Knopf, 1988), pp. 384, 438.

PAGE 37—*Hyacinthus*—Oscar Wilde to Lord Alfred Douglas. Wilde refers to a young Greek man loved by Zephyrus, the West Wind, the first man in Greek mythology to love another man. Apollo also fell in love with Hyacinthus, but one day killed him accidentally when the jealous Zephyrus blew into Hyacinthus's path a discus Apollo had thrown. The hyacinth first grew where the young man's blood fell.

PAGE 38— *"Carried out"*—Quoted in John P. Nettl, *Rosa Luxemburg* (London: Oxford University Press, 1966), p. 779.

PAGE 39—*Kautsky*—Rosa Luxemburg to Leo Jogiches. Luxemburg refers to Karl Kautsky, an influential German socialist theorist. A staunch Marxist, he was author of much of the "Erfurt Program" (1891), by which the German Social Democratic Party officially upheld revolutionary Marxism. He later condemned the Bolshevik Revolution as antidemocratic and lost influence after World War I.

PAGE 41— *"He was youth"*—Quoted in *The Letters of Jack London,* Vol. 1, ed. Earle Labor, Robert C. Leitz, III, and I. Milo Shepard (Stanford, CA: Stanford University Press, 1988), p. xviii.

PAGE 44—*Liguori*—Edith Wharton to Morton Fullerton. Wharton compares the misleading moral argument she is making to that of the eighteenth-century bishop familiarly known as Saint Alphonsus Liguori, well-known for this tactic.

PAGE 44— *"J'ai tué six loups"*—Wharton to Fullerton. The phrase is found in an offhand note from the King of Spain, absent on a hunt, to the Queen, in Victor Hugo's *Ruy Blas* (1838), act 3, scene 3: *"Madame, il fait grand vent et j'ai tué six loups* (it is very windy and I have killed six wolves). *Carlos."*

PAGE 45— *"How charming is divine"*—Wharton to Fullerton. From John Milton's *Comus* (1637).

PAGE 48— *"I should like"*—Quoted in *Letters of Wallace Stevens,* ed. Holly Stevens (New York: Knopf, 1981), p. 79.

PAGE 49— *"Harps Hung Up in Babylon"; "Though palmer bound"*—Wallace Stevens to Elsie Moll. Stevens refers to poems by Arthur Willis Colton (New York: Henry Holt, 1907).

PAGE 51— *"You came—like Summer"*—Quoted in *Correspondence of F. Scott Fitzgerald,* ed. Matthew J. Bruccoli and Margaret M. Duggan (New York: Random House, 1980), pp. 44–45.

PAGE 52— *"I love Mrs. Woolf"*—and subsequent quotes from *The Letters of Vita Sackville-West to Virginia Woolf,* ed. Louise DeSalvo and Mitchell A. Leaska (New York: Morrow, 1985), pp. 47, 217.

PAGE 52— *"mad and irresponsible"*—Quoted in Nigel Nicolson, *Portrait of a Marriage* (New York: Bantam Books, 1973), p. 112.

PAGE 54— *"is like watching"*—and subsequent quotes from *Loving Letters from Ogden Nash: A Family Album,* introduced and selected by Linell Nash Smith (Boston: Little, Brown, 1990), pp. vii, viii, 4, 17, 95.

PAGE 55—*Nelson Doubleday*—Ogden Nash to Frances Leonard. This is the publisher for whom Nash was working.

PAGE 57— *"I have loved"*—and subsequent quotes from *The Lives of Jean Toomer: A Hunger for Wholeness* by Cynthia Earl Kerman and Richard Eldridge (Baton Rouge, LA: Louisiana State University, 1987), pp. 193–194, epigraph, 199, and 205.

PAGE 61— *"wild and violent"*—and subsequent quotes from *Steinbeck: A Life in Letters,* edited Elaine A. Steinbeck and Robert Wallsten (New York: Viking Press, 1975), pp. 328, 329, and 686.

PAGE 62—*the skirts had arrived*—Steinbeck had sent as presents Chinese men's ceremonial skirts.

PAGE 64— *"Death is the stone into"*—From *Pablo Neruda: Five Decades. A Selection (Poems: 1925–1970),* ed. and trans. Ben Belitt (New York: Grove Press, 1974), p. 217.

PAGE 65— *"the only homosexuals I knew"*—Quoted in *The Letters of John Cheever,* ed. Benjamin Cheever (New York: Simon & Schuster, 1988), p. 16.

PART 2. LOVE'S INFINITE VARIETY

PAGES 69–71—*Marcus Aurelius to Fronto*—Reprinted and discussed in *Technologies of the Self: A Seminar with Michel Foucault*, edited by Luther H. Martin, Huck Gutman, and Patrick H. Hutton (Amherst, MA: University of Massachusetts Press, 1988).

PAGE 71—*"If you see my name"*—and subsequent quotes from Jeanne Boydston, Mary Kelley, and Anne Margolis, *The Limits of Sisterhood: The Beecher Sisters on Women's Rights and Woman's Sphere* (Chapel Hill, NC: University of North Carolina Press, 1988), pp. 48, 52, 53.

PAGE 74—*"She poured out"*—Quoted in *The Love Letters of Mark Twain*, p. 15.

PAGE 75—*"Her voice, her nobility"*—and subsequent quote from *Letters of Anton Chekhov*, ed. Simon Karlinsky; trans. Michael Henry Heim (New York: Harper & Row, 1973), pp. 360, 2.

PAGE 77—*"the Japanese"*—The Russo-Japanese War had just begun.

PAGE 78—*"How vain it seems"*—and subsequent quotes from Lillian Faderman, *Surpassing the Love of Men: Romantic Friendship and Love Between Women from the Renaissance to the Present* (New York: Morrow, 1981), pp. 174–175.

PAGE 80—*"with the sweep"*—Quoted in Candace Serena Falk, *Love, Anarchy, and Emma Goldman* (New Brunswick, NJ: Rutgers University Press, 1984), p. 3; see also, *The Feminist Companion to Literature in English: Women Writers from the Middle Ages to the Present*, ed. Virginia Blain, Patricia Clements, and Isobel Grundy (New Haven, CT: Yale University Press, 1990), pp. 435–446.

PAGE 81—*"How can I"*—and subsequent quote from Francis Steegmuller, *Cocteau: A Biography* (Boston: Little, Brown, 1970), pp. 3–4, 155.

PAGE 83—*"I loved him tremendously"*—Quoted in Alphonse Juilland, *A Célinian Trove: Elizabeth Craig's Jewelry Box* (Stanford, CA: Montparnasse Publications, 1991), p. 57. I am grateful to Professor Juilland for his assistance and generosity.

PAGE 83—*"didn't want to be"*—and subsequent quotes from *Céline: Letters to Elizabeth*, ed. Alphonse Juilland (Stanford, CA: Montparnasse Publications, 1990), pp. 7, 14–15.

PAGE 86—*"How pungent"*—Quoted in Phyllis Rose, *Parallel Lives: Five Victorian Marriages* (New York: Knopf, 1983), p. 255.

PAGE 87—*"O Carissima mia"*—and subsequent quotes from Lillian Faderman, *Surpassing the Love of Men: Romantic Friendship and Love Between Women from the Renaissance to the Present* (New York: Morrow, 1981), pp. 164–166.

PAGE 92—*"The ears being"*—Quoted in Richard Ellmann, *Yeats: The Man and the Masks* (New York: Macmillan, 1948), p. 159.

PAGE 93—*"That play is going"*—Maud Gonne to William Butler Yeats—She is probably referring to *The Player Queen*.

PAGE 94—*"You are the most wonderful"*—and subsequent quote from Philip Callow, *Son and Lover: The Young D. H. Lawrence* (Chicago: Elephant Paperbacks, 1975), pp. 182, 189.

PAGE 96—*"I behaves well"*—and subsequent quote from Arturo Sergio Visca, ed., *Correspondencia Íntima de Delmira Agustini y Tres Versiones de "La Inefable"* (Montevideo, Uruguay: Biblioteca Nacional, 1978). Special thanks to Silvia Tandeciarz for her translation and for information about Agustini.

PAGE 99—*"We talk, fencingly"*—and subsequent quotes from *Henry and June: From the Unexpurgated Diary of Anaïs Nin* (New York: Harcourt Brace Jovanovich, 1986), pp. 7, 14, 274.

PAGE 101—*"I am left alone"*—Quoted from *Selections from George Eliot's Letters*, ed. Gordon Haight (New Haven, CT: Yale University Press, 1985), p. 533.

PAGE 102— *"varium et mutabile semper"*—"Woman is ever fickle and changeable." In Virgil's *Aeneid,* this argument was made to Aeneas as justification for leaving Dido. However, the lovelorn Dido committed suicide by fire after Aeneas departed.

PAGE 102—*Beatrice*—Eliot signs with the name of the woman celebrated by Dante as the ideal of beauty and goodness. She had been reading Dante with Cross for some months.

PAGE 103— *"You tell me"*—Quoted in Candace Serena Falk, *Love, Anarchy, and Emma Goldman* (New Brunswick, NJ: Rutgers University Press, 1983), p. 199.

PAGE 105—*the Mercury. Nathan*—H. L. Mencken to Sara Haardt. In 1924 Mencken founded the *American Mercury* with G. J. Nathan. He was its editor until 1933.

PAGE 105— *"the Borglum affair"*—Mencken refers to the sculptor who did the heads of the Presidents on Mount Rushmore. He had begun working on a sculptured procession of Lee and his staff and soldiers in the Stone Mountain Memorial in Georgia. Borglum abandoned the project when those backing it refused to pay him more than originally agreed.

PAGE 106— *"Isaac Goldberg now proposes"*—The book was published as *The Man Mencken: A Biographical and Critical Survey.*

PAGE 107— *"He had taken me"*—Quoted in *Dear, Dear Brenda: The Love Letters of Henry Miller to Brenda Venus,* text by Brenda Venus, edited by Gerald Seth Sindell (New York: Morrow, 1986).

PAGE 110— *"Whenever I see"*—and subsequent quote from *Selected Letters of Charles Baudelaire: The Conquest of Solitude,* trans. and ed. Rosemary Lloyd (Chicago: University of Chicago Press, 1986), pp. xxi, xxii.

PAGE 113— *"I believe it a duty"*—and subsequent quotes from *Love Letters of the Bachelor Poet, James Whitcomb Riley to Miss Elizabeth Kahle* (Boston: The Bibliophile Society, 1922), pp. 11, 14, 158.

PAGE 116— *"so nice, and"*—and subsequent quotes from Michael Holroyd, *Bernard Shaw. Volume I. 1856–1898: The Search for Love* (New York: Random House, 1988), pp. 355, 348, 369.

PAGE 118— *"Arriving at school"*—Quoted in *The Brontës: Life and Letters,* ed. Clement Shorter (London: Hodder and Stoughton, 1958), I, p. 255.

PAGE 119—*Tantalus*—In Greek mythology, Tantalus, as punishment for trying to test the wisdom of the gods, was forced to stand up to his chin in water in Hades; whenever he bent to slake his burning thirst, the pool dried up.

PAGE 120—Cf. *The Letters of Herman Melville,* ed. Merrell R. Davis and William H. Gilman (New Haven: Yale University Press, 1960).

PAGE 122— *"most noble Festus"*—Acts 26:24–25: "And as he thus spake for himself, Festus said with a loud voice, Paul, thou art beside thyself; much learning doth make thee mad. But he said, I am not mad, most noble Festus; but speak forth the words of truth and soberness."

PAGE 122— *"Krakens"*—a huge, mythical fish

PAGE 123— *"Herman"*—The one occasion in his letters, except those to members of his family, when Melville signs his first name only.

PAGE 123—Cf. *Lydia Maria Child: Selected Letters,* ed. Milton Meltzer and Patricia Holland (Amherst: University of Massachusetts Press, 1982).

PAGE 126— *"Most every author"*—and subsequent quotes from *Five O'Clock Angel: Letters of Tennessee Williams to Maria St. Just, 1948–1982* (New York: Penguin Books, 1990), pp. ix, xviii, 7.

PAGE 128—Cf. *George Sand: In Her Own Words,* trans. and ed. Joseph Barry (New York: Doubleday, 1979).

PAGE 130—*Elizabeth Ramsey to Louisa Picquet,* see *Black Women in Nineteenth-Century American Life,* ed. Bert James Loewenberg and Ruth Bogin (University Park, PA: Pennsylvania State University Press, 1976), pp. 54–63.

PAGE 133—*"Susy was a rare"*—Quoted in *Mark Twain's Letters,* Vol. II, ed. Albert Bigelow Paine (New York: Harper & Row, 1917), p. 635.

PAGE 133—*"I didn't know"*—Quoted from *The Love Letters of Mark Twain,* ed. Dixon Wector (New York: Harper & Row, 1949), p. 15.

PAGE 139—*"Rats live on"*—Quoted from *Anne Sexton: A Self-Portrait in Letters* by Linda Gray Sexton and Lois Aimes (Boston: Houghton Mifflin, 1977).

PART 3. ABSENCE

PAGE 143—*"I began to think"*—Quoted from *The Letters of Abelard and Heloise,* trans. Betty Radice (London: Penguin Books, 1974), p. 15.

PAGE 145—*"wooing was aimless"*—and subsequent quote from *The Permanent Goethe,* ed. Thomas Mann, trans. Norbert Guterman (New York: Dial Press, 1948), pp. xxxvii and 598.

PAGE 146—*"Eyes that can feel"*—Quoted in T. J. Reed, *Goethe* (New York: Oxford University Press, 1984), p. 42.

PAGE 148—*"That little puss-in-boots"*—Quoted in Desmond Seward, *Napoleon's Family* (New York: Viking, 1986), p. 30.

PAGE 148—*"A kiss on your heart"*—Quoted in Correlli Barnett, *Bonaparte* (New York: Hill & Wang, 1978), p. 46.

PAGE 149—*"new and fresh and strong"*—and subsequent quote from Frances Richardson Keller, *An American Crusade: The Life of Charles Waddell Chesnutt* (Provo, Utah: Brigham Young University Press, 1978), pp. 165, 272.

PAGES 150–151—*"When I am no longer"*—and subsequent quotes from Jean Chalon, *Portrait of a Seductress: The World of Natalie Barney,* trans. Carol Barko (New York: Crown, 1979), epigraph and pp. 25, 38. See also, Shari Benstock, *Women of the Left Bank: Paris, 1900–1940* (Austin: University of Texas Press, 1986).

PAGE 152—*"Brave little Bevilacqua"*—and subsequent quotes from Leon Edel, *Henry James: A Life* (New York: Harper & Row, 1985), pp. 494, 497.

PAGE 155—*"On the back of"*—and subsequent quote from *Rat and the Devil: Journal Letters of F. O. Matthiessen and Russell Cheney,* ed. Louis K. Hyde (Boston: Alyson Publications, 1978), pp. 3, 19.

PAGE 158—*"years of nomadic"*—and subsequent quotes from Arnold Rampersad, *The Life of Langston Hughes* (New York: Oxford University Press, 1986), Volume I, pp. 4, 89–90, 264, 265, and 288.

PAGE 160—*"it was love"*—and subsequent quotes from Robert P. Newman, *The Cold War Romance of Lillian Hellman and John Melby* (Chapel Hill, NC: University of North Carolina Press, 1989), pp. 34, 39, and 268.

PAGE 162—*"The more abstract"*—and subsequent quotes from Václav Havel, *Letters to Olga: June 1979–September 1982,* trans. Paul Wilson (New York: Holt and Company, 1988), pp. 3–19.

PAGE 164—*"When I add"*—Quoted in Samuel Edwards [Noel Bertram Gerson], *The Divine Mistress* (New York: McKay, 1970), p. 1.

PAGE 164—*"How fortunate"*—and subsequent quotes from Joseph Barry, *French Lovers: From Heloise and Abelard to Beauvoir and Sartre* (New York: Arbor House, 1987), pp. viii, ix, 115.

PAGE 165—*"palace of Alcina"*—From Ariosto's *Orlando Furioso,* the palace of Alcina refers to the castle of a sorceress who imprisoned men.

PAGE 166—*Sullivan to Sarah Ballou*—see *The Civil War: An Illustrated History*, narrative by Geoffrey C. Ward (New York: Knopf, 1990), pp. 69–83.

PAGE 170—*"We saw [Hardy's] wife"*—Quoted in Michael Millgate, *Thomas Hardy: A Biography* (New York: Random House, 1982), p. 270.

PART 4. LOVE HURTS

PAGE 173—*"most admirable woman"*—and subsequent quote from Mary Kathleen Benet, *Writers in Love: Katherine Mansfield, George Eliot, Colette, and the Men They Lived With* (Boston: G. K. Hall, 1984), p. 124.

PAGES 178–179—*"I am yet young enough"*—and subsequent quote from *The Letters of Anne Gilchrist and Walt Whitman*, ed. Thomas B. Harned (Garden City, NY: Doubleday, 1918), pp. 6, xx.

PAGE 182—*"The personality of Federico"*—and subsequent quotes from Ian Gibson, *Federico García Lorca: A Life* (New York: Pantheon Books), pp. 123, 124, 129. My thanks to Pablo Yanez for bringing this letter to my attention.

PAGE 184—*"We are two"*—Quoted in *Anne Sexton: A Self-Portrait in Letters*, ed. Linda Gray Sexton and Lois Ames (Boston: Houghton Mifflin, 1977), p. 293.

PAGE 187—*"My Lord Herbert"*—Quoted in *The Letters of John Wilmot, Earl of Rochester*, ed. Jeremy Treglown (Chicago: University of Chicago Press, 1980), p. 10.

PAGE 189—*"The heart which blazes"*—Quoted in *To the Happy Few: Selected Letters of Stendhal*, intro. Emmanuel Boudot-Lamotte; trans. Norman Cameron (London: John Lehmann, 1952), p. 202.

PAGE 193—*"I have no spell"*—and subsequent quote from Dorothy Mermin, *Elizabeth Barrett Browning: The Origins of a New Poetry* (Chicago: University of Chicago Press, 1989), pp. 119–20, 127.

PAGE 196—Cf. Louise De Salvo, *Virginia Woolf: The Impact of Childhood Sexual Abuse on Her Life and Work* (Boston: Beacon Press, 1989).

PAGE 197—*"a life of passionate happiness"*—Quoted from *Letters of Leonard Woolf*, ed. Frederic Spotts (New York: Harcourt Brace Jovanovich, 1989), p. 484.

PAGE 199—*"You with your vegetable"*—Quoted in *Selected Letters of Conrad Aiken*, ed. Joseph Killorin (New Haven, CT: Yale University Press, 1978), p. xvii.

PAGE 202—*"a knight in"*—Quoted in *Selected Letters of Fyodor Dostoyevsky*, ed. Joseph Frank and David I. Goldstein; trans. Andrew R. MacAndrew (New Brunswick, NJ: Rutgers University Press, 1987), p. 520.

PAGE 203—*"Schreiben sie mier"*—Mier is misspelled; it should be *mir.* The phrase was a signal between Anya and Fyodor that he had lost at gambling and she should send him money.

PAGE 209—*"You will read me"*—and subsequent quote from *Marcel Proust: Selected Letters. Volume II*, trans. Philip Kolb (New York: Oxford University Press, 1989), pp. 41, 445–446.

PAGE 210—*"So often this week"*—Quoted in *Writers in Love*, p. 46.

PAGE 213—*"Yes, I well remember"*—and subsequent quotes from *The Letters of Vita Sackville-West to Virginia Woolf*, ed. Louise DeSalvo and Mitchell A. Leaska (New York: William Morrow, 1985), pp. 43, 424.

PAGE 214—*Sibyl Colefax*—Vita signs the letter with the name of a famous London hostess. She and Virginia often used the name when corresponding about social engagements.

PART 5. THE END OF LOVE

PAGE 217—*"mad, bad and dangerous"*—Quoted in George Paston and Peter Quennell, *"To Lord Byron": Feminine Profiles* (London: John Murray, 1939), p. 41.

PAGE 220—*"The man I once"*—and subsequent quotes from *The Letters of Percy Bysshe Shelley*, ed. Frederick L. Jones (Oxford: Clarendon Press, 1964), pp. 421, 520.

PAGE 224—*"I loved her once"*—Quoted in Scott Donaldson, "The Jilting of Ernest Hemingway," *Virginia Quarterly Review*, 65 (Autumn 1989), pp. 661–673.

PAGE 226—*"If I looked"*—Quoted in Joan Givner, *Katherine Anne Porter: A Life* (New York: Simon & Schuster, 1982), p. 202.

PAGE 228—*"Only truly passionate"*—and subsequent quotes from Deidre Bair, *Simone de Beauvoir: A Biography* (New York: Summit Books, 1990); and Claude Frances and Fernande Gontier, *Simone de Beauvoir: A Life, A Love Story*, trans. Lisa Nesselson (New York: St. Martin's Press, 1987), pp. 236–237.

PAGES 230–231—*"Amongst the feathered race"*—and subsequent quote from *Collected Letters of Mary Wollstonecraft*, ed. Ralph M. Wardle (Ithaca, NY: Cornell University Press, 1979), pp. 40, 43.

PAGE 231—*"I part with you"*—*Collected Letters of Mary Wollstonecraft*, p. 46.

PAGE 232—*"lasting estrangement"*—Quoted in *The Brontës: Life and Letters*, ed. Clement Shorter (London: Hodder and Stoughton, 1958), I, 255.

PAGE 233—*"the need of being loved"* and *"hunger, rebellion and rage"*—Quoted in *The Oxford Companion to English Literature*, ed. Margaret Drabble (Oxford: Oxford University Press, 1985), p. 13.

PAGE 236—*"The gay, gilt"*—and subsequent quotes from *Selected Letters of Oscar Wilde*, ed. Rupert Hart-Davis (Oxford: Oxford University Press, 1979), p. 117; and Richard Ellmann, *Oscar Wilde* (New York: Knopf, 1988), p. 389.

PAGES 238—*"The Idyll has seen"*—and subsequent quote from Jean Chalon, *Portrait of a Seductress: The World of Natalie Barney*, trans. Carol Barko (New York: Crown, 1979), pp. 49, 52.

PAGE 240—*"Thus I think of you"*—Quoted in *My Other Loneliness: Letters of Thomas Wolfe and Aline Bernstein*, ed. Suzanne Stutman (Chapel Hill, NC: University of North Carolina Press, 1983), p. 5.

PAGES 243–244—*Edith Wharton, Henry James*—Cf. Leon Edel, ed., *Henry James: Selected Letters* (Cambridge, MA: Belknap Press of Harvard University Press, 1987), pp. xxiii–xxiv.

PAGE 248—*"I don't believe"*—and subsequent quotes from Joy Harjo, *In Mad Love and War* (Middletown, CT: Wesleyan University Press, 1990), pp. 22, 36.

PAGE 252—*"I opened [the letter]"*—and subsequent quote from *Selected Letters of Charles Dickens*, ed. David Paroissien (Boston: Twayne, 1985), pp. 9–10.

PAGES 256–257—*"For the one I love"*; *"the most intense and"*; *"I shall have no show"*—Quoted in *Calamus Lovers: Walt Whitman's Working Class Camerados*, ed. Charley Shively (San Francisco: Gay Sunshine Press, 1987), pp. 36–41.

PAGES 259–261—Cf. *The Paul Laurence Dunbar Reader*, ed. Jay Martin and Gossie H. Hudson (New York: Dodd, Mead & Company, 1975).

PART 6. FALLING IN LOVE AGAIN

PAGE 265—*"women were attracted"*—and subsequent quotes from Ronald W. Clark, *Benjamin Franklin* (New York: Random House, 1983), pp. 42, 310, 311.

PAGE 268— *"If ever there was"*—and subsequent quotes from *Collected Letters of Mary Wollstonecraft,* pp. 46, 48.

PAGES 270—*"Pity me, but do not"*—and subsequent quotes from Francis Gribble, *George Sand and Her Lovers* (London: Eveleigh Nash, 1910), pp. 52, 56.

PAGE 271— *"lightly, healthily and well"*—Quoted in Joseph Barry, *Infamous Woman: The Life of George Sand* (Garden City, NY: Doubleday, 1977), p. 345.

PAGE 273— *"I am going to marry"*—and subsequent quote from *Writers in Love,* p. 228.

PAGE 274— *"Chiwawa"*—Chiwawa was Colette's nickname for Madame Bloch-Levallois, at whose house Colette met Maurice Goudeket over the Easter holidays in 1925.

PAGES 274–275— *"Henceforth I shall dream"* and *"I always held"*—Quoted from *The Letters of Jack London,* Volume 1, ed. Earle Labor, Robert C. Leitz, III, and I. Milo Shepard (Stanford, CA: Stanford University Press, 1988), 29 September 1902 and 28 September 1903, pp. 313 and 391, respectively.

PAGE 275— *"The hour is already"*—Quoted in Clarice Stasz, *American Dreamers: Charmian and Jack London* (New York: St. Martin's Press, 1988), p. 112.

PAGE 277— *"Where love may be"*—and subsequent quotes from *Sherwood Anderson's Love Letters to Eleanor Copenhaver Anderson,* ed. Charles E. Modlin (Athens, GA: University of Georgia Press, 1989), p. 2.

PAGE 280— *"I am just walking"*—and subsequent quotes from Nahum N. Glatzer, *The Loves of Franz Kafka* (New York: Schocken Books, 1986), pp. 58, 3.

PAGE 284— *"on little besides"*—Quoted in Carlos Baker, *Ernest Hemingway: A Life Story* (New York: Scribner's, 1969), p. 421.